PRAISE FOR

Helpless

ALSO BY CATHY GLASS

THE MULTI-MILLION COPY BESTSELLING AUTHOR

CATHY GLASS

Helpless

**Are Riley and his two little
siblings in danger?**

Certain details in this story, including names, places and dates,
have been changed to protect the family's privacy.

HarperElement
An imprint of HarperCollins*Publishers*
1 London Bridge Street
London SE1 9GF

www.harpercollins.co.uk

HarperCollins*Publishers*
Macken House, 39/40 Mayor Street Upper
Dublin 1, D01 C9W8, Ireland

First published by HarperElement 2024

1 3 5 7 9 10 8 6 4 2

© Cathy Glass 2024

Cathy Glass asserts the moral right to be
identified as the author of this work

A catalogue record of this book is
available from the British Library

ISBN 978-0-00-866366-7

Printed and bound in the UK using 100%
renewable electricity at CPI Group (UK) Ltd

ACKNOWLEDGEMENTS

A big thank you to my family; my editors, Ajda and Holly; my literary agent, Andrew; my UK publisher HarperCollins, and my overseas publishers who are now too numerous to list by name. Last, but definitely not least, a big thank-you to my readers for your unfailing support and kind words. They are much appreciated.

AUTHOR'S NOTE

At present, there are over 100,000 children in care in the UK. A further 50,000 are considered 'at risk' and 300,000 'in need'. These children are still living with their families and the parents are given support and monitored by the social services. Some parents are able to make the necessary changes so their family can stay together, but others can't, and the children have to be removed. I felt with Janie and her three children that it could go either way. This is their story.

CHAPTER ONE

EARLY ONE MORNING

It was still dark as I parked outside 32 Bridge Street. There were no lights on in the ground-floor maisonette I was visiting, which wasn't a good sign. Janie was expecting me. She and her three children should be up by now, getting ready to leave for school on time, which they hadn't been doing. Janie had received an official letter warning her that if she didn't ensure her children attended school regularly and on time, she could be prosecuted. It wasn't an idle threat. Over 10,000 parents are prosecuted for their children's non-attendance at school in England every year, resulting in fines and even imprisonment.

I opened my car door and got out. The chilly early-morning air hit me. It was 7.40 a.m. on a grey, overcast day in late January. The two-bedroom maisonette where Janie and her children lived was in a row of similar properties. Most of the occupants were local authority housing tenants; Janie didn't know any of them. A low brick wall and small patch of lawn separated each front door from the pavement. Janie had been given help finding this property, having fled an abusive partner. She was in receipt of financial support in the form of various benefits, and practical support in the form of me.

Having decided to retire from full-time fostering the year before, I was now working part-time as a family support worker (FSW), as well as doing occasional respite fostering. I'd been a foster carer for thirty years and felt I had something to offer. The local authority had felt so, too, for the role of FSW had been their suggestion. I'd taken a few months off last year after my last foster child had left, to spend more time with my family, catch up with friends and, with the help of my youngest daughter, Paula, redecorate most of the house. I'd then received the referral for Janie and, after an initial meeting, had begun visiting her six weeks ago. Janie was struggling and at present I wasn't sure if I was making a difference or not. It seemed to be one step forward and three back. But I was trying to stay positive and work out new strategies that might help Janie to keep her children with her and out of foster care.

I pressed the doorbell and waited. Janie, age twenty-six, wasn't a bad person but her parenting was giving cause for concern. She hadn't had much positive parenting herself, so had no role model. A number of unsuccessful relationships hadn't helped her confidence or self-esteem. Riley, seven, her eldest son, exploited the lack of firm and consistent boundaries, as many children would. His school had raised concerns and at home he'd put himself in charge and challenged or refused to do most things his mother asked of him. He'd also been in trouble with the police. Jayden, five, copied his older brother and together they presented a united front that overrode their mother. Lola, three, was cute and Janie's obvious favourite, which wasn't helping the boys' behaviour. As parents or carers, we can't have favourites and it was something I would work on with Janie at a later date. But for now, we just needed to get the boys to school on time and Lola to nursery.

I pressed the bell again. I could hear voices coming from the apartment above but nothing from Janie's. I pressed the bell for a third time, holding it down for what seemed like ages. As I released it I heard Riley shout: 'Mum! Door!'

It went quiet, then a light came on in the hall, a bolt slid and Janie opened the door. Yawning, dressed only in pants and a T-shirt and with sleep-dishevelled hair, it was clear she'd just got up.

'Oh, it's you. My alarm didn't go off,' she said, yawning again, and went back down the hall.

'Do you know it's nearly quarter to eight, love?' I said, following her into the small kitchen-diner. It was a mess. Open takeaway pizza boxes containing the bits no one wanted (strings of onion, etc.), empty crisp packets, beer cans, chocolate biscuit wrappers, paper plates Janie bought to save washing up and other debris littered the small table and work surface. A bottle of lemonade lay on its side, its sticky contents on the floor. Janie stepped in it before I could stop her.

'Shit!' she said. 'I told the kids to be careful!'

Why were they unattended in the kitchen? I thought but didn't ask. The children being unsupervised had already resulted in a number of minor accidents, which had added to the social services' concerns.

Riley appeared in his pyjamas.

'Hello, love,' I said, smiling.

'Mum, Lola's done a poo. It stinks,' he said, disgusted, and disappeared out of the room again.

Lola was still in nappies and all three children shared the double bedroom. Janie had the single room. It was cramped but this was all the council had available at the time. The boys slept in a bunk bed, and Lola a small cot bed. Now the door to their bedroom was open, I could smell poo.

'I need a coffee,' Janie said.

'I'll make you one and clear up the lemonade while you see to the children. Remember, they need to be eating their breakfast by 8.15 so you can leave for school at 8.30. Have they got their star charts?'

'Somewhere,' she said, rubbing her eyes. 'Liv was asking about them yesterday.'

Liv was the family social worker and the star charts, also known as reward charts, had been her suggestion. I'd helped Janie make them. The idea was that each time a child completed an age-appropriate task, like getting dressed, they were rewarded with a star.

'Liv was here yesterday?' I asked, looking around.

'Yes, after school. Don't worry, the place was tidy then – I knew she was coming, not like before.' Social workers make both planned and unannounced visits. 'I think it went OK,' Janie continued, making no attempt to get the children ready for school. 'When Liv went me and the kids celebrated with a takeaway and some beer.'

'Mum, it stinks!' Riley shouted from his bedroom.

'Janie, get the children ready,' I said. 'Then we can talk. The children need time for breakfast.' One of the issues the school had raised was that the children had been arriving hungry. They were all quite thin, as was Janie. I'd tried to put in place a morning routine to allow time for them all to have breakfast.

'Mum!' Riley shrieked again at the top of his voice.

'I'm coming!' Janie yelled back and finally went to them.

Careful not to tread in the pool of sticky lemonade on the floor, I opened the cupboard under the sink to get a bucket and cloth. I knew they were there, along with some cleaning products, as I'd taken Janie shopping to buy them, among other items. It had been decided I would help Janie budget as she was finding it difficult to make her money last. I was also showing her how to make simple, cheap and nutritious meals. She'd agree that in order to help save money she'd limit takeaways to a treat at the weekend, but it was only Wednesday and I knew the pizza, beer and lemonade would have made a big hole in her budget.

I filled the bucket, and on my hands and knees began cleaning the floor. I don't like housework any more than anyone else does, but it had to be done and Janie's social worker would note how clean her home was and that there was food in the cupboard. As I cleaned, I could hear chaos breaking out in the children's bedroom. Janie was now in the bathroom cleaning up Lola and the boys were in their bedroom fighting rather than getting dressed. We'd already agreed they would have their baths in the evening when there was more time. Janie was shouting at them to get a move on, and they were shouting back that they couldn't find their clothes and that the other one was kicking and punching. The boys were either working together against their mother or fighting each other.

'I can't go to school!' Riley shouted. 'You haven't washed my uniform!'

'Get it out of the machine then!' Janie yelled back.

I looked hopefully at the washer-dryer. One of the many reasons Janie had given for the boys not going to school was that they didn't have clean clothes to wear. The washer-dryer was full and silent, so I hoped it had completed its cycle during the night and the contents were ready to wear. My hope was short-lived. I paused from cleaning the floor and opened the door of the machine. It hadn't been turned on and was full of dirty washing including the boys' school uniforms. I'd been here on Monday and done a load, but with a young family it needed to be done every day. Riley ran into the kitchen followed by Jayden, both in their underpants.

'Be careful, the floor is still wet,' I said.

Riley pushed past me and began pulling the clothes from the washer-dryer. 'That's yours,' he said, throwing some items of school uniform at Jayden. Then he found his and began sniffing them. 'Not too bad,' he said.

Jayden copied him. I didn't know whether to laugh or cry. A seven- and five-year-old sniffing their dirty clothes to make sure they weren't too smelly. There was nothing I could do now, there wasn't time. The boys went off to get dressed while I finished cleaning the floor and then filled the kettle for Janie's coffee.

Once dressed, Riley and Jayden reappeared and went to the cupboard where the cereal was kept.

'Watch them while I get ready, will you?' Janie shouted from the bathroom.

'Yes!' I called back.

Over the six weeks I'd been visiting, I'd talked to Janie about the importance of routines and she had accepted that it was better if she was up, showered and dressed before the children. It made for a more relaxed start to the day, and also meant she could oversee them getting ready. It happened occasionally, but more by chance – when Janie couldn't sleep and got up early to watch television.

As I helped the boys get their cereal and milk, Lola wandered in barefoot but dressed and sucking a security blanket. I picked her up. Her hands and feet felt cold. In fact, the flat didn't feel warm. I felt the radiator and it was cold. I checked the thermostat on the wall and it had been turned off, presumably to save money.

'Janie, can I put the heating on for a bit?' I called. My role wasn't to take over but to support and assist Janie.

'I need to top up the card,' she replied.

Janie's home had a pay-as-you-go meter, so energy was paid for in advance using a smartcard. She got help towards her fuel, but the cost was going up. I left the heating off but went in search of socks and a cardigan for Lola. Then I made her some hot oak breakfast cereal, which I knew she liked. I talked to the children as they ate, taking every opportunity to praise them, although Lola didn't need praise from me as her mother continually told her what a good girl she was, how beautiful she was and how much she loved her, whereas the boys were continually told off and spoken to negatively. Praising them was something I was working on with Janie. I'd once heard Jayden ask his mother if she wished he hadn't been born, which was very sad.

But the time Janie came out of the bathroom the children had finished eating and she had just enough time for a coffee, but not breakfast.

'Make sure you have something to eat when you get back,' I said, as she rushed around trying to leave on time.

I did what I could to help. The star charts hadn't materialized and when I asked Riley if he knew where they were he said he'd ripped them up and thrown them in the bin. I didn't know if it was true, but he got another telling-off from Janie, who threatened to tell his teacher and social worker and told him what a bad boy he was. I saw him grin mischievously at Jayden, apparently satisfied that they'd wound her up again.

Yet despite the chaos and lack of routine, somehow the children were ready to leave at 8.30, so at least they wouldn't be late for school today, but the morning hadn't gone well. I was disappointed and I felt we'd taken another step back. I said goodbye to them all on the pavement and wished them a nice day. It wasn't part of my role to go with them to school.

'Are you coming tomorrow?' Janie asked.

'I could, although it's supposed to just be Mondays, Wednesdays and Fridays now,' I reminded her. The first four weeks I'd come early every weekday morning to help Janie establish a morning routine, but then it had been agreed that I'd just do three. At some point Janie would have to show she could manage alone or with minimum support.

'Don't worry then, I'll be OK,' she said, distracted by Riley and Jayden, who were now poking each other. 'Stop it!' she shouted at them.

'I think it might be an idea if we got together again for a chat to go over a few things, when the children are at school and Lola is at nursery,' I suggested.

'If you like,' Janie replied tensely, glaring at the boys.

'Good. I'll collect you tomorrow at ten o'clock. We can get your food shopping and have a coffee, then I'll drop you off after to collect Lola from nursery at twelve.' My role was pretty flexible, although I'd include a note of our meeting and anything significant that came out of it in my records.

'OK, text me a reminder,' Janie said. Then to the boys, 'If you don't stop it now, you won't play on my Xbox.' Which was something else I needed to talk to her about.

Riley and Jayden were underachieving at school and were often too tired to concentrate on their lessons. Riley had told his teacher more than once that he'd been up until midnight (after his mother had gone to bed) playing on the Xbox. He'd then described some very inappropriate adult material, which the teacher had noted.

I drove home wondering what else I could do to help Janie establish better routines and boundaries so that her children would flourish, and she could enjoy them as well as keep them safe.

CHAPTER TWO

FIGHTING

That afternoon I visited my daughter, Lucy, and my little baby grandson, Theo, who was just three weeks old. Lucy had come to me as a foster child and I'd adopted her. She couldn't have been more loved and cherished if I'd given birth to her, and I tell her story in *Will You Love Me?* Lucy saw her birth mother, Bonnie, about once a year, and in some ways Bonnie's chaotic lifestyle reminded me of Janie's. Bonnie hadn't been able to make the necessary changes to successfully parent Lucy and had agreed to the adoption.

As I sat in Lucy's living room with little Theo in my arms, I knew how lucky I was to have such a wonderful family. I'd been given kind and loving parents, now sadly dead, and although my husband had left when my children were little, they'd grown into well-adjusted, caring, compassionate adults of whom I was incredibly proud. I saw Lucy, her partner, Darren, their daughter, Emma, age four, and Theo as much as possible. Also, my son, Adrian, his wife, Kirsty, and their newborn daughter, Sophia. My youngest daughter, Paula, lived with me and was happy; she was doing well in her career working in the offices of a local manufacturing firm. She'd taken a bit of a dip during the lockdowns of Covid, like many young people, but now that time had passed she was back on track.

Yes, I felt very lucky and blessed to have my family and sorry for those who didn't enjoy what I did. I'd spent most of my adult life looking after vulnerable children and working with their parents, so I was aware of the challenges some families faced.

Lucy and Darren were early-years practitioners, both working in the same nursery. It was where they'd met. Lucy was now on maternity leave and Darren would be home between 5 and 7 p.m., depending on which shift he was on. While Theo slept, I helped Lucy with some housework, then went to collect Emma from school. She was in her second term and her little face was a picture when she saw me. She gave a cry of delight, ran into my arms and we hugged. I carried her school bag, which seemed rather heavy for a little one, and as we walked we chatted about her day at school.

Once home, I checked Lucy had everything she needed and then, kissing them all goodbye, I left. I knew Lucy had a routine she liked to keep to on school nights so that Emma had time to relax before dinner, after which she had a bath and bedtime stories. Darren helped once he was home. I'd see them again soon, but I didn't ever turn up without checking first it was all right, as it could have appeared intrusive. The same was true of Adrian and his family, and I was hoping to see them soon.

Still feeling the cosiness that came from being with my family, I got into my car and was about to start the engine when my mobile rang. Janie's number showed on the display. Unlike some of the children I'd fostered whose parents hadn't been given my contact details to protect the children, Janie and I had swapped numbers right at the start. She'd used it a few times, mainly to change an arrangement, and I assumed that's what she was now doing. She should be home by this time, having collected Riley and Jayden from school.

As soon as she spoke it was obvious something was wrong.

'You need to get here fast before I lose it completely!' she cried, upset and angry. 'You need to tell them to get off my back! I'm doing my best.'

'Are you at home?' I asked, wondering if the boys were playing up and making her so agitated.

'No, I'm still at the friggin' school! Can you come?'

'Yes, but why are you still at school?' I asked.

'The bitch wants the police involved and I can't have that. Can you tell them?'

'Tell who? What?'

'The headmistress. She's with me.'

'Can you put her on?' I asked, for clearly something had happened but Janie was too wound up to tell me. She sometimes reacted defensively, without forethought, taking a remark personally when it wasn't intended.

Ms Porter, the headmistress, however, was very level-headed. I'd met her at a team meeting when I'd first become involved with Janie's family. All the professionals had met to draw up a care plan to decide what support was needed to help Janie and her children. I'd also seen Ms Porter in the playground when I'd collected Riley and Jayden from school when their mother had been ill.

'Mrs Glass.'

'Yes. What's happened? Janie seems very upset.'

'I'm with her now. The boys are in afterschool club for the time being while I sort this out. Riley was in a fight with another child and the boy's mother wants the police involved. She is with my deputy and I will speak to her again soon, and hope we can sort this out without involving the police.'

'Was the boy badly hurt?' I asked, concerned.

'He's got a bruise on his cheek. I think it would be a good idea if you came to support Janie and maybe see her home.'

'Yes, of course. I'll come straight away, although it will take me about fifteen minutes.'

'Thank you. We are in my office. Come straight up.'

With a heavy heart I started the car and headed for Riley's school, the positive effects of a nice afternoon quickly vanishing. Janie was right, she didn't need the police involved. In fact, she didn't need this to happen at all. Although a child of Riley's age cannot be held criminally responsible – i.e. be arrested and prosecuted – there were other measures the police could take, and the matter would certainly be reported to the social services. Aside from that, Riley shouldn't be fighting in the first place, but this wasn't the first time. Riley had a history of attacking other boys and it was thought that some of it was due to the domestic violence he'd witnessed at home during his mother's previous relationship. That would almost certainly be a contributing factor. I was also concerned about the amount of aggression he saw on television and in the Xbox games he played. Young children's minds are very impressionable.

* * *

Now school had ended, the main gate at Riley's school wasn't security locked and I went straight in, through reception, and up a flight of stairs to Ms Porter's office on the first floor. I knocked on the door.

'Come in,' she called.

I tentatively opened the door and went in. It was a large office and Ms Porter and Janie were sitting on stacking chairs in the carpeted area to the right of her desk. Lola was on the floor between them, playing with a toy. She looked up as I entered and I smiled at her.

'Thank you for coming,' Ms Porter said, bringing over another chair. 'Do sit down. My deputy has persuaded the child's mother not to involve the police. Riley will apologize to the boy and he will also lose playtime tomorrow.'

I nodded, relieved. Janie seemed less agitated too.

'But Janie has told me she is thinking of putting Riley into care voluntarily,' Ms Porter continued. 'She feels she can't cope with him, and the situation at home would be more manageable if there was just Jayden and Lola. I'm inclined to agree.'

This was the first I'd heard of it and I didn't think it was such a good idea. I'm sure Ms Porter meant well, but she wouldn't necessarily appreciate the implications, nor the way the social services worked. It probably seemed like a quick-fix solution, but the whole point of me supporting Janie was to keep her children out of care.

'I think that could make Riley feel very rejected,' I said.

'Well, he should behave himself and do as he's told!' Janie said, immediately agitated again. 'He takes a delight in being a little shit and winding me up. Liv says he could have oppositional defiant disorder.'

Oppositional defiant disorder (ODD) is when a child is persistently angry, argumentative, resentful and defiant towards authority figures such as parents and teachers. They can also be deliberately vindictive to their peers. I didn't think Riley had ODD, but I kept quiet as I am one of the old school that believes a lot of behaviour – good or bad – is learnt.

'You'll need to discuss putting Riley into care with Liv,' I said to Janie.

'As Janie doesn't feel she is able to cope with the arrangements at present, are you able to put in more hours?' Ms Porter now asked me.

'I could, but again we would need to talk to Liv first and discuss how much and what form it would take. Another option might be for Riley to have some respite care,' I suggested.

'So he could stay with you at weekends?' Janie asked, clearly having thought it through.

'Weekends and school holidays are the times when Janie feels she needs most help,' Ms Porter added.

'It's possible that Riley could have some respite care at the weekends and during the school holidays,' I said carefully. 'But it would be for the social services to decide the exact nature of it and which foster carer would best suit his needs.'

'As he knows you it would make sense if he came to you,' Ms Porter said, again not fully appreciating the workings of the social services.

'I am registered for respite fostering,' I said. 'But it would be for the social worker to decide if coming to me is the best option.'

'I'll ask Liv,' Janie said.

'Yes,' Ms Porter agreed. 'And we also need to work on Riley's anger management. His teacher has talked to him about it.'

'So have me and Cathy,' Janie said. 'But it doesn't do any good. The ed. psych. [educational psychologist] sent Riley for therapy but it was boring so he didn't go.'

'A pity,' Ms Porter said.

'I can't force him!' Janie replied, taking it personally. 'His place has been given to someone else now.'

Which I knew would be true. There is a waiting list of children and young people needing to access NHS mental health services and it has risen in the aftermath of the pandemic.

We talked about boundaries to encourage good behaviour at home and school, with a system of rewards and sanctions. Janie said she'd tried most things and hoped Liv would agree to Riley having respite care as she was desperate. Ms Porter then took us to collect Riley and Jayden from afterschool club. They were clearly enjoying themselves. Riley was painting and Jayden was playing a game with another child. Both were reluctant to leave. I assumed there'd been nowhere else for them to wait but it had rather rewarded Riley for his bad behaviour.

'Riley, Jayden. Time to go,' Ms Porter said, and they both stopped what they were doing and came over.

'I wish they did what I told them first time,' Janie said. Then to Riley, 'You've got yourself into trouble again. You're not having the Xbox tonight.'

Riley shrugged as if he didn't care, then he saw Ms Porter looking at him.

'Sorry, Miss,' he said.

'You should listen to your mother, cooperate, and do as she says,' Ms Porter said.

'Yes, Miss,' Riley dutifully replied.

Ms Porter saw us out of the building. 'Tomorrow is a new day, so no more fighting, Riley,' she said as we parted.

'No, Miss.'

Going home in my car, Janie told Riley off big time and threatened to put him into foster care if he got in any more trouble.

'I'm talking to Liv about it tomorrow,' she said.

'Don't care,' Riley retaliated.

But I'm sure he did. I caught a glimpse of his expression in the rear-view mirror and he looked hurt. I appreciated Janie was stressed and at the end of her tether, but threatening to use foster care as a punishment wasn't helpful. As well as adding to Riley's feelings of rejection, if he ever did go into foster care it would start off on the wrong foot.

I pulled up outside their flat, saw them in, then continued home.

That evening when my daughter, Paula, returned from work we had dinner and talked about the day we'd had. I mentioned the incident at Riley's school and what had been said and asked her how she felt about giving Riley some respite care if we were asked. Fostering affects the whole family and would especially impact on Paula, as she lived with me. We'd recently looked after a little girl on respite and although she'd missed her mother there hadn't been any significant problems and generally it had gone well. But Riley was very different and would present a number of challenges, which I talked through with Paula. Like most foster carers, I share information about the child with my family on a need-to-know basis.

'Yes, that's fine with me, if you want to,' Paula said.

'It might not happen,' I pointed out. 'Janie needs to talk to her social worker first. And if Liv does agree to respite care, she might think another family is more suitable, one with a father figure or siblings – I don't know.'

'OK, but if we do have him perhaps start the weekend after next. We are going to see Adrian, Kirsty and little Sophia on Saturday.'

'Yes, I know, I hadn't forgotten, and it won't happen that quickly.'

Famous last words! The following afternoon Liv telephoned to ask if I could look after Riley on weekend respite, starting that weekend.

CHAPTER THREE

I SENSE HOSTILITY

I could have said no, but when I heard what Janie had told Liv I couldn't refuse. Janie was desperate and I felt some responsibility, as I was supporting her. She'd cancelled our meeting in the morning by text saying she was too tired, then Liv had phoned in the afternoon. Despite the promises Riley had made the previous day to try to control his anger and help his mother, he'd been confrontational and argumentative all evening. He'd refused to do what Janie had asked, swearing at her and goading Jayden to behave badly, and had then pushed over Lola. Janie had got angry with Riley and he'd answered back. She'd gone to bed, leaving Riley and Jayden watching the Xbox and they'd all been late for school in the morning.

'To be honest you're the only foster carer free with the experience to manage Riley's behaviour,' Liv admitted. I knew there was a shortage of foster carers, and it was true I was experienced in looking after children with challenging behaviour. Often children on respite care are given to new carers as a way of easing them in gradually, but that didn't seem to be an option here. If Riley was very challenging on respite it was likely to put them off fostering.

'What sort of arrangement are you thinking of?' I asked Liv.

'Janie has asked for you to collect Riley straight from school on Friday and then take him into school on Monday morning. But I've suggested he goes home first on Friday and you collect him from home, say around five o'clock. Janie has to go to school anyway for Jayden. Then on Sunday you return Riley home around five o'clock. We can trial it for a month and see how it goes.'

'All right. I'm visiting my son and his new baby on Saturday so Riley will have to come.'

'Sure, but keep an eye on him around the baby,' Liv said, which did nothing to ease my concerns.

'Liv, I would normally go to Janie early for the school run on Friday. Do you still want that to continue as I'll be there again after school?'

'Yes, please, for now, and we'll review. Janie needs all the help she can get at present.' Which was certainly true.

I messaged my family to let them know Riley was having respite care with us at weekends, and I checked with Adrian that he was happy for me to bring him.

Of course, Mum. Looking forward to seeing you all, he replied.

My children, now adults, had grown up with fostering and took it in their stride, welcoming each new arrival as family. But I could remember that some of the children we'd fostered had been very disruptive at family gatherings. I could understand why, as being with my family emphasized they weren't with theirs, although they were always made very welcome. I could also remember the anxiety I'd sometimes felt when a child had been particularly demanding and disruptive. It didn't exactly make for a relaxing time, but having said that, there are many positive aspects to fostering, which is why so many of us do it for so long. I hoped Riley wasn't going to be too challenging and we could all have a nice afternoon. To be honest, I would normally let a child settle in first before visiting my family and friends, but I wanted to see little Sophia again. She was only two weeks old and babies grow so quickly.

Friday morning, bright and early, I was at Janie's flat again to help her with the morning routine. It was better than last time. They were up, Riley was dressed, Jayden was getting dressed, and Janie was changing and dressing Lola. I waited in the kitchen while they got ready, and washed some dishes. Riley appeared first.

'I'm coming to stay with you!' he said, running in, upbeat and positive.

'Yes, for the weekend,' I said, with a big smile. 'We're looking forward to having you. Has someone explained what's happening?'

'The social worker,' he said, leaping onto the cabinet to reach the cereal. I took down the bowl. 'What's your house like?'

'I can show you some photographs,' I said.

If there's time, a child pays a preliminary visit to the new carer's home so it isn't so strange, but that hadn't been an option here. I sat with Riley while he ate his cereal (dry) and showed him some photos of my house and garden on my phone. He was interested and asked questions. He liked his bedroom, which Liv had already told him would be just for him. I knew that when Liv had spoken to Riley about coming to stay with me it would have been in a positive light, and I hoped he picked up my enthusiasm too.

Janie was also looking forward to Riley coming to stay with me but said things like, 'Peace and quiet for a whole weekend! I can't wait,' or, 'No aggro for two whole days!' It wasn't said with a smile, as a joke; it would be hurtful to Riley and do nothing for improving their relationship. I'm sure Janie had no idea how it sounded to her son – as though she couldn't wait to get rid of him. I appreciated she was looking forward to the break as she was struggling to cope and appeared continually stressed, but what she could have said, and what I would be saying, was, 'Mummy needs a bit of extra help.' Or, 'Cathy hasn't got any young children to look after so she can spend more time with you.' Or, 'Cathy is helping Mummy out.' Or similar.

Riley, of course, retaliated. 'I can't wait to get away from you!' he shouted, sticking out his tongue, which was covered in bits of cereal.

Jayden copied his older brother and stuck out his tongue at his mother.

'See what I have to put up with!' Janie exclaimed to me. Then to Jayden, 'If you don't behave you can go to Cathy's too.' Again, using the threat of foster care as a punishment.

With one eye on the clock, I steered the conversation onto safer ground and asked Riley what he liked to eat. I was going shopping and would buy some of his favourite food.

'Burger and chips,' he replied.

'You can have that for dinner tonight,' I said.

'And pizza,' he added. 'Chicken dippers and chocolate ice-cream.'

'That's a new one, I haven't heard of that before,' I said. 'Chicken dippers with ice-cream.'

'No! Not at the same time!' Riley said, then he realized I was joking and grinned.

Janie smiled too, which was nice to see as she didn't often smile.

They were ready to leave the house on time and outside we said goodbye and see you later. I stopped off at the supermarket on the way home and bought the groceries we needed. I was unpacking the shopping when my phone rang. It was Rania, my new supervising social worker (SSW). Every foster carer – including those who just offer respite care – have a supervising social worker. The role of the SSW is to support, monitor, advise and guide the carer and their family in all aspects of fostering. I'd had a number of SSWs in the past and had met Rania a couple of times. Although she wasn't directly involved in the support I was putting in to Janie's family, she was aware of it. Liv had now informed her that Riley was coming to me for respite care at weekends. As a respite carer I was still expected to attend training and meetings, complete appropriate records, have an annual review, follow the 'safer caring policy', and have a DBS (Disclosure and Barring Service) check for any criminal record.

Rania and I talked a bit about Riley and what I had planned for the weekend. She said she'd phone next week to see how it had gone, and reminded me that if I needed help or advice over the weekend to contact the duty social worker. There was now a social worker available out of hours to support foster carers, as in the past too many carers had been left without the help or advice they needed until the offices opened again.

Rania wished me a pleasant weekend and I finished unpacking the groceries, then I checked Riley's bedroom. I'd redecorated it a few months ago with Paula's help and had now put a duvet cover showing animal pictures on the bed. He should be bringing his clothes for the weekend, but I had extras in my box of spares – built up over years of fostering – if he forgot anything. I wasn't expecting him to bring toiletries; I would supply those.

Even after thirty years of fostering I'm still slightly anxious before a new child arrives, hoping they will be happy with us and that I can help them and their family. Riley and I knew each other from the support I was already involved in, but staying with me was a new experience for him. I wanted it to be positive and fun, as well as giving his mother a much-needed break. I was planning on taking him to the park in the morning to run off some energy before going to Adrian's in the afternoon. Then on Sunday I'd ask him what he wanted to do. I assumed he'd also have some schoolwork to complete over the weekend.

Satisfied I was as prepared as I could be, I spent a pleasant afternoon with a friend, before going to collect Riley at five o'clock.

Riley, wearing some of his school uniform, answered the door, clearly excited and eager to be on his way. He shot straight past me and headed for my car.

'Just a minute!' I called after him. 'We need to say goodbye. And where's your bag?'

'Forgot it!' he cried, and ran back, leaping over the doorstep and disappearing inside.

'Janie?' I called, going in.

'In here!' she replied from the living room.

I went in. A man with long hair in a ponytail was sitting on the sofa, looking at his phone. Lola and Jayden were next to him eating biscuits and watching a children's cartoon on the television.

'Lola's dad, Bowie,' Janie said, nodding in his direction. I knew Lola saw her father, but I hadn't met him before.

'Hello,' I said, assuming Janie had told him who I was.

He ignored me and concentrated on his phone. I sensed hostility.

'Bowie doesn't like foster carers,' Janie explained. 'His two older kids are in care.'

'Oh, I'm sorry,' I said, feeling uncomfortable, but not knowing what to say.

He didn't look up or in any way acknowledge me. Jayden and Lola continued to chew on their biscuits and watch television.

'We'll be off once Riley has his bag,' I said. 'Does he have schoolwork to do?'

'You'll have to ask him,' Janie replied. She was reading the instructions on a packet of microwave rice.

Riley appeared carrying a well-used plastic supermarket carrier bag, which I assumed contained what he needed for the weekend.

'Got everything?' I asked him.

'Yep.'

'What about your school bag with you weekend homework?' I checked.

'Forgot it,' he said, unfazed.

Janie sighed and glanced at Riley, but really at his age she should have checked he had his school bag when she'd collected him from school. There wasn't anything I could do about it now, so I told him to say goodbye.

Jayden left the sofa, came over and gave his brother a hug, which was nice. Lola was going to do the same, but her father stopped her by placing a restraining arm across her. 'Stay where you are,' he said gruffly, as if I might kidnap her into foster care. Clearly his experience hadn't been a good one.

'Bye,' Janie managed to say as he left.

I felt sorry for Riley, leaving without a proper goodbye, although he didn't seem bothered – his enthusiasm was undented.

I opened the car and Riley jumped into the back. I checked his seatbelt was properly fastened, then got into the driver's seat.

'Can we go swimming and to the cinema, and bowling?' he asked very excitedly, as I started the car and pulled away. 'A kid at school lives with foster carers all the time and he does loads of stuff with them.'

'Good. He's happy then?'

'Yes.'

Many children who come into care have had very little experience of family outings and activities, so it can seem like a bonanza. I explained my plans for Saturday – park in the morning and Adrian's in the afternoon, ending with, 'So you can choose what we do on Sunday.'

'Bowling,' Riley said.

'Fine, I'll book us a time slot. Have you ever been before?'

'Yes, lots of times,' he said at first, then, 'Not really. My mum keeps forgetting. She'll take us when she remembers.'

I glanced at him in the rear-view mirror and my heart went out to him. Like so many children whose families were involved with the social services, he was loyal to his mother despite her shortcomings. She was and always would be his mother. I think it would help parents with children in care to know this and that foster carers don't try to replace the parents; they just want to help.

CHAPTER FOUR

A GOOD START

'**Y**ou've got a nice house,' Riley said as I showed him round.

'Thank you, love. That's a nice thing to say.'

I always do a guided tour, as I call it, when a child first arrives or pays a preliminary visit. As well as familiarizing them with the house, it gives me the opportunity to mention a few rules that keep everyone safe. All foster carers have a 'safer caring policy' and follow similar guidelines – for example, not closing the door when alone in a room with a looked-after child. We don't know what experiences that child may have had, and leaving the door open means they can come out easily whenever they want to. A closed door to an abused child could be terrifying and trigger memories of previous ordeals.

'This is your bedroom,' I said, switching on the light as I showed him in.

'Cool.'

'It's a bit different to what you're used to. Here, our bedrooms are our own private spaces, and we don't go into each other's. We knock on the door if we want the person and wait. I will always knock on your door first before coming in.'

Riley nodded as he began opening and closing the wardrobe doors, and then the drawers. He was still carrying his plastic bag.

'You can leave your bag here and we'll unpack it later,' I suggested.

'We can do it now. There isn't much,' he said. And proved it by tipping the carrier bag upside down and shaking its contents onto the floor.

I looked at the sad little heap of belongings. A pair of faded pyjamas that looked far too small for him. Faded black socks, two pairs of faded blue underpants, a vest that might once have been white but was now grey. A tracksuit that seemed to have missed the wash completely and had stains on the front. I'd never seen Janie's children at the weekend, so I didn't know what they usually wore.

'Did you pack?' I asked him.

He nodded. 'Mum didn't have time and she says I have to make sure I take everything back with me, or rather Bowie did.'

'OK, don't worry, let's put your belongings in this drawer.'

Riley wasn't interested and looked through the window instead. 'Is that your garden?'

'Yes.'

'Can I go out?'

'If you wish, although it's rather cold and nearly dark now. You might be better waiting until the morning.'

'I'll watch television instead then,' he said. 'Have you got an Xbox?'

'No, love. But we can get children's games on the television and my tablet. Your clothes are here,' I said, showing him, before I closed the drawer. 'And I think tomorrow before we go to the park we'll go to the shops and buy you some clothes. You could leave them here, so you don't have to worry about forgetting anything next time.'

'Cool,' he said.

To be honest he didn't have anywhere near enough clothes to see him through the weekend. I could have lent him some from my spares, but it would be nice for him to have his own. I like the children I look after to look smart, and it helps their self-esteem. Riley would take his new clothes home with him when respite care ended. Of course, he might have had perfectly good casual clothes at home but just hadn't packed them, although I doubted it, as his mother was on benefits and struggled to make ends meet. She'd bought the boys' school uniforms for 10p an item from the school's second-hand box, now renamed *previously loved*. Foster carers usually add to the child's wardrobe or replace it completely.

I showed Riley the rest of the house and mentioned a few more house rules as we went. 'We always try to be kind, caring and polite to each other,' I said. 'If we are angry then we talk about our feelings rather than shout, and we never hit anyone. And lastly,' I said, as we passed the front door, 'either Paula or I will answer the door if someone calls.'

'I do it at Mum's,' he said.

'I know, but I am more cautious.' I had to be as a foster carer. Even having a child on respite was a huge responsibility.

We went into the living room, where Riley was interested in the photographs on the wall. I began telling him who they were.

'Who's that old lady?' he asked, with a child's frankness. 'She's in a lot of your pictures.'

'Yes, she was my mother,' I replied. But I'd never thought of her as old. Although she was in her late eighties when she died, she was still young at heart and sprightly – always ready to play a game with the children or come on a family outing.

'Where is she now?' Riley asked.

'She died, love, so she is with my father.'

'What, in heaven?'

'Yes.'

'Bowie says there's no such thing as heaven, it's a load of bollocks. He says when you die you rot in the ground and the worms eat you.'

'I like to believe something different,' I said, and changed the subject. I was becoming emotional talking about my dear mother. She'd died a few years previously, but my family and I still missed her and probably always would.

Riley turned his attention to the television.

'Where are the games?' he said, picking up the remote control.

I turned on the television and showed him what was available, but he wasn't impressed. 'They're for kids,' he said disdainfully.

'That's right.'

'Little kids.'

They were for Riley's age, but he was used to adult games.

'Show me your iPad,' he demanded.

'Please,' I added.

I fetched my tablet, turned it on and showed him the games. Some were educational and others purely for entertainment. But, of course, compared to the adult war and alien invasion games he was used to, mine were tame.

'Is that it?' he asked scornfully.

'Yes.'

He pulled a face.

'How about you have a look in our games cupboard?' I suggested. 'You might find something you'd like to do.'

'Like what?' he asked doubtfully.

'I'll show you.'

In the dining part of our kitchen-diner is a large cupboard containing games for all ages of children, built up from years of fostering and when my children were little. Puzzles, jigsaws, board games, arts and crafts, and so forth. Riley rummaged through, every so often pausing to examine a box.

'They're very old,' he said.

'Well loved,' I replied, with a smile.

'What's this?' he asked, examining another box.

'Modelling dough. I expect you played with something similar when you were younger?'

'Don't think so,' he said, and took off the lid.

'What do Jayden and Lola play with?' I asked.

'Nothing much,' Riley replied. 'Jayden has some cars and Lola just hangs around Mum.' Sadly, I thought this was probably true from what I'd seen.

'We'll cover the table with this plastic cloth if you're going to play with the dough,' I said, unfolding the cloth.

'Why?'

'To protect the table.'

He looked bemused as I shook out a brightly coloured PVC cloth and laid it on the table. He tipped out the contents of the box. Tubs of different-coloured doughs, a rolling pin, cutters, moulds and a spaghetti-making machine landed on the table.

'How does that work?' he asked, picking up the spaghetti machine.

'You put the dough in the top, there, turn the handle and the dough comes out in long strands.'

'And these?' he asked, picking up the moulds.

'You press the dough into the mould, then carefully take it out and it's in the shape of the dinosaur.'

I showed him, and from the expression on his face it could have been the first time he'd ever played with dough, which was sad. He knew how to kill an alien or enemy soldier from a hundred metres but didn't know how to model with dough. So many children from disadvantaged homes miss out on stimulating play. He sat at the table completely engrossed in what he was doing. Having made a pile of blue spaghetti and pretended to eat it, Riley began pressing dinosaur shapes. I made him a drink and said that we'd have dinner once Paula was home, which wouldn't be long. Burger and chips didn't need much preparation, so I sat at the table and modelled dough with Riley. Then we did a jigsaw together.

'Do you always play with your kids?' Riley asked.

'Yes, when I can.'

'My mum is too busy,' he replied loyally.

'Looking after young children is very demanding, which is why she needs your help. Do you help your mum?'

He didn't reply but I think I knew the answer.

'It would be nice if you could help her,' I said.

Further discussion on this matter was halted for the time being as we heard Paula's key in the front door.

'That'll be my daughter, Paula,' I told Riley. 'Hi, love, in here!' I called out to her.

Having taken off her coat and shoes, she came into the kitchen-diner.

'This is Riley,' I said.

'Hi. You're playing nicely,' she said.

'That's what your mum keeps saying,' Riley replied in his cheeky way.

'Well, it's true,' I said.

Paula went to wash and change from her work clothes while I cooked the burger and chips. I also chopped some salad and placed it in a bowl on the table for us to help ourselves.

'Nah,' Riley said when he first saw it. But then he took some cucumber and tomato, and then some more.

As we ate, Paula and I made conversation that included Riley. Sitting at a table and eating with strangers can be quite daunting for a child. Riley knew me a little but not Paula, and he'd never had a meal with us before. Customs vary between households and what one family considers the norm can be quite foreign to a visitor. Most parents who have had their child's friends to tea will have noticed this. On the first few visits they glance around nervously, taking cues from what others are doing.

'Do you always sit here to eat?' Riley asked part way through the meal.

'Usually,' Paula replied.

'We have our food in front of the television.'

Foster carers are expected to take family meals around the table. Not only does it make it easier to check that the children or young people are eating enough, but it also brings the family together. Sometimes the evening meal is the only time a busy family can sit down together.

'Do you stay here often?' Riley then asked Paula.

I'd mentioned who Paula was but there'd been a lot for him to take in and he must have forgotten.

'Yes, I live here,' Paula said.

'You're lucky. It's nice,' Riley said again, bless him. 'You got a dad?'

'Yes, but he doesn't live here.'

'Like me.'

Riley ate all his burger and chips and wanted ice-cream for pudding, which I took from the freezer. It wasn't the same as he was used to at home but after some deliberation he decided to have it anyway. Once we'd finished eating, I asked Riley to help clear the table. He pulled a face but did as I asked, then went to the toy cupboard and took out more games. The three of us spent the next two hours at the table playing various board games and cards. Riley was fascinated with what the cupboard held and kept returning to it over and over again, all thoughts of the Xbox and iPad gone. I was pleased he was enjoying himself. His behaviour wasn't at all challenging as I'd warned Paula it could be, but then there were two adults giving him all the attention he needed – a very different situation to that he had at home. The only resistance came at eight o'clock when I said it was his bedtime.

'No, it isn't,' he replied forcefully.

I wasn't going to get into a 'yes, it is'/'no, it isn't' debate, so using an authoritative tone and the closed-choice technique, I said firmly, 'Bedtime, Riley. Do you want a bath or a shower?'

'None,' he replied, equally firmly.

'What do you have at home? A bath or shower?'

'A bath. The shower broke. But not on Friday. That's when Jayden and Lola have theirs.'

'OK, so you take it in turns at home, but here you can have a bath every day. How lucky are you? So would you like your bath now or first thing tomorrow morning? I think now would be better as it will mean you'll have more time in the park tomorrow.'

'Now then, get it over with.'

He came with me upstairs where I ran his bath, gave him a sponge and checked he had everything he needed. Drawing the bathroom door to, I waited on the landing while he washed. I always give a child age-appropriate privacy, but I would never leave a child his age in a bath completely unattended. After a few minutes I heard a big splash and guessed Riley had tipped in all the bath toys that were in a mesh bag stuck to the tiled wall. Intended for younger children, I listened to him playing with them – dive-bombing the plastic ducks, sending the wind-up fish zooming across the water, and generally having fun like a child should. In some ways Riley often appeared older than his years, burdened and world-weary, perhaps from being aware of his mother's problems and not having a carefree childhood. But now he appeared much younger. After a while, when I assumed the bath water would be cooling, I called for him to get out, dry himself and let me know when he was ready. Once he shouted, 'I'm dressed!' I knocked on the door and went in, then spent some time mopping up the water that had pooled on the floor and was running down the walls and around the edges of the bath.

'You had a fun time,' I said.

'It was OK.'

I waited while he brushed his teeth to make sure he did them well. He'd already lost some teeth through decay, which was sad for a child. I'd provided him with a toothbrush, paste, bath sponge, flannel, towels, etc., as he hadn't packed any.

'Well done,' I said.

'What for?' he asked.

'Having a bath nicely and doing your teeth.'

He shrugged off my praise as though it didn't matter, but we all grow from praise, and it was especially important for a child like Riley, who was used to getting into trouble and being told off.

I saw Riley into his bedroom. On the first night I always ask the child how they like to sleep: the curtains open or closed, the light on or off, the bedroom door open or shut. It's little familiar details like these that help a child settle in a strange room. Riley closed his curtains himself, pulling them so hard I thought they might fly off the rail. He then spent some time playing with the dimmable light switch, eventually leaving it on low. He said I could leave his door open. I asked him if he wanted a goodnight kiss but he pulled a face.

'Kisses are for sissies,' he said, and jumped into bed.

I told him to call me in the night if he needed anything and I'd come to him as I didn't want him wandering around. Then, saying goodnight, I came out of his room, relieved the evening had gone well. I was optimistic that this had set the mood for the weekend, but the following day I was very quickly proved wrong.

CHAPTER FIVE

CAN'T BE SQUEAMISH

During all my years of fostering as a single parent I've made sure I was up and dressed, and had ideally had my first coffee before the child woke. I then felt ready to face the day and whatever challenges lay ahead, of which there had usually been plenty. Also, some of the children I'd looked after – the very young, those with additional needs or challenging behaviour – couldn't safely be left alone, not even for a few minutes while I showered.

I'd set my alarm for 6 a.m. on Saturday morning, which I assumed would be plenty early enough to give me a head start on the day. However, I was jolted from sleep not by the alarm, but the sound of the television blaring from the living room.

I sat bolt upright. The clock showed 5.20 a.m. Good grief!

'Riley!' I called out, as I scrambled into my dressing-gown. I ran downstairs. 'Riley, whatever are you doing?' I felt light-headed from the shock of suddenly waking. I went into the living room. 'Switch it off now, please. You'll wake Paula.'

'No,' he replied defiantly.

I reached for the remote control, but he snatched it away. 'Now, please, Riley.'

He hid it behind his back, so I manually switched off the television.

'You can't do that!' he shouted angrily. I needed this like a hole in the head first thing in the morning.

'Riley, listen to me,' I said calmly but firmly. 'It's only 5.20, far too early to be up, and that television was on too loud.'

'No, it wasn't,' he said, his face setting in anger.

'I could hear it upstairs. Now, calm down and listen to me. You'll wake Paula.'

'Don't care.'

I put a bit of distance between us in case he lashed out, and I perched on the edge of the sofa. What a contrast to last night, I thought, and all before I'd had a coffee! I spoke in an even, non-confrontational voice.

'Riley, last night, when I saw you into bed, I said I didn't want you wandering around the house by yourself, but to call for me,' I reminded him.

'No, you didn't,' he said, jutting out his chin. 'I can do what I want.'

'I'm afraid you can't. None of us can do what we want all the time as we have to consider others.'

'I can. I want the television on. I always have it on when I'm at home. I'm allowed.'

'Not at this time, surely.'

'Yes! You don't know. You're not there. I watch this programme on a Saturday morning.'

I realized it was possible. I didn't know what time Riley got up at weekends. Many children who struggle to get out of bed on a school day can rise ridiculously early

at the weekends. In the past, when I'd looked after children on respite, I'd asked their parent or carer for an
outline of their routine, but Janie didn't have a routine –
that was something we were trying to establish. In truth,
I had no idea what happened in their home at weekends.

'So talk to me in a nice voice like the big boy you are,
and explain what happens at your home on a Saturday
morning,' I told Riley.

He pulled a face, folded his arms across his chest and,
when he realized I would wait for as long as it took, he
began to tell me.

'I wake up and I have to leave the bedroom quietly so
I don't wake Jayden and Lola, then I watch television
with the door closed. It doesn't matter what time as long
as I don't wake anyone.'

'And where is your mum?'

'In bed. She gets up when Lola wakes.'

'I see. Thank you for explaining that.'

'Can I have the television on now?' he asked.

'In a minute, but listen to me first.' He was calmer
now, open to reason. 'As your foster carer, I need to be
downstairs when you are to make sure you are safe. If
you wanted to come down this morning, you should have
called out to me.'

'I get told off if I wake anyone,' he replied earnestly.

'I understand, but it's different here. Now, I need to
get dressed so I want you to go to your bedroom until I –'
Riley went to interrupt. 'No, love, listen to what I have to
say.' He pulled a face but fell silent.

'I'll give you my tablet so you can watch the same
programme in bed until I'm ready,' I continued. 'Then,
once I'm showered and dressed, we can both come down

here. And tonight I will leave my tablet by your bedroom door so if you wake before I am up you can quietly watch it in bed.' I'd installed parental controls so he couldn't access inappropriate material online.

'Or I could keep it with me at night,' he suggested cutely.

'Outside your door will be fine,' I said. 'Now, let's go upstairs quietly without waking Paula.'

Indeed, I was surprised Paula hadn't woken. I guessed she must have been very tired after a week at work. I gave Riley my tablet and, in a more compliant and cooperative mood, he came with me upstairs, his too-small pyjama pants flying at half-mast. He used the toilet and then returned to bed, and I left him watching his favourite programme while I showered and dressed. I had just finished when I heard him shout: 'The battery's gone!'

We went downstairs where I made a much-needed coffee and watched children's television at 6.15 a.m. I'd make sure my tablet was fully charged for tomorrow!

The positive side of being up very early was that we arrived at the shops as they opened at 9 a.m. With the promise of a visit to the park as soon as we'd finished, Riley was quite cooperative. Not many young children like shopping but Riley didn't really have a chance to grow bored as we flew around the children's clothes section in the department store, dropping into the basket what he needed. Two pairs of pyjamas (he chose some with pictures of dinosaurs on them), two tracksuits with Superman logos on the tops, underwear, trainers and a blue padded jacket. We were finished in under an hour, just as the shops were growing busy. Riley said he was hungry, which wasn't surprising as we'd had a very early breakfast. I picked up a couple of wraps and we ate them in the car before we set off for the park.

I was pleased with the way the day was going, but the park wasn't the success I'd hoped for. Riley simply wasn't interested in playing on the apparatus, although there was plenty for his age group, including a mini obstacle course, a climbing net, rope ladders, slackline with rings and a monkey bar, a suspended rope bridge and a tunnel to crawl through. Other children his age would have a great time, but Riley wanted to go back to my house as another of his favourite programmes was on the television. I assumed he spent most Saturday mornings watching television.

'Do you go to the park when you are with your mum?' I asked, trying to encourage him onto the equipment.

'No, Mum says I'm too young.'

'I meant with her, not alone.'

'No. Can we go now? I'm done here.'

'Yes, if you've had enough.' He'd had one turn on the roundabout and that was all.

'Your tablet will be charged now,' he said as we headed for the exit.

I thought it was sad that a seven-year-old would rather be indoors playing games on a tablet or watching television than running free in the park, but I knew it was a battle many parents and carers faced. I wasn't sure how often Janie took them out at weekends, but it seemed as though Riley wasn't used to going out. I would mention it to her when I had the chance, as the parks are free and if children play in the fresh air they often settle more easily once home.

Paula was up when we got back and she suggested to Riley that they play one of the games we'd all played last night. Families who foster want to give children on respite a good time and make it like a mini holiday, but Riley wanted to watch the television.

'One more programme, then I want you to do something else,' I said.

'Why?' he asked, astonished.

'Too much television isn't good for you.'

'My mum let's me.'

'It's different here.'

'So you keep saying,' he replied in his cheeky manner.

But I kept to my word and once the programme had finished I asked Riley to switch off the television.

'It's on all day at my mum's,' he protested.

I appreciated that some families had their television on in the background for most of the day – I guess it's comforting, but children can become very reliant on simply watching, which is a passive activity. It's fine for unwinding at the end of the day, but young minds need stimulating in order to develop so they can reach their full potential. As much, if not more, learning takes place away from school as it does in school, and I would be failing in my role as Riley's respite carer if I allowed him to spend hours in front of the television or endlessly playing games on my tablet.

I switched off the television. Riley glared at me, threatened to tell his mother what a nasty person I was, then said he was going to the toilet. He stomped off upstairs. I heard the door to the toilet close. Ten minutes later, when he was still in there, I grew suspicious he was up to mischief. He wouldn't be the first child I'd looked after to take out their anger by stuffing whole toilet rolls and other items down the pan and then watch the water rise over the edge. I went upstairs.

'Riley, have you finished in there?' I asked through the door.

'No,' he groaned. 'I can't go.'

'Oh. Are you trying to do a poo?' I asked.

'Yes, but it won't come. I'm constipated.'

'OK, love. Don't sit there straining, you'll hurt yourself. Get off now and try again later.'

Foster carers can't afford to be squeamish, and I'd dealt with worse: a child who'd smeared faeces on the walls (faecal smearing is known as scatolia), and a girl who'd hidden heavily used sanitary towels in her bedroom for months.

'When was the last time you went?' I asked Riley as he came out of the toilet.

'Can't remember,' he said, pulling a face. 'I get constipated at Mum's.' The poor kid was obviously feeling very uncomfortable.

'Don't worry. Come down and I'll cut up some fruit and give your mother a ring.'

I thought Riley might object to eating fruit – he had when I'd offered it the night before after dinner and also at breakfast – but now he didn't.

'Will it make me go?' he asked.

'It should help.'

He ate the halved grapes, sliced apple and segmented tangerine I'd put in a bowl, while I called his mother. Severe constipation in children may need medical help.

'You want to bring him back early,' Janie semi-joked as she answered.

'No.' I explained the problem.

'I give him a laxative when he's constipated,' she said. 'I've got some here. I had to take him to the doctor and he said it was his diet.'

'He's having some fruit now, so hopefully that will help.'

'He won't eat fruit here, so I'll give him the medicine tomorrow if he hasn't been.'

'All right, Janie.'

I was satisfied that Janie had sought medical help and was treating Riley's constipation. He ate all the fruit and then we had a game of cards. We were due at Adrian and Kirsty's at two o'clock and would have lunch before we went. With Riley's condition in mind, I decided to make a thick vegetable soup and suggested he might like to help. If a child helps in the preparation of their food, they are more likely to eat it. After some protestation about not liking vegetables or cooking and that he'd rather watch television, he became interested in the process and enjoyed peeling and cutting the vegetables and putting them in the pot. I added seasoning and Riley stirred it. When the soup was ready we served it with warm wholemeal rolls, all of which provided good fibre and normally Riley hated.

'Why am I having to eat this?' Riley asked as we sat at the table with Paula.

'Because it's good for you. As well as containing vitamins, it is high in fibre, which is good for pooing.'

'Too much information!' Paula exclaimed, grimacing.

But it worked. An hour later, just as we were about to leave for Adrian and Kirsty's, with Riley looking smart in his new clothes, he shouted, 'I need a poo!' and shot upstairs to the toilet.

Paula waited in the hall while I went up to check he was all right, and that he had washed his hands.

'It stinks in here,' he said, finally coming out.

He wasn't wrong. I went in and opened the window. As I said, foster carers can't afford to be squeamish!

CHAPTER SIX

MUM'S BOYFRIEND

One of the reasons I'd decided to stop full-time foster-ing was to spend more time with my family. My third grandchild, born to Adrian and Kirsty, was their first child, little Sophia – beautiful, adorable, so small and prefect, a miracle. Even Riley was interested, for about two minutes, then with all the attention focused on Sophia he became disruptive. Nothing gains attention faster for a child than negative behaviour.

Adrian and Kirsty had made a fuss of Riley when we'd first arrived, as they did all our looked-after children. Adrian had grown up with fostering and Kirsty was a teacher, at present on maternity leave, so they knew how to talk to and engage with children. They had asked Riley about his interests, school, family and so forth, and had showed him around their flat. I'd also brought my tablet and a bag of games for him to play with. But Riley didn't want to engage with the games, and as soon as attention slipped from him he began playing up: pressing the television buttons on and off in quick succession; wandering into the bedrooms, which he knew were private, just as they were at my house; going into the kitchen and opening the drawers and cupboards;

repeatedly flushing the toilet although he hadn't used it. I kept bringing him back and settling him with a game, which lasted about one minute. Generally, negative behaviour is best ignored as much as possible and good behaviour rewarded, although this was becoming increasingly difficult. Then, in a loud voice, Riley declared he was very bored and wanted to go now.

'We're staying for a little while longer,' I said evenly, and found him something else to do. I'd planned on staying for about two hours.

Adrian and Kirsty made us drinks and sliced cake while I held Sophia. Eating and drinking kept Riley occupied for a short time, then he began attention-seeking again, disappearing from the room, making loud noises and talking over us, and effectively making conversation impossible. I apologized for his behaviour and warned him of the consequences if he didn't settle down. He'd been losing screentime and now I said we wouldn't be going bowling tomorrow if his behaviour didn't improve.

'I'll go home early then,' he said. 'I can do what I like at home.'

And that, of course, was part of the problem. Riley did do what he wanted at home. He ruled; it was the easiest option for his exhausted mother. I knew it would help if she and I put in place similar boundaries for good behaviour so we were both on the same page. It would be hard work for her to begin with but would pay rewards in the long term. Putting in place boundaries for good behaviour is a sign of caring and as a family support worker I wanted to do all I could to help Janie and her children. Unruly behaviour isn't socially acceptable, and as well as causing Janie stress it could lead Riley into more and more trouble as he got older. I made a mental note to add discussing boundaries with Janie when we got together.

I apologized again to Adrian and Kirsty for Riley's behaviour, as did Paula, who was very disappointed we couldn't all just have a nice afternoon. We weren't staying for dinner (just as well) and left as planned after a couple of hours.

On the way home I didn't so much tell Riley off – I'd been doing that all afternoon – but patiently went over what he'd done wrong and why it wasn't acceptable, for it was possible he didn't fully appreciate how disruptive his behaviour had been.

'Don't care,' he said, but it was said quietly, without attitude, so I hoped he was thinking about what he'd done.

Riley had lost his television time for the evening due to his disruptive behaviour, and I saw this through. I had to, so he remembered next time. Children soon spot idle threats.

'Am I still going bowling?' he asked.

'We'll see how well the evening goes,' I said.

Paula played a game with Riley while I made us dinner and the evening passed without incident. I praised him.

'Can I have the television on?' he asked.

'Not this evening, love, but you can have my tablet first thing in the morning,' which he accepted. Riley was starting to realize I meant what I said.

We looked at some books together and I said it was a pity he'd forgotten his schoolwork as we could have done that. 'Remember it next time and I can help you.'

At bedtime he had a bath and dressed in his new pyjamas, which he liked. I put my fully charged tablet just outside his bedroom door and reminded him it was for the morning. 'I trust you not to use it during the night,' I said.

I think giving him this little bit of responsibility helped. 'I'm sorry I was naughty when we saw the baby,' he said. I was very touched. Riley put on such a hard, couldn't-care-less attitude most of the time, but there was a gentle, kind child beneath.

'So am I, so don't do it again, please,' I said. 'And you need to think about your behaviour at home.' For what he learnt with me needed to be transferable to home, otherwise it would be a waste of time. 'Your mother needs your help and cooperation as much, if not more, than I do, Riley.'

'Why?' he asked, climbing into bed.

'Because she doesn't want to keep telling you off. It's hard work. Your mum loves you and wants to have fun with you, Jayden and Lola.'

'I'm not sure Mum loves me,' he said ruefully. It was sad, although I could see why he might think that.

'I'm sure she does, but she has a lot on, so it would be helpful if you could do as she asks. Jayden will copy you.'

Ultimately, though, Janie would need to change too. Parenting doesn't have to be perfect but 'good enough'. It's a recognised term in social work and in essence means that parents have to put their children's needs first by providing routine and care to meet their health and developmental requirements, and to ask for help when necessary. Parenting requires unconditional love of the child, and I knew that Janie had been advised by her social worker to attend a parenting class. It's a suggestion made to many parents whose family is involved with the social services, and, while not compulsory, it is advisable. As well as talking about strategies to help the parent, it also offers a platform to discuss issues and listen to and support others. I hoped Janie would attend as she would be expected to.

My tablet was still outside Riley's bedroom door when Paula and I went to bed around 11 p.m. and he was fast asleep. I slept well and didn't wake until I heard the toilet flush, then Riley's bedroom door close, shortly after 6 a.m. It went quiet and so, putting on my dressing gown, I went to check on him, lightly knocking on his door before going in. He was sitting up in bed playing a game on the tablet with the volume on low.

'Good boy,' I said, pleased.

He was so engrossed he didn't reply.

'I'll tell you when it's time to get up.'

I came out, pulling the door to. It was a much better start to the day. I had time for a coffee, and to shower and dress, and Paula had a lie-in.

After breakfast the three of us set off for bowling. It was the first time Riley had been and he was very excited, but in true Riley style he was convinced he knew all about bowling and had nothing to learn. Bowling shoes on, he wouldn't listen to our suggestions and quickly became frustrated when his ball bounced heavily a short way down the lane and then went straight into the gulley. His frustration grew when Paula and I bowled. I explained we had been bowling for years, and eventually he accepted my suggestion of using a lighter-weight ball, and allowed Paula to show him some techniques for sending the ball low and straight. The first time he hit one of the pins he exploded with delight.

We had two games; Paula won both, but Riley's skill had improved and he wanted to come again the following week. However, his joy of bowling was matched by seeing a child from school on our way out.

'He's in my class,' Riley hissed excitedly. 'He must come bowling too! Hiya!' Riley shouted across the foyer.

I smiled at the boy's parents, who looked at me a little oddly.

They presumably knew who Janie was from the school playground so could be wondering who I was. It would be up to Riley what he told the boy, if anything. Some children with a foster carer are happy to admit who they are, while others pass us off as an aunt/uncle or friend of their parents.

Once home, I made us a drink and a snack and as soon as Riley finished he grew restless. He didn't know how to amuse himself other than to watch television. Paula had done her fair share of entertaining him. I knew she didn't mind, but it was her weekend too, so I enlisted Riley's help in preparing dinner for later. Like many families, we usually have a roast on a Sunday. As we peeled and chopped vegetables, I told him a bit about where the food came from – carrots and potatoes grow underground, peas in pods on vines. I was doing roast chicken, as I knew Riley liked chicken, but he was surprised at what the raw meat looked like, having only ever seen it covered in batter or breadcrumbs and reshaped to form nuggets or drummers.

While we waited for the meal to cook we sat at the table and I showed him how to play draughts and then noughts and crosses – a simple game that just needs pen and paper. He wasn't used to all the attention and really responded. After dinner I let him play on my tablet while I cleared up, and then I packed his bag ready to take him home. I'd bought a holdall while we'd been shopping rather than using the old plastic carrier bag he'd come with. I'd washed his school uniform ready for Monday, as well as the clothes he'd been wearing. I would send all those home. Riley was wearing a set of new clothes and he'd wear those to go home in.

Just after 4.30 we said goodbye to Paula, who said she'd see him again next weekend. Overall I felt the weekend had gone well. It had been hard work but no more than I'd expected. There is only so much a foster carer can achieve during respite care and I felt Paula and I had done our best. Riley must have felt relaxed in my company, for as I drove he suddenly said, 'You know your bloke doesn't live with you?'

'My husband? Yes, I'm divorced.'

'Is that because he used to beat you up?' he asked.

I was taken aback. Not by the directness of his question – children do ask difficult questions and make inappropriate comments; they don't have the same filter as adults. What had shocked me was that domestic violence was the first reason he could think of for my ex not being with me. I knew his mother had fled an abusive relationship, but not the details.

'No, love,' I said, glancing at him in the rear-view mirror. He was looking serious and deep in thought. 'My ex-husband didn't hit me. He left me to live with another woman. What made you ask?'

'Mum's boyfriend, the one we lived with, used to beat her up. He used to hit me too, but I showed him.'

I knew that bravado was masking his fears. It's petrifying for a child to witness or be caught up in violence at home – the place that should be safe and caring.

'That was very wrong of him, and frightening. What was his name? Do you remember?'

'Rhys.'

'Does your mother see him now?' I asked. Sadly, some victims of domestic violence are coerced and threatened back into the abusive relationship they've fled.

'No.'

'What about Bowie?' I asked, taking the opportunity to learn as much as possible. I'd found before that children often disclose while I'm driving. I think it's something to do with my concentration being elsewhere so that I am not looking directly at them.

'Bowie doesn't hit us, but I don't like him,' Riley replied.

'Why not?' Janie had been in the abusive relationship with Rhys after her relationship with Bowie, Lola's father, had ended. I didn't know if she had restarted a relationship with Bowie or if he was simply visiting Lola. I'd make a note of what Riley had said as I was supposed to, in case it became relevant in the future.

'Why don't you like Bowie?' I asked again.

Riley shrugged. 'Just don't. He thinks he's all it, and tells us what to do and it's not his job.'

'I understand. Is he kind to you?'

'Don't know.'

'Does he stay the night?' I asked. If he was in a relationship with Janie, their social worker would need to be satisfied it wasn't detrimental to the children's well-being or safety.

'Don't know,' Riley replied again.

'OK, love. The way Rhys treated you all was very wrong. Nobody should be cruel to someone or hit them, and certainly not in a relationship.'

'I had to tell the social worker and the police what happened,' Riley said. 'Jayden and Lola were too young.'

'Yes, that would be usual. You did the right thing.'

'I wouldn't hit a girl,' Riley added.

'Good. Best not to hit anyone,' I replied, thinking of his altercation with the boy at school. 'You've met my son, Adrian. He wouldn't hit anyone. If he doesn't agree with someone, he tries to talk about it or says nothing and walks away.'

'That's what my teacher tells us to do.'

'She's right. Do you still think a lot about the bad things Rhys did?' I asked, concerned.

'Sometimes.'

'Have you talked to your mother about it?'

'No. She hasn't time. She's always stressed.'

'I think you should tell her, or I could say something to her.'

'You tell her.'

'All right. Is there anything else you want to talk about?' I asked. We were close to his home now.

Riley shook his head but then said, 'Thanks for taking me bowling.'

'You're welcome, love.' I was touched that he'd thanked me. 'We had a nice time.' I could see how much it had meant to Riley. 'We can go again next weekend if you like.'

'Can we bring Jayden?' he asked, which caught me on the hop.

'I'm not sure, love. I'll need to ask your social worker and your mother. Let me see.'

'He'd like it. I could show him what to do.'

'I'm not making any promises. I'll find out.' *Under-promise and over-deliver* is my maxim when it comes to children, to avoid disappointment.

I parked in the road outside Riley's home and opened his car door, which was child-locked. He ran down the path, apparently looking forward to seeing his family again, which was good. I followed with his bag. I hoped their time apart had given them all the break they needed, and that Janie had benefited from just having two children to look after. However, when she answered the door, it was not with a smile, but with: 'Oh, it's you.'

Thankfully Jayden and Lola were outwardly pleased to see Riley and ran down the hall to greet him, hugging him hard, which made Riley smile. Lola wanted kisses.

'Everything all right?' I asked Janie.

'Same old,' she replied drearily. So I assumed she hadn't benefited from the break.

'Riley's had a good weekend,' I said positively. 'I'm sure he'll tell you all about it. I bought him a few extra clothes and a bag for his belongings.' I passed it to her. 'The clothes he came with are in there and I've washed his school uniform ready for tomorrow.'

'Thanks,' she said. 'You know you said about meeting for a coffee when the kids are at school?'

'Yes.'

'How about tomorrow morning after I've taken them to school and nursery? There's something I need to talk to you about.'

'Yes, I can do that. Do you still want me to come early in the morning to help with the routine?'

'Yes, you'd better.'

'I'll see you about quarter to eight then. Have a good evening.'

I called goodbye to the children and came away, wondering what Janie wanted to talk to me about. I had a number of matters I wanted to discuss with her, but her request had seemed urgent. I hoped it wasn't something bad that could affect her or the children.

Once home, I wrote up my log notes for the weekend and emailed Liv a résumé, copying in Rania, so they'd both see it on Monday morning. I also asked about taking Jayden bowling with Riley next Sunday.

CHAPTER SEVEN

BOWIE

As a foster carer looking after someone's children, I was sometimes seen by the parents as the enemy – on the same side as the social services. It's a great pity the system has become so adversarial, for surely we should all be on the same side, working for the good of the children considered at risk? Not many parents are truly evil, intent on abusing their children. Most who come to the attention of the social services are lacking, often due to mental health issues, and drug and alcohol abuse, and have little family support. I've seen the social worker's role change over the years. Some of the old-style social workers used to be more hands-on, spending hours with the family and helping them rather than paying visits and observing. In my role as family support worker I seemed to bridge that gap a little, and was generally viewed differently by the parents, who usually appreciated I was there to help, although they knew I would report any concerns I had. I felt it was a sign of the rapport I'd established with Janie that she wanted to talk to me.

There was no point in me returning home after seeing Janie and the children off to school, and then coming back three-quarters of an hour later, so I went with them to school and waited outside the gates while Janie took them in. Lola attended the nursery at the same school as the boys. Once in, Janie and I walked to a local café in a small block of shops not far away. It was a cold but dry day, and Janie seemed a bit more upbeat than she had the evening before.

'Riley liked bowling,' she said as we walked.

'Good. We had a nice time.'

'He says you're going to take Jayden too, next Sunday,' Janie said.

'I told him I'd need to ask you and Liv.'

'It's fine with me.'

'Good. I've emailed Liv and asked her.'

'I guess Lola is a bit young to go?' Janie tried hopefully.

'Yes.'

'Bowie said he'd take us all bowling when he has a job.'

I nodded.

'He's good with kids, you know.'

I didn't comment, for that wasn't the impression I'd formed so far from Riley.

'The boys can be rude to him, but Riley can be rude to anyone,' Janie said. 'Bowie doesn't let them get away with it. He tells them off. Riley doesn't like it.'

'All children need boundaries,' I agreed. 'Although discipline might be better coming from you – their mother.'

'No, Bowie is good with them,' she said again. 'They don't answer him back.'

Janie continued to talk about Bowie in a positive light all the way to the café, but it was only once we were settled at a corner table with coffee and toasted tea cakes that she came to the point.

'The thing is – the reason I need to see you is to ask you what you think about something.'

'Yes?'

'You know how the social services work and Bowie wants to get his older kids out of care. So we thought if he moved in, and lived with us proper-like, he'd stand more chance of getting them back. What do you think?'

A lot of thoughts crossed my mind. 'Did he apply for custody of his children at the time of the hearing?' I asked.

'Yes, but his ex told a pack of lies about him, and the social worker wrote a report saying he wasn't suitable, so his kids are in long-term foster care. He only sees them for two hours three times a year at supervised contact. It's disgusting,' she said indignantly. 'He's their dad!'

'I know it's not much but that's to allow the children to settle with their permanent carers, as they are in long-term care,' I said. I paused and looked at my cooling coffee. 'Janie, can I speak honestly to you even if it's not what you want to hear?'

'Yes,' she replied, frowning.

'I think you need to concentrate on your children. The court decided that Bowie's older children would be better off in long-term foster care and they would have had their reasons.'

'But his ex lied and things have changed now,' she said adamantly.

'How have things changed?' I asked. If the situation really had changed then Bowie might be able to apply to the court for custody of his children.

'Me and Bowie are going to get together so we can give them a proper home,' Janie said. 'It's right that all his kids are together. Lola never sees her half-siblings.'

It wasn't enough, but I was gentle in what I said. 'Janie, you are finding it challenging looking after three children. How would you cope with five? And you only have two bedrooms.'

'We can apply for a bigger council house,' she said.

I didn't want to break the bond Janie and I had built, or the trust she had placed in me, but I did have to be honest. She'd asked me for my opinion and it was no good giving her false hopes.

'Janie, I don't know Bowie, but the court would have had good reasons for making the decision they did, after speaking to all parties and looking at all the reports. He could ask a solicitor for legal advice, but unless something has dramatically changed, I don't think he will be given custody now, even if you were all living together. Why did you two split up?'

'Not sure,' she said, shrugging, and took a sip of her coffee. 'I guess we both met other people. I met Rhys, and look where that got me! The bastard. I had a miscarriage after he kicked me in the stomach.'

I couldn't help but grimace. 'I didn't know. I am so sorry. That's dreadful.'

'Bowie would never hurt me. I mean, we argue, but so do all couples.'

I nodded. 'Riley has some bad memories from that time with Rhys,' I said. 'He began talking about it yesterday afternoon on the way home. He asked me if my husband ever beat me up.'

'He's never said anything to me,' Janie said, surprised.

'No. He probably thinks you have enough to cope with. Maybe you could sit down and have a chat with him, just the two of you? Reassure him it won't happen again and that you will protect him and his brother and sister.'

'Or Bowie can,' Janie said. 'I'm not much good at talking to my kids.'

'Maybe this is the time to start?' I suggested. 'I think it would be good. It's usually a matter of seizing the opportunity or steering the conversation in the direction you want. Maybe at bedtime when Jayden and Lola are in bed?'

'You think it will help?' she asked.

'I do. And, Janie, there's a few other things I think might help I'd like to bring up while we're having this chat.'

'Go on, but if it's about the star charts, they've gone. Sorry, but Riley admitted he and Jayden ripped them up and threw them away.'

'It's OK, but we need to establish a system of rewards to encourage good behaviour, otherwise you're just telling them off all the time.'

'Tell me about it!' Janie said, and finished off her tea cake.

'We could try a marble jar,' I suggested. 'Some teachers use them in the classroom. I've used them in the past to encourage good behaviour. Each time the child does something positive – for example, something you've asked them to do – they add a colourful marble to a jar. The jar needs to be somewhere prominent, so it reminds them of their target. They watch it slowly fill and once it has they get a small reward, like an outing to the park.'

'Or a chocolate bar,' Janie suggested.

'Yes. You'll need to be very enthusiastic for it to work. Make a big thing of it and praise them as they add their marble. They have to feel it's worth doing. Lola can join in, but her behaviour isn't causing you concern.'

'What if they still don't do as I say and play up?'

'Then sanction whoever is responsible. From what I know of Riley, I would suggest stopping his screentime. He likes playing games online and watching television, so stop fifteen minutes at a time, and make sure you see it through. Also, Janie, I think you need to keep a close eye on what Riley is accessing online, particularly on the Xbox. You have the parental-control software we talked about?'

'Yes, but Riley knows the password.'

'So change it. It is important, Janie. Some of Riley's behaviour could be from watching inappropriate material.'

'I'll tell Bowie,' she said.

I looked at Janie carefully. 'I know you want to make it work with Bowie, but the children are primarily your responsibility,' I reminded her. 'Liv will want to see you making the changes we've all discussed, taking charge and being proactive in their care. I wouldn't place too much emphasis on Bowie at this stage.'

'Don't you like him?' Janie asked.

'I don't know him,' I replied.

'The boys need a man,' Janie said.

'They need you. I know it's not easy being a single parent – I've been there and done it. It's hard work, but doable. Praise them when they have done something well and sanction their negative behaviour along the lines we have talked about. They could resent Bowie telling them what to do so early in your relationship.'

'I know him from before, and some days Riley and Jayden don't do anything right.'

'Find something, even if it's finishing their dinner. Riley is a good eater. Tell him. It's obvious to me that Lola is your favourite, and Riley and Jayden will feel it,' I said, moving to something else I needed to talk about.

'But she's good. I don't have to tell her off all the time.'

'Janie, as a parent, you can't have favourites. The boys will feel unloved. Riley told me that he doesn't think you love him. Do you ever tell him and Jayden you love them?'

'They're a bit old for that,' she said.

'No. A child is never too old to hear their parents say, "I love you." My mother always said it to me.'

'You don't think Riley has that oppositional defiant disorder Liv mentioned?'

'It's not for me to say, but I think a lot of Riley's behaviour can be changed. Also, he's had an unsettling time in the last few years with the moves and the trouble Rhys caused.'

'It'll be better once we all get together and Bowie lives with us,' Janie replied.

I took a breath. I could see that Janie was fixated on Bowie being the answer to all her problems, and life isn't like that. 'Janie, it's you who can make this better. You're the children's mother. Have you signed up for the parenting class Liv mentioned?'

'I will.'

'As soon as possible, Janie. It should help with techniques for managing the children's behaviour.' I then talked more about strategies, and putting in place bound-aries as so many of the problems Janie was having seemed to be about the boys' behaviour. 'And try to have fun with them,' I said. 'Take them out at the weekend. Let them run off some energy. At the moment it is all hard work for you. Before you know it, they'll be grown up. Your children need you. I know you can do this, Janie.'

'Do you really think I can?' she asked, surprised.

'Yes.'

'You're the only person who's ever had faith in me,' she said, and her eyes filled.

My heart clenched and I reached for her hand, but she took it away.

'My mother wasn't bothered about me and kept putting me into care. It might have been better if she'd left me there, but each time she got a new boyfriend she got me out again. I hated all her blokes and some of them tried to molest me.'

'I am so sorry. You had such a rough time. Where is your mother now?' I asked.

'Don't know and don't care,' she said, her face growing hard. 'We fell out years ago. She only ever thought about herself and didn't give a shit about me. I vowed I'd give my kids what I didn't have – a proper home with loving parents, including a dad who did fun things with his kids. Bowie says he wants that too.'

'And maybe he can fulfil that role in the future, but for now Liv will want to see *you* parenting your children. Can I suggest you talk to the children about how they feel about Bowie? Not while he's there, of course. Listen to what they say.'

'But they can't rule my life,' Janie said.

'No, but what they feel should be part of your decision-making if you are thinking about making Bowie their stepfather. They have to be your priority. Just like your mother should have made you hers.'

'So how long do you think I should wait before I can move Bowie in?' Janie asked. And I wondered if she'd listened to a word I'd said.

CHAPTER EIGHT

MOTHER'S PRAISE

Janie and I were in the café for about an hour, then we walked to her flat, where we said goodbye. I got into my car and was going to go straight home, but on the spur of the moment I decided to drive into town instead, where I bought a marble jar, and also a bunch of flowers for Janie. I'd been thinking about what I'd said and hoped Janie appreciated I had spoken directly with her best interests at heart. I certainly didn't want to ruin her chances of future happiness in a committed, loving relationship with Bowie, if that was what he was offering. But they'd had one failed attempt at a relationship already. How much had changed? And it remained true that she needed to concentrate on her own children before offering a home to him and his children.

It was late morning when I returned to Janie's and gave her the marble jar and the flowers. She was grateful and said no one had ever given her flowers before. Her eyes filled as she thanked me, and I was really touched. It was such a small act of kindness but one that clearly meant so much to her. I didn't go in as she had to leave shortly to collect Lola from nursery, so I said I'd see her on Wednesday morning. She thanked me again and I left feeling pretty choked up. I was rooting for Janie and hoped she'd do what was necessary to keep her family together. I thought part of it was helping her to take responsibility; for most of her life she'd been at the mercy of others – her mother, the social services and then the men she'd had relationships with.

On Tuesday morning Liv phoned.

'I got your email,' she began. 'It's fine with me for Jayden to go bowling with you on Sunday if he wants to. I've told Janie. She phoned me this morning. I'll leave the two of you to make the arrangements. I understand Lola's father, Bowie, is back on the scene?'

'Yes,' I said.

'Janie tells me she and Bowie want to apply for custody of his older children who are in long-term foster care.'

My heart sank. 'Yes, she mentioned it to me yesterday.'

'I've told her I won't back it,' Liv said bluntly. 'I'm afraid it's not what she wanted to hear. Janie is barely coping with her own three, so goodness knows why she thought she could cope with two more.'

I'd only met Liv a couple of times before. She was young – I guessed late twenties or early thirties – but she was straight-talking and down to earth in her approach. Unfortunately, Janie, who'd had a lot of involvement with social workers in her life, tended to view all social workers hostilely – as interfering busybodies who were out to get her.

'I understand Bowie is there a lot now,' Liv said.

'I don't know. I've only seen him there once and that was on Friday when I collected Riley.'

'Janie originally told me he only saw Lola every few months and that was away from the family home. Now, suddenly, she wants to move him in so they can apply to the court for custody of his children. It's not going to happen. His children are settled with their foster carers. The court won't give Bowie custody. He was refused last time, and he has no job and has served a prison sentence for drug dealing.'

My heart fell further. Janie had clearly omitted to mention that yesterday when we'd spoken at length about Bowie. Family support workers are given information on a need-to-know basis by the agency they work for.

It was about to get worse.

'I have concerns about Bowie being in the family home at all,' Liv said. 'There was an incident when Janie and Bowie lived together when she called the police. She claimed Bowie had assaulted her and pushed her so hard she'd fallen and hit her head. He wasn't prosecuted, and Janie is now telling me it was just an argument that got out of hand when they were breaking up. But it was logged as domestic violence.'

'Oh, dear me,' I said, appreciating the wider implications. The social services would be very concerned if an adult with a history of domestic violence was living in a household with young children.

'Yes, exactly. I'm going to see Janie later today,' Liv said. 'But apart from this, how is it going? I've read your reports.'

'I thought it was going all right until this,' I said. 'Janie can ask for help when necessary and is open to suggestions about how to improve her parenting skills. We had a long chat yesterday morning about strategies for managing the children's behaviour.'

'She mentioned you'd bought a marble jar to replace the star charts.'

'That's right, and we're working on routines and so forth.'

'No problems at the weekend with Riley?'

'A little. We went to my son's, and Riley wasn't the centre of attention so he played up.'

Liv gave a small laugh. 'I can imagine. He told his mother he'd had a nice time.'

'Good.'

'So, we'll continue with the arrangements as they are and then review at the end of four weeks. You're in tomorrow morning?'

'Yes.'

'They were late for school this morning. Janie said her alarm didn't go off. Also, can you have another look at her finances? She says she's struggling.'

'I will, and I'll see what I can do about the alarm,' I added. We said goodbye.

I was sad and disappointed in Janie, not so much because she hadn't managed to get the children to school on time, but because she was acting irresponsibly. Bowie had a criminal record for drug dealing, which she hadn't thought to mention when she'd been singing his praises to me, and there'd been an incident of domestic violence with him when they'd lived together. Had I known these things, my reaction to her question would have been very different. By having Bowie in the home, she was placing her children at risk. I knew she'd just taken a step closer to losing them all and I hoped Liv gave her another chance and talked some sense into her.

* * *

On Tuesday afternoon I had some me-time. I did some writing as well as catching up with the housework, and preparing the evening meal for when Paula came home from work. I also found a bedside alarm clock I'd used when I'd fostered a teenager who couldn't get up for school. I replaced the batteries and tested it, and nearly jumped out of my skin. I'd forgotten how loud it was. It rang for a minute, then every two minutes, until it was silenced. I remember I'd heard it from my bedroom at the front of the house and she'd slept at the back. Even if Janie managed to sleep through it, I felt sure the children would hear it and wake her. I knew Janie had problems sleeping and often played on the Xbox until the early hours, then struggled to get up on time.

The following morning, I left Paula getting ready for work and headed for Janie's again. It was another clear, cold winter day. The lights were on in her home, which was a good sign. When I pressed the doorbell Riley answered it in his pyjamas.

'Hi, love, is Mum up?' I asked.

'She's in the kitchen,' he said, and began down the hall.

I followed but had only taken a couple of steps when I nearly lost my footing. The floor was moving. I looked down and saw marbles everywhere. Riley kicked a few out of the way, sending them crashing against the skirting board with a loud thud.

'We'd better pick those up, love,' I said. 'Where's the tub they came in?'

'I dunno,' he said. 'I've got to get dressed.' He disappeared into his bedroom.

I found Janie in the kitchen feeding Lola. There were

71

marbles running all over the floor in there too. I hadn't realized the box held so many.

'Good morning,' I said.

Janie shrugged.

'Everything OK?' I asked. 'Apart from the marbles.'

She shrugged again. There was an atmosphere.

I spotted the tub the marbles had come in on the work surface beside the empty marble jar and the flowers I'd given her in a large beer glass. 'I'll clear up the marbles,' I said, taking the tub, and I began picking them up.

'Liv was here yesterday,' Janie volunteered, her voice flat. 'The nasty cow said I may have to choose between Bowie and my kids.'

I left the marbles and looked at Janie. She was very tense, holding in her anger and upset. I wasn't convinced that was how Liv would have phrased it, although I thought it was likely to be the gist of what she'd said. At that moment Jayden and Riley ran into the kitchen, skidding on the marbles. Riley was fully dressed in his school uniform but Jayden just had his pants on.

'Shall we have a chat once they're in school?' I suggested to Janie. 'You don't want to be late again.'

'If you like,' she said, off-hand. Then to Jayden she yelled, 'Will you get dressed! It was your fault we were late yesterday.'

'No, it wasn't!' he shouted back. 'It was yours!' He ran off, kicking the marbles as he went. I began to wonder if the marble jar had been a good idea.

Riley helped himself to cereal and I continued picking up the marbles, working my way across the kitchen floor and then down the hall. I snapped shut the lid on the tub and by the time I'd returned to the kitchen both boys were having breakfast.

'Only your mother touches this,' I said to the boys in a firm, authoritative voice. I placed the tub on the shelf out of reach. 'Does everyone understand?'

'You can't tell us what to do,' Jayden said defiantly.

'Yes, she can,' Riley told him. 'She's here to help us, so listen.'

I was taken aback but pleased. To have Riley on side would help. 'Thank you, love,' I said. 'And it's important you both do what your mother asks as well.'

'Am I going bowling with you and Riley?' Jayden asked.

'If you have a good week,' I replied.

Not bribery, but an incentive for positive behaviour, just as the marble jar was supposed to be.

'As Riley and Jayden are both dressed and eating their breakfast nicely, I think that deserves a marble each, don't you?' I suggested to Janie.

'If you want,' she replied, with a complete lack of enthusiasm. Thankfully the boys didn't notice.

'Yes, a marble!' Riley said. 'And when the jar is full we get a chocolate bar.'

'That's right. I want one too,' Jayden said.

As they finished their breakfasts I reached for the tub of marbles and the jar and, placing them ceremoniously on the table, allowed the boys to choose one colourful marble each and drop it into the jar.

'Well done, both of you,' I said.

'Yes, well done,' Janie added.

And the looks on their faces at hearing their mother's praise said it all. They'd done something right and had achieved her approval. Children need praise – they thrive on it – as much as, if not more than, correction for negative behaviour.

CHAPTER NINE

A SURPRISE!

That morning I went with Janie to take the children to school as she wanted to talk about Liv's visit. I waited outside the school gates while she took them in, then on the way back she heatedly told me what Liv had said about Bowie: that he shouldn't be coming into her home and having contact with the children, given his history of drug dealing and the incident of domestic violence. Janie was adamant that Bowie no longer 'did drugs' and the domestic violence was a 'one-off', when an argument had got out of hand. Janie was indignant, saying everyone deserved a second chance, and was angry that Liv wouldn't give him that chance, which was fair enough. However, I could see Liv's point of view as she needed to safeguard the children. I appreciated what a difficult job the social worker had in getting the balance right and knowing when to act. Supposing Liv did nothing and one of the children was harmed as a result? She would be held responsible. Liv had told Janie she would look into setting up supervised contact so that Bowie could see Lola away from the family home. But that wasn't what Janie wanted to hear as she had her sights set on him and his children living with them as one big happy family, which as far as I could see wasn't going to happen in the foreseeable future.

Janie let off steam on the way home and once we'd arrived I asked her if it was a good time to have another look at her finances as Liv had asked me to. Janie said now was as good a time as any. She made us a mug of tea each and then we sat at the small table in the kitchen-diner to look over her finances again. Managing money had always been a problem for Janie, as it is for many who rely on benefits. The first week I'd been involved with Janie and her family I'd gone through her income and expenditure and drawn up a simple plan to help her budget. I'd asked her to keep receipts, as it's easier to see where money is going with receipts, and she had been doing this – paper and digital. We checked her direct debits but none of those had gone up. Using the calculator on my phone, we added up her expenditure and income and there was a deficit of over £200 – a lot for someone on a low income. Janie had effectively run out of money and wouldn't get any more until the end of the week.

'Are these all the receipts?' I asked her, puzzled.

'Yes. I swear.'

I went through it all again, searching for something I'd missed, but I couldn't see where over £200 had gone.

'You're sure you haven't bought anything and forgotten?' I asked. 'Maybe something for your home?'

'No,' she said, shaking her head vehemently, and continued to drink her tea.

I gazed at the figures, trying to work out why she'd run out of money. It was tight, but according to my calculations she should have had enough to see her through to the end of the week, with a little left over.

'Oh, hang on a moment,' Janie suddenly said. 'I remember now. I lent Bowie some money.'

'How much?' I asked.

'Well, it could have been two hundred quid, I suppose. But not all at once, of course. I've been giving him twenty here and there. It adds up.'

'Yes, it does. They were loans?'

'Yes, although I haven't seen any of it back yet,' she admitted.

'You think it could have added up to two hundred pounds?'

'Yes, I guess it could. I lost track.'

What could I say? Janie found it difficult to manage anyway and Bowie had taken money that should have been spent on her and the children. I wondered if she'd remembered the loans earlier but hadn't liked to say.

'I've told Bowie that's all he's having,' Janie said. 'There's no more because I can't manage on what I get. I've got to feed and clothe my kids.'

'Yes,' I said, and hoped she meant it.

'Will you tell Liv?' Janie asked.

'Only if she asks.'

'Shall I keep these?' she said, collecting up the paper receipts.

'I would for now.'

Janie busied herself for a few moments returning the receipts to the kitchen drawer, which acted as a filing cabinet. I felt sorry for her. She knew what she'd done was irresponsible, effectively depriving her children, but she couldn't help herself.

'Have you got food to last for the week?' I asked.

'Not a lot, and I'm out of milk.'

'We'll make a list of what you need to see you through to the end of the week and I'll drop it off later.' I wasn't going to give her cash in case that went to Bowie, but I wouldn't stand by and let her and the children go hungry.

'Thanks,' she said.

'Liv told me your alarm didn't go off yesterday,' I said, 'so I wondered if this would help?' I took the alarm from my bag. 'We don't use it any more. It's very loud.' I gave her a demonstration.

'I should hear that!' she exclaimed with a smile.

'As long as you remember to set it,' I said.

She laughed. 'Yes, that's true. I think you know me better than I know myself. You're a good sort. Can you tell Liv I'm doing my best?'

'I will.'

There always seemed to be a new challenge or hurdle to overcome in Janie's life. As fast as we dealt with one issue, another appeared. Janie found it difficult to take these problems in her stride, presumably because she was only ever just about coping, rather than being in control of life. It didn't take much to throw her off course and into a panic, when she would go on the defensive, became agitated and blame everyone else, instead of taking on board what she was being told.

At 12.15 that Wednesday morning, I hadn't long since returned from looking at Janie's finances when she phoned. I knew she would have collected Lola from nursery at this time and be on her way home.

'Is everything all right?' I asked.

'No, it isn't! Mrs Sykes asked to have a word with me when I collected Lola,' Janie began, all het up. 'She's just

given me a lecture about how I need to start toilet training her so she's ready to start school in September. She
said she needs to feed herself better too, as they haven't
got the staff in reception to feed and change the children.
Cheeky moo! Telling me what to do! She said most of
Lola's age group are out of nappies and feeding themselves. Well, good for them, I say!'

Janie had taken it personally, but of course Mrs Sykes,
the head of the nursery, was right. Lola would be four
when she started Reception and so should be out of
nappies and feeding herself by then. Most children are
toilet trained by the age of three. I'd read a comment in a
report that Janie tended to 'baby' Lola, so that rather than
encouraging age-appropriate self-care, she kept Lola
dependent. It was thought to make her feel wanted. I'd
seen this too in Janie. Lola was her baby and she wanted
to keep her like that for as long as possible. But while that
fulfilled a need in Janie, it wasn't good for Lola's develop-
ment.

'I bet she's told Liv!' Janie ended.

'When were the boys toilet-trained and feeding themselves?' I asked.

'I don't know. I can't remember. As soon as I could, I
guess.'

'Janie, it will be a lot less work for you and cheaper
when Lola is toilet-trained. Nappies are expensive. And
she will need to feed herself before long.'

'So you agree with Mrs Sykes!' Janie snapped.

'Well, yes, I do.'

'Thanks for nothing!' she said, and ended the call.

I didn't take it to heart. Janie tended to react
before she'd had time to think. She was like a firecracker

sometimes. A big bang, a whoosh, then quickly fizzling out. I gave her ten minutes to calm down and then texted.

I'm going shopping soon. I'll drop off what you need around 2pm if that's OK. Cathy

She replied: *Thanks x*

I went supermarket shopping and bought what was on Janie's list, plus a few extras for her and the children. I arrived at her home shortly after 2 p.m. As she let me in all previous animosity had gone, as I thought it would be. I followed her into the living room where Lola was sitting on the sofa watching television and eating a banana. I think it was the first time I'd seen her feeding herself. Usually, Janie spoon-fed her or popped bits of food into her mouth like a mother bird.

'That looks yummy,' I said to Lola. 'Good girl.'

'I've found the potty I used with the boys,' Janie said. 'I'll start tomorrow.'

It seemed that, despite Janie's anger and indignation at Mrs Sykes's advice, she was following it.

'Well done,' I said. 'Remember it's the three Ps when it comes to potty training – potty, patience and perseverance.'

'And piss!' Janie exclaimed with a smile. I smiled too. 'I'm doing my best,' she said. 'I just wish everyone would get off my back.'

'I think Mrs Sykes only meant well and wanted to help,' I said. 'Better to know now than have a problem when Lola starts school in September.'

'Maybe.'

Janie didn't need any advice from me on potty training as she'd done it twice before with the boys. I stayed for about fifteen minutes, then said goodbye and that I'd be back as planned at 7.45 on Friday morning. Bowie wasn't mentioned.

I was seeing more of Janie and her family than originally planned, as do many family support workers. We bond with the family and do what is necessary to help them to a better future. Like fostering, it wasn't a 9-to-5 job and I often took Janie's problems home with me. In the evening I found myself thinking about her and wondering how she was doing. Now I hoped she wasn't letting Bowie into her home again.

I didn't hear from Janie again until Thursday evening when she texted.

We've got a surprise for you. Show you tomorrow x

I naively assumed it was regarding Lola feeding herself or potty training, as that had been the focus of my last visit. I texted back: *Great. Look forward to it. Don't forget to set the alarm clock.*

On Friday morning when I arrived all the lights were on – a positive sign that someone was up. I pressed the doorbell and immediately a dog began barking – the high-pitched yap of a puppy. To begin with I thought it was the television, which was often on in the morning, sometimes quite loudly. But when the yapping came closer to the other side of the front door I thought it might be a new toy Janie had bought for the children. Some of them are very realistic and life-like. But then Riley opened the door in his pyjamas with a real, live puppy in his arms – a Staffordshire bull terrier.

CHAPTER TEN

MAX

'Is that yours?' I asked, hoping he would say no and that they were looking after it for someone.

'Yes. He's called Max,' Riley replied, kissing the top of the dog's head.

I tried to hide my concerns as I went down the hall to the kitchen-diner. I love animals and my family has had plenty of pets over the years. Our last cat, Sammy, had died from old age at the end of the previous year. But I knew that pets, especially puppies, took a great deal of looking after, and it was another mouth for Janie to feed on a tight budget.

'Bowie wanted to call him Killer,' Riley said as we entered the kitchen. 'But I've called him Max.'

Janie shot Riley a censoring look at the mention of Bowie as it suggested he'd seen them recently.

'We've got a puppy,' Jayden told me, delighted.

'Yes, so I see.'

They were supposed to be dressed or at least getting dressed at this time, but they were all still in their night-wear, including Janie. The puppy's needs had clearly taken precedence over the routine I'd been working on with Janie.

'Doggy,' Lola said, trying to reach him in Riley's arms. 'My doggy.'

'No, he's not!' Riley said, snatching him away. 'Mum said he's everyone's, didn't you, Mum?' Riley lifted Max high into the air so Lola couldn't possibly reach him, even on tiptoes.

She screamed and burst into tears. Janie was trying to make herself a mug of tea but turned from what she was doing to shout at Riley.

'Let her stroke him! I've told you before. Now!'

Riley lowered Max to just within Lola's reach and she petted him. Janie stirred her tea and looked at me. 'Well? What do you think?' she asked. 'You're not saying much.'

'About the dog?'

She nodded.

'I'm just a bit surprised,' I admitted. 'I didn't know you were thinking of buying a pet.'

'I wasn't,' Janie said. 'I bumped into someone I know who breeds Staffs [a common name for Staffordshire bull terriers]. She got left with that one in the litter and she's going away tomorrow for a month so had to get rid of him quickly.'

'So you're just looking after him while she's away?' I asked, wondering if I'd misunderstood.

'No. I bought him – well, not all at once,' Janie said. 'She usually sells them for five hundred quid, but she knows I'm hard up so let me have him for two hundred. I'm paying her off at ten pounds a week – more if I can afford it.'

'What about vaccinations?' I asked, as chaos erupted around us. Riley had put Max on the floor and all three children were trying to excite the puppy and make him chase them by jumping around and yelping in front of him. Max was also yelping.

'I think puppies like some quiet time,' I said to the children. They ignored me.

'He's had his puppy vaccines. The next one is a booster at six months,' Janie replied over the noise.

'I think vet bills can be expensive.'

'There's a place does it for nothing it you are on benefit,' Janie replied. 'You're just asked to make a donation. I'll get him a proper bed when I can afford it.' There was a cardboard box with a towel in it acting as a makeshift bed in one corner of the kitchen.

The children were still on the floor winding up Max, now trying to make him jump. Max got so excited he peed on the floor, as puppies do. Janie laughed. 'It's non-stop widdle and poo here.'

And sure enough, right on cue, Max squatted and began to strain.

'Take him outside!' Janie yelled at Riley.

Too late. As Riley picked up Max, pellets of poo dropped to the floor.

'He's pooed on the floor again!' Jayden shouted.

'Poo!' Lola cried.

'Take him out!' Janie yelled again. Riley disappeared down the hall as Janie tore off a strip of kitchen towel and used it to pick up the poo, dropping it in the rubbish bin in the kitchen.

There wasn't a back door to their property, so Riley had to go out the front door and then around the back. There was a small piece of communal lawn at the rear and we could see Riley through the window in the kitchen-diner. Janie banged on the glass to get Riley's attention. 'Make sure Max doesn't run off!' she yelled, for he wasn't on a lead.

I was more concerned that Riley was out there in his pyjamas in the middle of winter. I still had on my coat and shoes; I hadn't had a chance to take them off.

'I'll take him his coat and shoes,' I said. I knew where they were in the hall. 'You'd better start getting the others ready for school,' I reminded Janie. 'It's after eight o'clock.'

I found Riley's coat and shoes in the box in the hall where they kept them and went outside. I waited with Riley but Max didn't want to go to the toilet again so we returned indoors.

'You need to get ready,' I told Riley.

He disappeared into his bedroom with Max in his arms. Jayden was already in there, hopefully getting dressed. I could hear Janie with Lola in the bathroom. I went into the kitchen-diner and took out the bucket and cleaning products from the cupboard under the sink. I ran some hot water, added disinfectant, took a cleaning cloth and wiped the floor where Max had gone to the toilet. The children played on the floor so it seemed sensible to make sure there was no residual bacteria left behind.

Janie and Lola appeared, dressed first. I could hear the boys in their bedroom playing with Max.

'I didn't need your alarm clock to wake me,' Janie said, sitting Lola at the table. 'Max was whining and yelping all night. I guess he missed his mother so I took him into my bed, but he weed on the duvet. I'll have to wash that later.'

I nodded and checked my watch. 'It's eight-fifteen, love.'

'Riley! Jayden! Are you ready?' Janie shouted.

And so the chaos continued. I did what I could to help and eventually they were all washed and dressed and had had some breakfast, but they were late leaving for school. I didn't say what I was thinking to Janie: that this wasn't the right time in her life to buy a puppy and she should be concentrating on her children.

Liv, however, didn't have the same reluctance to share her thoughts. Janie phoned me later that morning – I seemed to be her first point of contact when anything went wrong. She had just phoned Liv to tell her the children had been late for school, feeling it was better that she told her rather than Liv finding out from school. She'd used Max as the excuse, saying that 'a new addition to their family' was the reason for them being late, assuming Liv would be pleased she had a pet. It seemed Liv had the same concerns I did and had expressed them. How was Janie going to afford to look after a dog? Was the dog safe with young children? How would it fit into their routine and lifestyle? Who was going to walk it? Train it? And so forth. Janie had told Liv that as Lola was getting older and more independent, and was starting school in September, she wouldn't need her so much so she'd have time to look after the dog, and that without Max she would be lonely. It was sad and simplistic. Liv had concluded by telling Janie she'd need to visit and complete a dog assessment form.

'A dog assessment form! Daft cow!' Janie had scorned when she'd phoned to tell me.

'They're also used to assess foster carers' dogs,' I told her. 'To make sure the children are safe with the dog and it won't bite them.'

'Max wouldn't harm anyone.'

Having let off steam, Janie hurriedly said she needed to go now as she was meeting a man about a dog bed.

'I'll see you tonight then at five o'clock,' I said. It was Friday, so I would collect Riley later as he was staying with me for the weekend.

'Oh, yes, see you later,' Janie said, clearly preoccupied. And the phone went dead.

When I returned at five o'clock to collect Riley it was a while before the door was answered, this time by five-year-old Jayden. He literally flung it back and ran inside. I closed the door and went into the kitchen-diner where they all were. Janie was at the cooker and the children were on the floor playing with Max. My gaze went to the new, luxurious fur-lined dog's bed, which had replaced the cardboard box. In it were some puppy toys, including a comforter much like those babies have. Other toys were near the bed. Max was wearing a smart red collar, and a matching lead hung over a chair. My first thought was: how much had all this cost?

'I'm knackered, I've been out all day,' Janie said, adding pasta to a pan of boiling water. 'But I did well. Look what I got.'

'Yes, Max will be very comfortable,' I said.

'And it didn't cost me a penny!' Janie continued. 'Well, apart from the bus fare and the McDonald's that Lola and I had for lunch. I saw an advertisement on Gumtree [a website for buying and selling items locally]. I phoned and arranged to go after I collected Lola from nursery. It was the son of an elderly lady. Her husband had died and she was lonely so he'd bought her a puppy to keep her company, but she couldn't cope with it and he'd had to have it rehomed. He was asking for forty quid for all the stuff but when I said I was on benefits and couldn't afford to pay him until next week he told me I could have it for nothing. He said his mother was upset and he just wanted rid of all the stuff. I did well, didn't I?'

'Yes. That was a good find,' I said. I guessed new the items would have cost over a hundred pounds.

Yet while Janie had done well, my thoughts went to the son and his mother. In an act of kindness, he'd bought her a puppy to keep her company, but it had backfired, as it does for many. On average 130,000 dogs need to be rehomed every year in the UK, and one in ten puppies after only a month. The numbers went up after the pandemic when puppies and dogs bought during lock-down didn't fit in with the family's lifestyle once normality returned.

'I told him to thank his mother and tell her I'd put the things to good use,' Janie said. 'It was a struggle bringing them home on the bus, but worth it.'

'Yes, indeed. I can give Riley dinner at my house,' I said, as Janie strained the pasta.

'Oh, I forgot to tell you. He isn't going to you this weekend. He wants to stay with Max.'

Riley didn't have to stay with me. He wasn't in care as a result of a court order, which would have been very different. The weekend respite had been put in place to help Janie.

'Sure?' I asked.

'Riley, do you want to go to Cathy's for the weekend?' she said.

'No,' he replied decisively, his attention on Max.

'What about bowling on Sunday afternoon?' I checked. 'I think the boys were looking forward to it.'

'Riley, Jayden, do you want to go bowling with Cathy on Sunday?'

'Can Max come?' Riley asked.

'No, love,' I replied. 'Dogs aren't allowed in the leisure centre, apart from assistance dogs.'

'I'm not going then,' Riley said adamantly.

'Me neither,' Jayden added.

'All right. Have a good weekend and I'll see you as usual on Monday morning.' And, saying goodbye, I let myself out.

With the weekend now suddenly free, I texted my family's WhatsApp group: *Are you able to come for lunch tomorrow? Love Mum xx*

By the time I was home they'd replied saying they were. So Friday evening I took the ingredients I needed from the freezer, then on Saturday morning, instead of entertaining Riley, I cooked. Chicken casserole followed by apple pie and custard – a real winter warmer. It was a lovely day, my children and grandchildren all together. As often happened when we were together our conversation turned to my parents – Nana and Grandpa, and how they used to love our family gatherings. We looked at some photographs and video clips.

I played with Emma and held the babies, and we took more photographs. I'll admit, with only a touch of guilt, that without having to watch Riley the whole time and keep him amused, it was far more relaxing than the previous weekend had been. I hoped he and his family were having a nice day, although I could imagine it could be quite stressful and full-on with the puppy as well.

I was right. On Sunday morning Janie texted me: *Can you take the boys out? They're doing my head in!*

CHAPTER ELEVEN

A WORRYING PHONE CALL

I could have said no to Janie's request to take Riley and Jayden out that Sunday afternoon, and if I'd had a prior arrangement I would very likely have done so. Although I wanted to help Janie, I wasn't at her beck and call, and she'd cancelled the bowling trip. However, I didn't have anything pressing to do so I texted back: *I'll collect the boys after lunch at 2pm. I'll take them bowling and bring them back after.*

Paula decided to come bowling with us but waited in the car while I went in and collected the boys. They were ready and just had to put on their shoes and coats. Max was asleep in his bed and Lola was watching television.

'I know I have to clear up,' Janie said. 'Once the boys are out of the way, I'll have a chance to do it if Max stays asleep.'

I wasn't going to say anything, but the place was a mess. Plates, dishes, cups, empty crisp packets, children's toys and discarded clothes lay where they'd been left. There was a pile of dirty washing on the kitchen floor waiting to go into the machine, and the sink and draining board were littered with other items.

'I've booked the bowling for two-thirty,' I said. 'So I'll bring them back around four-thirty to five.'

'Can you get them something to eat? They've only had breakfast,' she replied.

'All right.'

'But don't tell Liv,' Janie added, as she often did.

Janie seemed to imagine that I spent my free time reporting her latest transgression to her social worker – 'Liv, Janie didn't give the boys lunch on Sunday ...' and so forth. I always wrote or spoke of Janie in as positive terms as possible, so, for example, today I would include in my log that I took Riley and Jayden bowling and gave them lunch as Janie had asked me to, so it wasn't an issue.

The boys needed no encouragement to put on their coats and shoes as they were eager to go bowling now. I told them to say goodbye, and we left.

'Mum says you're going to buy us burger and chips,' Riley told me as soon as we were outside.

'Yes, if you're hungry, at the leisure centre.'

'I want chicken nuggets and chips,' Jayden said.

'OK.'

I opened the rear door and they clambered into the back of the car. I checked their seatbelts were fastened. Paula was in the front passenger seat and made conversation with them as I drove, asking them about Max and school and so on. They were chatty, excited to have a puppy, and to be going bowling. Riley was wondering if he would see the boy from his school again at the leisure centre, but their conversation kept returning to Max.

'I'm the only one who's allowed to take Max outside,' Riley announced proudly. 'Jayden and Lola are too little.'

'No, I'm not,' Jayden retaliated.

'Yes, you are,' Max said. 'Mum said I'm in charge of him outside.'

'But inside we are all in charge,' Jayden said.

'Yes, but Lola can't be in charge, she's too small.'

'Lola is too small,' Jayden agreed. 'But we aren't.'

And so their conversation continued as they do between young children.

Once at the leisure centre we went straight to the café where I ordered the boys the meals they wanted, as they were hungry. They had just enough time to eat it before it was our turn to play on lane five. Riley was still looking out for the boy he'd seen last week, but I explained that he probably didn't come every week, just occasionally as a treat.

'Can we come every week?' Riley asked.

'We'll have to see,' I said.

Riley had remembered some of the bowling technique Paula and I had taught him the week before and didn't feel he needed our help until his bowls started bouncing straight into the gulley. He got annoyed and finally allowed Paula to show him again. This was Jayden's first time bowling, so we helped him as we had Riley. Paula won both games, although we said it was close. Riley and Jayden wanted to go into the amusement section before we left – an area with video games, pinball machines, claw cranes, coin-pushers and so on. We limited our time there to half an hour, so it was approaching five o'clock by the time we arrived back at their home. The boys were in a jubilant mood and looking forward to seeing Max again.

'I hope Max hasn't done another smelly poo-poo,' Riley said, grinning and pulling a face.

'Poooooo! Poooooo!' Jayden laughed, pinching his nose. Like many young children, they found toilet-talk amusing.

I was expecting Janie to have benefited from an afternoon with just her and Lola.

Paula said goodbye to the boys in the car and I went with them to their front door.

'I'm telling Mum I nearly won bowling,' Riley said.

'I came second,' Jayden said.

I smiled, but as Janie opened the door she looked upset. The boys didn't notice. They shot in past her, eager to see Max.

'Are you all right?' I asked Janie.

'Not really.'

'What's the matter?'

She shrugged despondently.

'Is it something I can help with?'

'No. I'll phone you later,' she said. 'I can't talk about it now.'

She hadn't invited me in, so I had to accept she didn't want my help, although I was concerned. It took a lot to upset Janie. If there was a problem, she usually reacted with anger and indignation, but now she looked down and close to tears.

'Are you sure you'll be OK?' I asked.

She nodded. 'I'll phone you later.'

I came away puzzled and troubled. It couldn't be anything to do with Liv or the social services – a common reason for Janie reacting – as it was Sunday, so only the duty social worker was on call for emergencies. The children were all right, so I wondered if Janie was ill, and had perhaps received the results of medical tests. But again, it was unlikely on a Sunday. I couldn't work out what had upset her.

It was nearly 9 p.m. when Janie called my mobile. I was in the living room and Paula was in her bedroom.

'It's me,' Janie said, her voice flat.

'Hello, love. What's the matter?'

'Bowie,' she said.

'What is it?'

'He's left me.'

'Oh, I see.' But I'm sorry to say, my first thought was: that might not be a bad thing.

'He's gone back to live with the mother of his older kids,' Janie said. 'She's pregnant again.'

'With his baby?' I asked, taken aback.

'That's what he says. He sent me a text this afternoon – couldn't even tell me to my face.' I understood why she was taking it so badly.

'So he's been seeing her while he's been seeing you?' I said.

'Spot on. I phoned him when I got his text, and he said his other kids were in care and he wasn't going to let it happen to this one. He said as he couldn't move in with me, he would live with her.'

Fickle and selfish were just some of the words that came to my mind about Bowie, but I kept them to myself. I try not to be judgemental – you can't afford to be in fostering – but Bowie's actions were irresponsible and deceitful. What about the long-term happiness and stability of the children he'd fathered and their mothers? He appeared not to have given them a second thought.

'I am sorry, Janie,' I said. 'He's behaved despicably. I know you were hoping you'd be together properly at some point.' Indeed, as far as I knew that had been their plan only a few days ago, despite Liv's cautionary words.

'Bowie said he's going to get custody of his other two now. He's obsessed with it. It's like he owns them. He says he'll stand more chance if he's living with her.'

'I doubt it,' I said. 'The same criteria will apply, and his older children are settled with their foster carers.'

'I told him not to come here any more, but he says he has a right to see Lola. I don't want him here again.'

'Liv mentioned setting up supervised contact at the Family Centre,' I reminded her.

'He won't like that.'

'To be honest, Janie, it will be what is in the best interests of Lola, not Bowie.'

'He can get nasty if he doesn't get his own way.'

'You won't have to see him. If Liv sets up contact at the Family Centre, a contact supervisor could collect Lola from you and bring her back. I'm aware of similar happening in other families. And if Bowie starts to harass you then call the police.'

'They'll be sick of me,' she said. The police had been called to incidents of domestic violence in her previous relationship with Rhys – the one she'd fled from. 'I'll phone Liv tomorrow,' Janie said in the same depressed tone. 'When I told Riley and Jayden they wouldn't be seeing Bowie any more they were pleased.'

'Riley told me he didn't like Bowie when he stayed with me last weekend. I told him to tell you.'

'He might have done,' Janie said lethargically. 'I probably didn't take much notice. I wouldn't have anything bad said against Bowie then. I thought he deserved another chance. I believed what he said about wanting to be a family and being sorry for the way he'd acted in the past.' Her voice broke and she began to cry.

'Oh, Janie, you're upset.' I would rather have heard her being angry and calling Bowie names. 'Are the children in bed?' I asked, my first thought going to them.

'Yes,' she said through her tears. 'I can't seem to do anything right. Others treat me like shit. Perhaps I deserve it.' Janie had faced many ordeals and issues in her life, and while I hadn't known her long – just over six weeks – it seemed Bowie's deceitful actions were the final straw.

I waited while she recovered a little, concerned she was by herself.

'Do you have a friend or neighbour who could come in and be with you for a while?' I asked. She'd mentioned she'd made friends with some of her neighbours.

'I don't want to see anyone right now,' she replied.

'Do you want me to come over?'

'No, not even you. Thanks anyway.'

'What will you do?'

'What I usually do when the shit hits the fan: have a few beers and go to bed.'

'Are you sure you don't want some company?' I asked.

'No. I'll see you in the morning.'

She said goodbye and ended the call.

I felt sorry for Janie. Despite my feeling that Bowie being out of her life was for the best, he had betrayed her, undermining her confidence even further.

I was worried, so fifteen minutes later I texted: *Are you OK?*

She didn't reply. I tried to phone but it went through to voicemail, so I left a message: 'Just wanted to make sure you're OK. Please text if you are awake, otherwise see you in the morning.'

It was difficult to know what to do. If Janie had been very distressed when she'd called me, threatening to take her own life, and now wasn't answering her phone, I would have called the emergency duty social worker and probably gone to her home. She'd been down, but not enough to make me think she was severely depressed and at risk of suicide. I tried to phone her again before I went to bed but it went through to voicemail again. I convinced myself that she'd had a few beers and an early night as she'd said, and hoped she'd feel brighter in the morning and realize she was better off without Bowie.

Having said that, I checked my phone in the night. There was nothing from Janie, but I told myself I was worrying unnecessarily, which I am prone to do. I think it comes from being a parent, as I know others react similarly. I can imagine all sorts of dreadful scenarios if my children are late or not answering their phones, even though they're adults. I can easily transfer these concerns to others I care about or are responsible for.

The following morning when I checked my phone there was still nothing from Janie, but as I was seeing her shortly I didn't phone again. I showered and dressed and drove to her house on another cold day. The sky was overcast and rain was forecast later. I parked outside Janie's flat at 7.40 a.m. There were no lights on. My concerns increased. I went up the path, pressed the doorbell and waited. Someone should be up by now. Max began yelping. I pressed the bell again and a few moments later the light went on in the hall. Riley opened the door in his pyjamas with Max in his arms.

'Mum says she's staying in bed and you'll have to take us to school,' he said.

'Why? What's the matter?' I asked, going in.

'I don't know,' Riley said. 'But there's a lot of Max's poop to clear up.'

I could smell it, and further up the hall I spotted a lump of dog poo. Lola and Jayden came out of the children's bedroom. 'Mind where you walk,' I said, and went to them.

'Yuck,' Jayden said, pulling a face.

'Where's Mummy?' Lola asked.

'In bed, love. I want you all to start getting ready for school while I speak to Mummy, then I'll clear up,' I said.

'Mummy,' Lola said.

'She'll be up soon,' I said. 'I want you to be a big girl and start getting dressed.'

'I'll help her,' Riley offered.

'Good boy.'

Riley took Jayden and Lola into their bedroom and I knocked on Janie's bedroom door, then slowly opened it.

'Janie, it's Cathy,' I said, taking a step in.

There were no curtains at the window in her bedroom, and by the early-morning light coming from outside I could see Janie lying in bed on her side, duvet pulled up and partially covering her face.

'Janie, it's Cathy,' I said again. I stepped over the clothes and other items that littered the floor and went to her bed. 'Janie.'

'What?' she said groggily.

'It's Monday. Are you ill?' She kept her eyes closed.

'Can you see to my kids?' she mumbled. 'I'm not getting up.'

'Why? Have you got a hangover?' There were three empty beer bottles on the floor beside her bed.

'No. I just can't face another day. You can tell Liv if you want to.'

And at that point I knew we had a big problem.

CHAPTER TWELVE

WHAT'S WRONG WITH MUMMY?

'Janie,' I said, perching on the edge of her bed. 'I think you should get up and have a shower, then see how you feel.'

'No,' she replied, her eyes still closed.

'Why not?'

'Because I can't,' she mumbled from beneath the bed covers.

I could hear Riley, Jayden and Lola in their bedroom, hopefully getting dressed, and Max yelping.

'Your children need you,' I said.

'No, they don't. They're better off without me.'

This wasn't like Janie, not the person I knew. She was a fighter.

'Janie, have you ever felt like this before?' I asked. 'Really low.'

She gave a small nod.

'What did you do to feel better?'

'Went to the doctor. He gave me tablets.'

'Antidepressants?'

'Yes.'

'Do you still take them?'

She nodded again.

'You took one yesterday?'

'Yes.'

'Just one?'

'Yes.'

'Then drank all this beer?' I asked, keeping the censure from my voice.

She didn't reply. I picked up one of the bottles and looked at the label. They were large bottles of a strong-brew beer containing 7 per cent alcohol. I knew from my foster-care training on substance misuse that antidepressants shouldn't be combined with alcohol. It can be dangerous and worsen the symptoms, causing the person to become more depressed and anxious. Was this what had caused Janie's depression?

'Did you drink all these last night?' I asked.

'Yes. I needed to get Bowie out of my head.'

And while I could understand Janie's need to self-medicate after Bowie's deception, it had been the wrong decision.

The children's voices were getting louder in the bedroom and Max was yelping continuously.

'If you can get up and have a shower, I'll see to the children,' I said.

There was no response.

If someone is feeling low, there are strategies to help them out of it, but Janie was on medication for depression and had drunk a lot of alcohol. While her life wasn't in danger – she wasn't unconscious – I felt she needed medical advice.

'I think you should phone your doctor,' I said.

'Not now,' she mumbled. 'Get the kids to school.'

I hesitated. 'All right. But speak to your doctor later. Do you want a drink and something to eat?'

'Just water.'

I left Janie's room, checked on the children, who were getting ready despite all the noise, and then, walking round the poo in the hall, went into the kitchen-diner. There were puddles of what I assumed was Max's urine on the floor. I stepped over those and poured a glass of water, which I took to Janie.

'I'll leave your water by your bed,' I said, putting the glass on the floor.

'Ta,' she mumbled, half asleep.

'Have a drink and see if you can get up.'

I left her to it and went into the children's room. They were nearly dressed, just putting on their socks. Riley was helping Lola.

'Well done. I want you to stay in here until I've cleared up Max's mess,' I told them.

I returned to the kitchen where I put on rubber gloves, tore off kitchen towel and collected up the dog poop from the hall. I put it into the bin, sealed the bag and took it to the wheelie bin outside. Indoors, I ran hot water into the bucket, added disinfectant and on my hands and knees began cleaning the floor again. It was now after 8 a.m. and the children should have been having their breakfast. As I worked I felt annoyed with Janie. Of course I was concerned for her well-being, but I also felt irritated that she'd drunk all that beer, and bought a puppy, which had caused all this extra work. What would she have done if I hadn't been on hand to help?

Once I'd cleaned the floor, I told the children they could come out of their bedroom and have breakfast.

'Is Mum getting up?' Riley asked.

'Later,' I said.

'Are you taking us to school?' Jayden wanted to know.

'I think so.'

Lola went to find her mother and I brought her back. 'You'll see Mummy later,' I said. 'We need to get you to nursery.'

The boys were used to getting their own cereal and I asked Lola what she wanted. She didn't know.

'Banana,' Riley replied.

I found some bananas in a bag of shopping on the countertop in the kitchen. Unzipping one, I gave it to Lola together with a drink of milk, which I'd seen Janie give her. The boys had some milk on their cereal and a glass of juice. Leaving them eating, I checked on Janie. She was still in bed but had drunk some of the water.

'Are you getting up?' I asked.

'No.'

'The children are having breakfast. Do you want me to take them to school?'

'Yes.' Which I'd assumed.

'I'll have to phone the duty social worker to let them know what's going on. Liv won't be in yet.'

'Suit yourself,' she said testily.

I needed to phone the social services for advice and to cover myself. As the children ate their breakfast, I called the number for the duty social worker. He answered straight away and I gave my name, and explained my role in respect of Janie, her family and the current situation.

'She's conscious and talking so doesn't need immediate medical assistance?' he checked.

'No. I don't think so. She's drunk some water too.

After I've taken the children to school, I'll come straight back and make sure she contacts her doctor.'

'Yes. I'll pass this on to their social worker to deal with, as she will be in shortly.'

'Thank you.'

I said goodbye and turned my attention to the children, who were all looking at me.

'What's wrong with Mummy?' Riley asked.

'She's not feeling well, love. Don't worry, I am sure she'll be better later.'

'Mummy,' Lola said, her little face sad.

'She's having a rest. Let's get you all ready for school and nursery.'

'Can we have a marble then?' Jayden asked.

'Thank you for reminding me. Yes, if everyone brushes their teeth and has a wash, then you can each put a marble in the jar,' I said, checking it was still on the shelf. It was.

'I need to feed Max,' Riley suddenly remembered.

He took a can of dog food from the fridge and spooned some into Max's bowl, then gave him some clean water.

'Good boy,' I said. 'Do you take him outside for a wee in the morning?'

'No.'

I thought that once Janie was up and feeling better, we'd need to look at incorporating Max into their routine so they could house-train him.

I went with them to the bathroom. The boys were very independent and didn't want my help, but Lola just stood there waiting for me to brush her teeth in place of her mother. They put on their shoes and coats; I did Lola's. I gave them the promised marble each and returned the jar to the shelf.

'Well done,' I said again.

'Can we say goodbye to Mummy?' Jayden asked.

'Yes, love.'

They rushed into her bedroom where the boys shouted goodbye and then rushed out again. Lola kissed and hugged her mother, then wanted to stay.

'Go with Cathy,' Janie said from beneath the covers. 'I'll get up soon.'

I took Lola's hand and led her gently from the room, then we all had to walk very quickly to school. We were late. It was 9.10 when we arrived. The playground was empty, as lessons had begun.

'You have to sign us in at reception,' Riley told me. He knew the procedure from all the previous times they'd been late. I'd once fostered a child who had been late for school so often before coming into care that they thought signing in late was normal procedure; they had been amazed when we arrived on time to find children in the playground before school began.

I apologized to the school secretary for the children's lateness, giving the reason as their mother being ill.

'I hope she is feeling better soon,' the secretary said.

'Thank you.'

The boys went to their respective classrooms. I didn't know where the nursey was so the secretary said she'd take Lola.

'Will Janie be collecting Lola at lunchtime?' she wanted to know.

'I'm not sure. I'm going to see her now. If she doesn't then I will.'

I said goodbye to Lola and came away.

* * *

It was 9.30 when I arrived at Janie's again and pressed the doorbell. She didn't immediately answer so I wondered if, instead of getting up, she'd gone back to sleep. I'd never had a key as there hadn't been a need, until now. I was considering banging on her bedroom window when I heard her voice from the other side of the door. She slowly opened it, still in her nightwear and talking on her phone. I followed her into the kitchen-diner where Max was asleep in his bed, the floor still puddle-free. Janie sat heavily on a chair at the table, and I sat opposite her as she continued the phone call, listening and sometimes speaking, her voice flat. 'Yes … no … I don't know.' Then, 'She's here now.' So I assumed she meant me. 'Yes, I will. Bye.' She ended the call.

'It was Liv. You phoned the duty social worker,' she said, clearly having forgotten I'd said I would.

'Yes, I told you I would.'

'Liv says she'll speak to you another time. She's due in court soon.'

'All right.'

'She's not happy with me,' Janie said, in the same despondent voice. 'She asked me what I would have done if you hadn't arrived. I told her I'd probably have stayed in bed, which was true, and let the kids get on with it. It's happened before, but it won't happen again. Bowie has gone for good. I'm OK now.'

She didn't look or sound OK. She seemed very low.

'Have you phoned your doctor's surgery?' I asked.

'No, I've got to do it now. Can you make me a coffee?'

'Yes, of course.'

As Janie called her doctor's surgery and then waited in a holding queue, I made us both a mug of instant coffee and took it to the table. As I did, Max slipped quietly from his bed and peed on the floor. Janie raised her eyebrows in exasperation, and while she waited for her call to be answered I filled the bucket with hot water, added disinfectant, and with rubber gloves on cleaned the floor again, keeping a watchful eye on Max, who had returned to his bed.

Doctor's appointment made, Janie ended the call and, looking at me, said, 'It wasn't a good idea getting a puppy, was it?'

'No, love,' I replied honestly. 'But you have one now, so we need to see about house-training him.'

'How the hell do you do that?' she asked.

'I don't know, but I'm sure, like most things, we can find the answer online.'

CHAPTER THIRTEEN

THAT POOR CHILD

Janie took her coffee with her to shower and dress while I put the laundry into the washing machine, then I sat at the table and used the internet on my phone to research house-training a puppy. By the time Janie reappeared, hair towel-dried, she looked a bit brighter, and I had a number of webpages bookmarked that I wanted to show her.

'Sorry for all the trouble I'm causing you,' she said, sitting opposite me. 'The way Bowie treated me really got to me.'

'I understand. I know what it feels like,' I said. 'My husband left me for another woman many years ago.'

'Really? I didn't know that.'

I nodded stoically. 'My children were little, but I can still remember the pain, the betrayal, the deceit. I was angry, not only for me, but for my children.'

'I know, I've been there before,' Janie said with a sigh.

She then told me more about the relationships she'd had in the past, most of which had ended acrimoniously. I listened and sympathized, but mindful the morning was quickly passing I drew her attention to the articles I'd found online about house-training a puppy. I pointed out the salient advice, reading some of the lines: 'Dogs are creatures of habit so it's best to get them into a routine by taking them outside to go to the toilet when they wake, after they eat, at night-time, when they are going to be left, and if they start sniffing around to find a spot to pee or poop.'

One article said that the time it took to house-train a puppy depended largely on the owner being diligent and keeping to the routine – not Janie's strongest point. The advice emphasized that when the puppy got it right and relieved themselves where they were supposed to, it was important to praise them and give them a treat. 'With patience and perseverance they will remember, but be prepared for accidents.'

'It sounds like hard work,' Janie said as I finished.

'Yes, but so is raising children. Putting in the hard work now will bring rewards later.' I then told her how cooperative her children had been earlier with the promise of putting a marble in the jar.

'That's good,' she said. 'I just need to remember to do it.'

Max got out of his basket and we both looked at him carefully.

'Come on, let's start now,' I said, 'and take him outside.'

Janie picked up Max while I got his lead, and we went outside and then round the back of the building to the patch of grass. He sniffed around for a few minutes, then to our delight he did a poo. I think it was more luck than anything, but we praised him and Janie was pleased. I asked if she had any bags for his poo as we needed to clear it up. She didn't, but she did have some nappy bags, so we used one of those instead. I suggested buying some doggy treats to give him as a reward when she next went shopping.

'Not a marble then?' she asked in a deadpan voice.

I looked at her and for a moment thought she might be serious until I saw the smile playing on her lips. I laughed.

'Had you there!' she said.

'You did.'

I was pleased to see Janie hadn't lost her sense of humour and I hoped that with time it would be able to surface more often.

We returned indoors where I helped Janie tidy up the children's bedroom – with three of them sharing a room it soon got very cluttered. As 11.30 approached I asked her if she would be all right to collect Lola from nursery as I had some things to do at home. She said she would. I checked she had groceries and something for dinner and said I'd see her on Wednesday morning as usual, but if she needed me before – even just to talk – then she could phone.

I drove home occupied by thoughts of Janie and her children, as often happened. When I'd decided to become a family support worker I'd naively assumed it wouldn't impact on me as much as when I'd fostered full-time and the children had lived with me. In some ways I worried more now because they didn't live with me, so I had little influence over what was going on but still felt responsible. Having said that, I was enjoying the work and hoped I was making a difference.

I hadn't been in long when Rania, my SSW, phoned.

'How did respite go?' she asked brightly. It took me a moment to realize what she meant, so much had happened.

'Riley didn't stay this weekend,' I said.

'No? I thought that was the plan?'

'It changed at the last minute.'

I explained that Janie and her family had a new puppy, Max, and that when I'd arrived on Friday to collect Riley he'd wanted to stay with Max rather than spend the weekend with me. Then Janie had phoned yesterday and asked me to take both boys bowling, which I had done. I mentioned the upset with Bowie, that I'd arrived to find Janie in bed, and that Liv was aware and had spoken to Janie.

'I see. Is Riley staying this weekend?' Rania asked.

'I don't know.'

'If not, I can put your room to good use. We have a teenage girl who may need respite this weekend. When will you know if Riley is staying?'

'I'm really not sure,' I replied.

'I'll call Liv and see what's going on and then get back to you.'

'All right.'

That afternoon I video-called Adrian and family, and then Lucy and family, for a chat and to see if they needed anything. They didn't, but I got to see the babies again. Sophia was sleeping, but Theo was awake and I'm sure he smiled at me. We said we'd all get together again soon.

Half an hour later Rania phoned back. 'Can you take Tia Wednesday night?' she asked, coming straight to the point.

'Who's Tia?'

'The fifteen-year-old girl I told you about earlier. It turns out the respite isn't for the weekend but Wednesday night. Her foster carers will be out until late, but Tia can't be left alone. Their usual sitter isn't available.' Foster carers can nominate a family member or close friend as a sitter, and they are vetted for suitability to offer support to the carer. Paula and Lucy are mine. But if the sitter can't help then respite can be requested, although it is not guaranteed.

'Yes, I can look after Tia on Wednesday night,' I said. 'Why can't she be left alone?' I was half expecting tales of partying when the carers had left her alone in their home before, but what Rania said took my breath away.

'She's considered a suicide risk.'

My heart clenched. That poor child. 'Oh dear. Yes, I can take her, but I would like to know some more details. Why is she considered a suicide risk?' This was a huge responsibility, even for one night, and I needed to know as much as possible to make sure I kept Tia safe and met her needs.

'She's been depressed and has talked about taking her life. She is receiving therapy. Would you like to speak to one of her carers?'

'Yes, please. I think I should.'

'It's Bev and Rob Hutchins,' Rania said. 'I'll ask them to call you. I understand the respite will be needed from about five o'clock on Wednesday. The carers will drop Tia off and then collect her the following morning at whatever time suits you.'

'Tia isn't in school then?' I asked.

'Not at present. I don't know the details. You can ask Bev or Rob when they call you.'

'Thank you.'

How dreadfully sad that a young person with their whole life ahead of them should be considered a suicide risk, I thought as the call ended. At fifteen, Tia should have so much to look forward to, although I was aware of the challenges and pressures that many young people faced. The pandemic hadn't helped. The worry of falling ill or losing a loved one, and the isolating lockdowns, had taken a toll on many. Young people had been particularly affected, but whether this had played a part in Tia's depression I didn't yet know.

I thought I probably knew Bev and Rob at least by sight from foster-carer training and other functions foster carers attended. I couldn't place them until Bev phoned that evening. She knew me.

'You semi-retired last year, didn't you?'

'Yes, that's right.'

'Rob and I take it in turns to attend training,' Bev said. 'You'll know Rob even if you can't remember me. He's the one with the bushy beard with a blond streak in it.'

'Yes, I know who you are,' I said.

She gave a small laugh. 'Everyone does when I mention the beard. Thank you so much for agreeing to look after Tia. My sister is my nominated support but she's busy with her mother-in-law, who is very sick. Bob has won an award at work and they are presenting it on Wednesday at a meal. There's going to be about fifty of us and management will be there. They've booked us in to a hotel for the night, all expenses paid. Bob has done well and we wanted to go, but we can't take Tia, and nor can we leave her alone.'

'I understand. It's fine. I'm happy to help, but please tell me what I need to know about Tia.' I sat on the sofa in the living room. It was 7 p.m. and Paula was in the kitchen making us a cup of after-dinner tea.

Bev told me of Tia's distressing childhood when she'd lived with her abusive mother, who was now in prison for an unrelated offence. The social services had been involved but Tia had been eleven when she'd finally been brought into care, angry and upset. She'd had three foster carers before being placed with Bev and Rob two years ago and would be with them long-term. After an initial settling-in period, she'd seemed to be doing all right, but then a string of events, including the pandemic, had plunged her into depression.

'During lockdown she started a relationship with a similar-aged local lad online, and that seemed to be going well,' Bev said. 'But when lockdown rules eased and they were allowed to meet he ended the relationship, saying Tia was too intense and not his type. She took it badly. When school returned she struggled to cope and became increasingly anxious. She felt others were talking and laughing about her. We contacted the school. There was no evidence she was being bullied in school or online. I think her past suffering had finally caught up with her and she found it overwhelming. From what I know she should have been taken into care sooner. She hasn't been in school for six months, but they set work for her, which she does at home. We're hoping she will start part-time after Easter.'

'And how is her mental health now?' I asked.

'That's the problem,' Bev said with a sigh. 'It's so diffi-cult to know. What Tia shares with the therapist is between them. We attend the family sessions, but they aren't often. Generally, Tia seems brighter and is coping better, or we would never have considered leaving her even for one night. Sometimes she goes very quiet, which is worrying. We try not to keep asking her how she is and checking on her, as it can irritate her. But it's very difficult not to.'

'I can imagine,' I empathized.

'Just keep an eye on her. It's only for one night,' Bev said, as if reassuring herself. 'But if you have any concerns then call us and we'll come straight back. Tia trusts us to be there for her, so that's something.'

'Good. What about food? What does Tia like to eat?'

'Anything veggie. She eats dairy products but not meat. Pasta or quiche are her favourites.'

'Fine. Any allergies?'

'No, and she's not on any medication.'

'Anything else I should know?'

Bev paused. 'I don't think so. Rob and I have talked to Tia about staying with you for the night and she says she's OK with it, although she feels she could be left alone. I've told her I'll check my phone regularly and to text me whenever she likes. And perhaps you could text and tell me how she's doing.' I could hear the anxiety in her voice.

'Yes, but try not to worry. She'll be fine. Enjoy yourselves.'

'Thank you. We'll try.'

But I could appreciate Bev and Rob's concern for Tia and the responsibility they felt. Foster carers often worry more about the children they look after than they do about their own. Without a shared history, we rely on the information we're given, which can be incomplete. So we empathize with their suffering and often overcompensate for what they have been through, although Bev had every reason to worry about Tia. She confirmed she and Rob would bring Tia to me at 5 p.m. on Wednesday, and from my house they would go straight to the venue, which was about a forty-minute drive.

'What time shall we collect her on Thursday?' Bev asked.

'It's up to you,' I said.

'If we leave before breakfast, we can be there by eight o'clock.'

'There's no need to come that early. If there is a problem, I'll phone or text you. Why not stay at the hotel for breakfast and then collect Tia mid to late morning? I expect it's a while since you have been out together.'

'Yes, it was before the pandemic,' Bev admitted. 'If you're sure that's all right, it would be lovely to have breakfast made for us in the hotel.'

'I'm sure.'

'We'll leave straight after. Thank you so much.'

'You're welcome. Text me if you think of anything else I should know, otherwise see you on Wednesday.'

She thanked me again before saying goodbye.

Paula came in with a cup of tea for me, having waited until I'd finished on the phone.

'Thanks, love. That was Bev, Tia's carer.'

I told Paula what she needed to know. She was as concerned for Tia as I was and sympathetic to what she had been through. During one of the pandemic lock-downs, unable to go to work or socialize and with her job under threat, Paula had become low but had confided in me and we'd got her through it together.

As we talked and I drank my tea I checked my phone. A message had arrived from Janie with a thumbs-up emoji: *Max peed on the floor and also outside, Lola peed in her potty for the first time!*

I texted back, *Well done*. Clearly Janie's day was ending significantly better than it had begun and I felt very relieved, if you'll excuse the pun.

CHAPTER FOURTEEN

A WONDERFUL AFTERNOON

On Tuesday morning I changed the bed linen in the room I was using for respite fostering so it was ready for Tia's overnight stay on Wednesday, then I caught up with some paperwork, writing and house-work. Later that afternoon I went grocery shopping and made dinner for Paula and myself: cottage pie with vege-tables and lashings of thick gravy – another favourite winter warmer of ours. As we ate Paula told me of her day at work. That evening we watched some television and were both in bed at a reasonable time as we had to be up early – Paula to go to work and I was due at Janie's again to help with their morning routine. That routine would now have to allow time to take Max outside to go to the toilet and for Lola to use her potty.

I arrived at Janie's as usual on Wednesday at around 7.45 a.m. It was mild for February but drizzling. I pressed the doorbell and heard Janie before I saw her. 'Riley!' she shouted. 'See to Max, will you, while I let Cathy in!'

Janie opened the door, dressed but clearly stressed. 'Riley is refusing to take Max outside because it's raining,' she said, annoyed.

'It's not raining much,' I said, going in. 'Does Riley know dogs have to be walked in all weathers?'

'I've told him. He's in a bad mood,' Janie replied. 'He persuaded me to let him stay up late last night gaming with me. But don't tell Liv.'

I followed Janie into the kitchen-diner. Riley was dressed and Lola was wandering around with just her pyjama top on. Janie scooped her up and sat her on the potty. 'Do wee-wees for Mummy, good girl.'

There are various approaches to potty training; leaving off a child's nappy and sitting them on the potty at regular intervals is often successful. It's luck to begin with, but once they've used the potty a few times and received lots of praise, they start to recognize when they want to go and ask for the potty.

'Riley! Will you take Max out! Now!' Janie cried at him.

He looked at her sullenly and didn't move.

'I'll come with you,' I told Riley. 'Good boy. We can't have Max using the floor in here as a toilet.'

'He already has,' Janie said, putting Lola back on the potty. 'I cleaned it up.'

'Are you taking us bowling at the weekend?' Riley asked me.

'I can. Come on, let's take Max out, then you can add a marble to the jar.'

'Now!' Janie cried, annoyed by Riley's attitude.

'I'm going!' he retaliated moodily. 'Keep your hair on.'

'Don't be rude to me. That's the last time you stay up late!' she cried.

Not the best start to the day, but I knew how tiredness can affect a child's mood, just as it can an adult's.

With his face set, Riley clipped the dog lead to Max's collar.

'Good boy,' I said.

We went into the hall where Riley put on his coat and shoes. Hoods up, we went outside, round the back of the building, and then stood on the grass as Max began sniffing around.

'Hopefully he'll remember he went here before,' I said.

Riley just looked very grumpy.

'Are you tired or is there something bothering you?' I asked him after a while.

He shrugged. 'Like what?'

'I don't know. Anything. Is school going all right?'

'I guess. My teacher keeps asking me that.'

Schools are so much better now at keeping an eye on children considered vulnerable or at risk.

'Everything OK at home?' I ventured as Max continued to sniff the grass.

'I guess,' Riley replied without much conviction.

'So what is it, love?'

'I was worried about Mum on Monday when she couldn't get out of bed. That's why I stayed up late last night to keep her company. I know she's not the best mum, but I don't want anything bad to happen to her. I don't mind staying at yours at the weekend, we have fun, but I don't want to be there all the time if anything happened to Mum.'

Bless him, I thought. Children often internalize their feelings and fears, so they can build up and burst out as anger. Riley had been up late gaming with his mother, so it wasn't all sacrifice, but even so, I saw the truth in what he'd said. He was worried he might be placed in care permanently.

'I don't think it will happen again,' I said. 'Your mother was upset on Monday. Do you know why?'

'Because of Bowie,' Riley replied.

'That's right. She realizes now that the way she dealt with it was wrong. She felt very unhappy but has made an appointment to see the doctor so it shouldn't happen again.' I couldn't promise it wouldn't ever happen again, so this was the next best thing.

'If I did have to go into care, would I live with you?' Riley asked, clearly having thought about it.

'It would depend on which foster carer was available,' I replied honestly. 'Have you told your mother you're worried?'

'No. She never listens to me.'

'Could you try to tell her?'

He shrugged. 'You can.'

'All right. I think it's important she knows how you feel.'

The conversation abruptly stopped and Riley's mood immediately lifted as Max went to the toilet.

'He's been!' Riley cried, delighted, and glanced towards the kitchen window, hoping his mother was there to see, but she wasn't. 'Well done, Max,' Riley said, and bending down, he patted his back and ruffled his short fur.

Max looked very pleased with himself; so did Riley. We returned indoors.

'Mum! Max did a wee!' Riley yelled from the hall, presumably hoping for a well done. But there wasn't one.

He unclipped Max's lead and the dog shot into the kitchen.

'He's got wet paws!' Janie shouted. 'All over my clean top!' So I guessed Max had jumped up at her, but poor Riley couldn't seem to do anything right.

We took off our shoes and went into the kitchen-diner.

'It might be worth keeping a cloth by the front door to wipe Max's paws on,' I suggested.

'I need to get Lola dressed,' Janie replied, stressed, and carried her out of the room.

I found a cloth in the cupboard under the sink and placed it in the hall by the front door. I then made sure Riley and Jayden were eating their cereal before going to talk to Janie. She was in the children's bedroom getting Lola dressed. I told her what Riley had just said – that he was worried that what happened on Monday could happen again, and he would be placed in foster care permanently. I also said he felt she never listened to him – it was important she knew.

'I've told him I won't do it again,' Janie said, concentrating on Lola.

'Maybe reassure him. He's obviously worried. And, Janie, I know we've talked about this before, but Riley needs more of your attention in a positive way.'

'He can wind me up just like his father did,' Janie said tightly. 'I see so much of his father in him.' I knew from what Janie had told me that her relationship with Riley's father had ended as badly as most of the others had.

'Riley is his own person,' I said. 'And he needs you, although he may not show it.'

'I hear you,' Janie said as she finished dressing Lola.

There wasn't time for any further discussion now, so we returned to the kitchen.

'You forgot my marble for taking Max out,' Riley told me accusingly.

'Sorry,' I said.

I took down the box of marbles and let Riley drop one into the jar. It fell on top of the others with a satisfying ping.

'Well done. Now Jayden's turn,' I said.

'He didn't help with Max,' Riley was quick to point out.

'No, but he got dressed and ate his cereal nicely,' I replied.

Jayden proudly took a marble and dropped it into the jar. Then I turned to Lola.

'Well done for using your potty,' I said.

'She hasn't this morning,' Janie said.

'But she's been sitting on it, which is good.'

Lola took a marble from the box and dropped it into the jar.

'Well done, everyone,' I said with an encouraging smile.

Sometimes you have to find a reason to reward a child; it's always possible to find something, even if it's small, which I'd previously explained to Janie. There is a famous poem by Dorothy Law Nolte, which you may have read, entitled 'Children Learn What They Live'. It starts:

If children live with criticism,
They learn to condemn.
If children live with hostility,
They learn to fight ...
If children live with praise,
They learn to appreciate.
If children live with acceptance,
They learn to love.
If children live with approval,
They learn to like themselves ...

As relevant now as when it was first published in 1954.

It was a rush to get them out on time and as Janie finally opened the front door Riley asked why they couldn't take Max to school with them. He'd had all his vaccinations so could go out, otherwise we couldn't have started toilet training him outside.

'I've already told you, dogs aren't allowed in the playground!' Janie said, instantly losing patience with Riley. I guessed he'd asked before.

'I can go in by myself, so can Jayden,' Riley replied.

'Doh! But Lola can't,' Janie said, slamming the door behind us with a lot more force than was necessary.

'So tie him up outside,' Riley persisted.

'I can't! I'm going straight to the doctor's.'

'Tomorrow then,' Riley said.

'I don't know. Stop going on,' Janie snapped, and began walking along the pavement.

I called goodbye after them and returned to my car. I hadn't interfered but Janie was sending mixed messages to Riley about taking Max to school. If she'd made the decision not to take Max at all then she needed to make that clear to him. If it was just today she couldn't take him because she was going straight to the doctor's, then she should have said that. It's easy as a parent to inadvertently give a child mixed messages by assuming they are following our thought processes. Children process information differently to adults and need clear instructions and a simple reason for a decision, otherwise it can appear unfair and a child of Riley's age is likely to challenge what is being said.

Aware that I would probably have Riley at the weekend, I decided to phone Lucy to see if she was free so I could pop in and see her and Theo. Emma would be in school and Darren's paternity leave – like Adrian's – had already ended, so he would be at work. Lucy answered her phone in the playground where Emma went to school.

'Hi, Mum,' she said brightly. 'Are you OK?'

'Yes, love. I wondered if you were free this morning. I thought I might drop by.'

'Yes, that would be nice. Kirsty is coming at eleven for some lunch so why not join us?'

'Fantastic. Do you need anything from the shops?'

'You could bring something for dessert.'

'Sure, anything else?'

'I don't think so. I went shopping yesterday.'

'I'll see you later then.'

My heart sang with happiness, and I felt truly blessed to have such a wonderful, loving family. Lucy and Kirsty got on well, as did Adrian and Darren. I was touched that Lucy had so easily included me. I also felt slightly guilty at the contrast with Janie and her struggles. I so wanted her life to be better, with the hope that she could find happiness and contentment.

I went home briefly and then left for Lucy's, stopping off at the supermarket on the way. I bought a selection of desserts and cakes, and a potted plant for each of them. It was just after 11 a.m. when I arrived at Lucy's. The rain had stopped, and Kirsty let me in.

'Lucy's changing Theo,' she said as we kissed cheeks and hugged. 'Sophia is asleep, but she'll be awake soon.'

'OK, love. I'll put this shopping in the kitchen,' I said. 'And here's something for you.' I gave her a plant.

'Thank you. That is nice.'

'Hi, Mum!' Lucy called from the bedroom.

'Hi, love,' I returned quietly, not wanting to wake Sophia.

I took off my coat and shoes and then went through to the kitchen where I put the desserts in the fridge and the rest of the shopping and Lucy's plant on the work surface. I joined Kirsty in the living room. She was standing beside the Moses basket where Sophia was fast asleep.

'She's gorgeous,' I said.

Sophia was on her back with her head turned slightly to one side and her little mouth relaxed open in sleep – the epitome of the contented baby.

We continued to gaze at her. 'She's the image of Adrian, don't you think?' Kirsty said.

'I can see it more now than when she was first born,' I replied. 'But I can see you in her too.'

'That's what my mother said.'

A few moments later Lucy came in carrying Theo. We kissed cheeks. 'Go to Nana,' she told Theo, and placed him in my arms. 'He's just been fed and changed so he's a happy fellow.'

He looked it. He was wide awake and seemed to be watching me. I sat on the sofa and rested him in the crook of my arm, smiling and talking to him as Lucy took some photos. It was at moments like this that my thoughts went to my dear parents. They would have doted on their great-grandchildren, just as they had their grandchildren. Presently Sophia woke and Kirsty fed her. We then took turns holding the babies, passing them around. When Theo fell asleep Lucy and Kirsty left me holding Sophia and keeping an eye on Theo while they went into the kitchen and made lunch.

It was a wonderful afternoon, memory-making, but at 2.45 Lucy said she needed to start getting ready to collect Emma from school. The school was within walking distance. I offered to go but Lucy wanted to and suggested I went with them. Kirsty said she had some things to do at home and said goodbye, thanking Lucy for a nice time. I carried her belongings to the car as she carried Sophia in the car seat. We hugged goodbye and I saw her off, then returned indoors. I washed up our lunch dishes as Lucy got Theo ready for our outing, then we walked to Emma's school, with me pushing the pram. We waited in the playground for her class to come out.

Emma's face lit up when she saw me. She cried, 'Nana!' ran to me and gave me a big hug.

'Have you had a good day?' I asked her.

She nodded, then held my hand all the way home, telling me about her friends. Creating friendship bonds and socializing at school is as important for children as their education. I saw them into the flat. Emma wanted me to stay so I had to explain that I needed to go home as I had someone coming shortly. I gave her a big hug and lots of kisses, then thanked Lucy and said we'd meet up again soon.

It was 4.30 when I arrived home and I immediately began making a quiche for dinner, which Bev, Tia's foster carer, had said Tia liked. Once it was in the oven, all I could do was wait. My usual nervous anticipation kicked in, so it was a relief when shortly after five o'clock the doorbell rang.

CHAPTER FIFTEEN

TIA

B ev stood beside Tia, and Rob was just behind them; the blond streak in his beard looked freshly high-lighted.

'Welcome,' I said with a smile. 'Come in.'

'This is Cathy,' Bev told Tia.

'Lovely to meet you,' I said as Rob closed the front door behind them.

Tia was of average height and build for her age and looked at me from under her fringe with a nervous smile. They all slipped off their shoes and Tia took off her jacket.

'You can hang it on the stand,' I said.

'Shall I leave her overnight bag here?' Rob asked.

'Yes, please.'

Bev took off her coat. Beneath it, she was wearing a lovely royal-blue evening dress, Rob was wearing a sleek light-grey suit. They were dressed to go straight to the function.

'You both look very smart,' I said.

'Thanks, I had my beard done specially,' Rob replied mischievously.

Bev sighed indulgently.

'He's so embarrassing,' Tia said, as any younger person might in respect of a parent who was drawing attention to themselves.

'It covers the grey,' Rob said.

'Is that why you do it?' I asked, leading the way down the hall and into the living room.

'Yes, I've had a grey streak in my beard since I first grew it,' Rob said. 'It made me look old, so I started dying it. Now I look trendy rather than old, don't you think?'

'Absolutely,' I said, while Bev and Tia sighed again.

Bev and Rob were in their late forties with a grown-up son who was away at university. Tia seemed comfortable with her foster parents, which I thought would help her through the challenges she was facing in her mental health.

In the living room Tia and Bev sat on the sofa and Rob took an easy chair. I offered them drinks and Rob said he'd like a coffee, 'White, no sugar, please.'

Bev and Tia didn't want anything.

I made Rob's coffee and also switched off the oven as the quiche had cooked, then returned to the living room and placed his cup on the occasional table within his reach.

'Thank you,' he said. 'I'll drink this and then we'll be off.'

I sat in the other easy chair. 'I'll show you around later,' I said to Tia.

'Where's your daughter?' she asked me.

Bev would have told Tia a little about me. 'Paula is at work,' I said. 'She'll be home in about an hour.'

Tia nodded. 'Can I go to my room now?' she asked.

'Stay down here for a while,' Bev said. 'Have a chat with Cathy before you disappear into your room.'

'What do you like to do in the evenings?' I asked Tia.

'Watch television,' she said with a small shrug. 'Do schoolwork sometimes.'

'Do you have any schoolwork to do this evening?' I asked.

'No.'

'She did it earlier,' Bev added.

There was a small silence, so I filled the gap. 'Well done for getting the award,' I said to Rob. 'What's it for?'

'I devised a new app for the company.'

'So you're an IT boffin?' I asked with a smile.

'That's me,' Rob agreed.

'He's good,' Bev said. 'He's been teaching Tia and me. If you want to know anything about computer software or have problems with any of your devices, ask Rob.'

'I'll remember that,' I said.

We talked for a while longer as Rob finished his coffee, then, checking his phone, he said they should be going and stood.

'Bye, love,' Bev said to Tia, and gave her a big hug.

'Bye, Mum,' she said, hugging her back.

'See you tomorrow,' Rob said. 'Be good and don't trash the place.'

'Rob!' Bev admonished. 'Cathy won't know you're joking.' Then to me she said, 'Tia is always good. It's Rob's weird sense of humour.'

'Dad's just weird,' Tia said fondly, pulling a face. Again, I saw how comfortable Tia was with Bev and Rob. She called them Mum and Dad – unusual for a child who'd come into care at the age Tia had, having lived with her birth mother for many years.

Tia stayed in the living room while I saw Bev and Rob out.

'Keep an eye on her,' Bev said quietly to me in the hall. 'And phone me if there's a problem.'

'I will. But try not to worry. Enjoy yourselves. I'm sure she'll be fine.'

I watched them go and then returned to the living room.

'Would you like a drink now?' I asked Tia.

'No, thank you.'

'It must be useful, Rob being an expert in IT,' I said, sitting down and making conversation.

Tia nodded.

'I've made a quiche for dinner – Bev said you liked it. I'll do new potatoes, peas and salad to go with it. Is that OK?'

'Fine.'

'What do you usually have for dessert?'

'I don't mind.'

I knew I was trying too hard, but I wanted Tia's over-night stay to be a success, not only for her sake, but for Bev's and Rob's too. They deserved a night out, and if they had to return early or Tia told them she'd been very unhappy, it would ruin it for them. I doubted they'd ever go out again.

'Shall I show you around the house now?' I asked.

'OK,' she said and stood.

'So, this is the living room,' I began. 'The kitchen-diner is through here.'

I then showed Tia the front room and, collecting her bag from the hall, we went upstairs and into her bedroom first. I set the bag on the floor. She didn't say anything and I found it difficult to judge what she was thinking.

'It won't be as nice as your room at home with all your things in it,' I said.

'It's OK,' she said.

I showed her where the toilet and bathroom were, and pointed out Paula's bedroom and mine.

'I leave a night light on in the landing in case you want the toilet,' I said. 'But call me if you need anything during the night.' It was something I said to all the children and young people I fostered to help them feel safe and at ease sleeping in a strange room in an unfamiliar house.

'Can I go to my room now?' Tia asked as I finished the tour.

'You can, or come downstairs with me,' I suggested, which I would have preferred. 'I'll be in the kitchen seeing to dinner, so you can come and talk to me or sit in the living room if you want peace.'

'I'll sit on my bed and watch a film on my laptop,' she said.

'All right, love. You'll need the Wi-Fi code.'

She nodded.

'Just a minute. I'll get it.' I went downstairs. It was an eleven-digit code, a mixture of numbers and upper- and lower-case letters, which I could never remember.

I returned upstairs where Tia was taking her laptop from her bag. She sat on the edge of her bed and opened it. I waited until she was ready and then read out the long code. I waited again to make sure it connected. 'All right?'

'Yes.'

'I'll be in the kitchen then.'

I left Tia sitting on her bed with the bedroom door open and went downstairs, where I checked my phone. There was already a text from Bev: *How is Tia?*

They'd only been gone twenty minutes.

I replied: *She's fine. I've showed her around and she's watching a film on her laptop.*

Thank you x, came Bev's immediate reply.

I washed the new potatoes and set them in a pan of boiling water, then prepared the salad. It was about fifteen minutes since I'd left Tia in her bedroom, so I went up to check she was all right. Her bedroom door was still open and she was on her bed, propped up by the pillows, earpieces in and concentrating on her laptop. She saw me, pressed pause and took out one earpiece.

'Everything all right?' I asked.

'Yes, thank you,' she replied in a quiet voice.

'We'll have dinner when Paula returns around six o'clock.'

'Can I have mine up here?' she asked.

'I'd prefer it if you came down. There'll just be Paula and me. See how you feel.'

I smiled reassuringly and returned downstairs. I wouldn't make an issue of it if she really did want to have dinner in her room; she was only with me for one night. But it was just Paula and me, and Bev had asked me to keep an eye on her and had encouraged her to stay downstairs when she'd wanted to go to her room earlier.

I laid the table and had just added the peas to the boiling water when I heard Paula's key go in the front door. I went into the hall.

'Hi, love,' I said as she took off her shoes and coat. 'Have you had a good day?'

'Yes, thanks, and you?'

'Yes, I have. I went to Lucy's for lunch. Kirsty was there too.'

'Lovely. I'll see them again soon.'

'Tia is here. She's in her room. She's a bit quiet. Can you bring her down with you when you're ready?'

'Sure.'

Paula liked to have a wash and to change out of her office clothes when she came home from work.

As Paula went upstairs I returned to the kitchen where I strained the potatoes and checked the quiche was still warm. Once the peas had cooked, I went to the foot of the stairs and called up that dinner was ready.

'Won't be a minute,' Paula replied.

I returned to the kitchen and listened to the movement on the landing above. There are some loose floorboards under the carpet up there that I'd never got around to having repaired, as it meant taking up all the carpet. They'd proved useful in the past for letting me know when a child was out of bed. I heard Paula go to Tia's room, then voices, although I couldn't hear what they said. If Tia didn't come down with Paula, I would go up and try to persuade her, as I really didn't want her sitting up there the whole evening.

To my relief, a few moments later I heard Tia and Paula come downstairs. I put the food into serving dishes and set them on the table so we could help ourselves.

Paula isn't an extrovert and can appear shy on first meeting until you get to know her. She is good with children but can take longer to warm to adults. She seemed to be just what Tia needed, for as they came into the kitchen-diner she was talking to Paula in a way she hadn't to me. Perhaps it helped that Paula was closer to her in age, although there was still a thirteen-year gap. Tia was asking Paula about her job and their conversation continued as we ate. Tia said she'd like to do something in IT like her dad but recognized she'd have to get back into school first, then study at college.

'I think college will be better for me than school,' she said. 'I haven't got a really good friend there, and you have to study subjects you're not interested in.'

I nodded, pleased that Tia was talking to us, although she'd need a good general education and to pass exams in the core subjects to go to college, which I'm sure Bev and Rob had explained to her.

Talk of school and college continued. Tia ate all her main course but didn't want a pudding, saying she might have a yoghurt later. The three of us cleared the table and I was pleased she came with Paula and me into the living room. I checked my phone and there was nothing from Bev.

'Where are your sisters?' Tia asked Paula.

Paula told her they lived close by and a little about her nieces and nephew.

'And your dad?' Tia asked.

'He hasn't lived here for a long time,' Paula replied. 'Not since I was little.'

'At least you've got your mum,' Tia said, her manner suddenly becoming serious. 'Mine is in prison.'

'Oh, I am sorry,' Paula said. I hadn't told Paula this, feeling there was no need to go into that much detail as Tia was only with us for one night.

'I'm not sorry,' Tia said fervently. 'I hope she stays there forever. She's evil. The social worker wants me to visit her, but I've refused. Mum and Dad are on my side, and I know it got them into trouble. Foster carers are supposed to do what the social worker says. But I would rather die than see her again.'

Paula was looking concerned at what Tia was saying and the vehemence in her words. It was a long time, if ever, since we'd heard a child or young person express such negative feelings towards their birth mother.

'She never wanted me,' Tia continued. 'She used to lock me in a cupboard when she'd had enough of me. She said I was naughty, but I wasn't. I just got in the way. I don't know why they [the social services] left me there for so long. Surely, they could see what was going on? I should have been taken into care when I was little.' Bev had said similar.

As Tia continued to tell us of her suffering at home with her mother – or rather telling Paula, as she was looking at her as she spoke – my thoughts went to Janie. Support had been put in place to help her keep her children, but in the future might they think they should have been taken into care? I sincerely hoped not, but it was a sobering thought. It's sometimes said of social workers that they are damned if they do and damned if they don't, meaning they can never get it right, which I can in part understand. You can't take children away from their parents without a very good reason, and yet if they aren't removed soon enough from an abusive or neglectful home then the outcome can be horrendous.

Tia's words had come out in a torrent, as though a valve had been released. She finished with, 'At least I have Mum and Dad now,' meaning Bev and Rob, then she sat back and suddenly changed the subject, as if that was the end of it.

'I like this room,' she said. 'It's cosy.'

'Thank you, love,' I said.

Tia couldn't be drawn into further conversation on any matter, despite Paula and me trying. It was as though she'd purged herself and had nothing more to say about anything. I suggested we put on the television or play a game of cards.

'I think I'll finish watching the film on my laptop upstairs,' she said.

'You could watch it on this television here?' I said. 'It's connected to the internet.'

'No, I'm a bit tired. Thanks for dinner. It was nice,' she said, and stood.

'You're welcome, love.'

I watched her hurry from the room.

'Are you all right?' I asked Paula. She'd come home hoping to relax after a day at work and instead had listened to Tia's suffering.

'Yes, but poor Tia,' she replied.

'I know. I'll go and check on her before long.'

Paula went upstairs to wash her hair while I stayed in the living room wondering what Tia was thinking. Was she now embarrassed that she'd disclosed so much to Paula and me – relative strangers? We can all do that. Or possibly she was simply tired, although it was only 7.30. I checked my phone again and there was another message from Bev: *About to sit down for dinner but I'll check my phone regularly.*

We've had ours, I replied. *Tia ate well. She's fine.* Which I hoped was true.

I didn't like the way Tia had opened up to us so dramatically, then shut down and left the room. Bev had said she could go quiet, and it became difficult to gauge how she was feeling. Had telling us reopened old wounds? Was she now reliving in her mind's eye the abuse she'd described?

I gave her fifteen minutes, then went up. Her bedroom door was shut so I knocked and waited for her to call 'come in'. She didn't respond and my anxiety quickly increased. She had after all threatened to take her own life before. I knocked on the door again and when there was no reply I opened it. Of course she couldn't hear me: she had her earpieces in!

Tia had changed into her pyjamas and was in bed with her laptop open. She saw me and took out an earpiece.

'Sorry to disturb you, love. Have you got everything you need?'

'Yes, thank you.'

'Do you want a shower before you settle down for the night?'

'I'll have it in the morning.'

'All right, love. Tell me if you need anything.'

She nodded and I came out.

I checked on her every half an hour or so during the evening and each time she was concentrating on her laptop. I didn't pry, and assumed that Bev and Rob had talked to her about staying safe online and were aware of what she was accessing, as I would have done had she been staying with me permanently.

I last looked in on Tia at 10.30 p.m. on my way to bed.

'I'm fine, really,' she told me. 'I'll finish this box set, then go to sleep.'

I reminded her to call me in the night if she needed anything, then I said goodnight and came out, closing her door. I also looked in on Paula, who was just getting into bed, and we kissed goodnight.

I texted Bev before I went to bed: *Hope you're having a nice time. We're all in bed. Tia is watching a box set on her laptop in her room. x*

Bev replied: *Thanks. She loves her box sets. I'll text you once we're up in the morning x*

I lay in bed with my lamp on listening out for Tia, my thoughts going over some of the things she'd told us. Most foster carers will tell you that disclosures a child or young person makes are rarely forgotten and can haunt you, even if they are of historic abuse. At some point I must have dropped off to sleep for when my eyes opened my bedside clock showed 1 a.m. and my lamp was still on. The house was quiet and I crept silently round the landing to Tia's room. It was quiet in her room too, but I gently opened her bedroom door to check she was asleep. She was on her side, eyes closed, her laptop shut and on the floor. Satisfied she had settled for the night, I returned to my room and was finally able to sleep properly.

CHAPTER SIXTEEN

A WEEKEND GUEST

The following morning I woke at 7 a.m. when I heard Paula getting ready for work. Yawning, I checked my phone and there was already a text message from Bev. *Good morning. Hope you are all OK. Breakfast is at 8 a.m. so we'll leave straight after. Aiming to be with you by 10 a.m.*

I replied: *All good here. See you around 10 but don't rush x*

I heard Tia get up to use the toilet, then return to her room. Throwing on my dressing gown, I went round the landing and knocked on her door.

'Come in!' she called.

'Hi, love, did you sleep well?' I asked, poking my head round the door.

'Yes, thank you. Mum and Dad should be here by ten,' she said, and picked up her laptop. 'I'll watch the last episode in this series and then get up.'

'OK, love.'

I left Tia sitting up in bed with her laptop, and I had breakfast with Paula. She said goodbye to Tia before she left for work.

Tia got up shortly before 9 a.m., showered and dressed, and then came down. She just wanted muesli and a glass of juice for breakfast. She took it up to her room, saying she needed to pack, then reappeared at 9.30 and put her bag in the hall. She sat with me in the living room and I made light conversation as we waited for Bev and Rob. We'd both received a text to say they were on their way.

Fifteen minutes later the doorbell rang.

'That'll be them!' Tia cried and shot down the hall.

Arriving just ahead of me, Tia opened the door and fell into Bev's arms, then gave Rob a big hug.

'That's a nice greeting,' Bev said.

I smiled. 'Come in.'

'There's no need for you to come in, I'm ready,' Tia said, and proved it by picking up her overnight bag, leaving Bev and Rob standing outside.

'I was going to offer you a coffee,' I said to them.

'We're OK,' Bev said. 'We'll go and I'll give you a ring tonight.'

'If you're sure.'

'Tia, say goodbye to Cathy,' Bev said.

'Bye,' she called over her shoulder, heading down the front path.

'Bye, love. It was nice having you to stay,' I replied.

'Thanks,' Bev said to me.

Tia was now on the pavement waiting for Rob to unlock the car. 'Thanks, Cathy!' he called.

'Tia's been fine,' I told Bev.

'We'll speak later,' she said, and went to their car.

I gave a little wave as it pulled away, then I closed the front door.

It was a good sign that Tia had developed a strong attachment to Bev and Rob. Some children who have been badly abused or neglected struggle to form attachments even into adulthood. There's a lot of research and writing on attachment theory and it's covered in foster-carer training. Yet, while Tia had been able to form a strong attachment to her foster parents, I could see how difficult it would be to gauge her feelings. From what I'd seen of her in the short time she'd been with us, her mood was unpredictable, going from complete openness and non-stop talking to silence and shutting others out. Some of this could be due to her age – the teenage years, with all their hormonal changes, can wreak havoc on the emotions – but undoubtedly some of it was due to her harrowing past. Thankfully, she had Bev and Rob, who had helped her so much in the past and would see her through whatever lay ahead.

I stripped what had been Tia's bed, put the linen in the washing machine, then gave the room a clean, because although Tia had only used it for one night I was expecting Riley for the weekend. I put the rest of the day to good use and spent a large part of it at my computer in the front room where I wrote up my log notes, completed a module of foster-caring training, then worked on the book I was writing. Writing had always been part of my life, even before my fostering memoirs and my Lisa Stone thrillers were published. Now, I also spent time online answering emails and comments on social media from my many wonderful readers.

I prepared dinner for when Paula arrived home and we sat at the table and talked as we ate. That evening Bev telephoned. She began by thanking me for all I'd done for Tia, apologized for their abrupt departure, then said Tia had been telling them what a lovely time she'd had.

'She hasn't stopped talking about you and Paula,' Bev said.

'Really? I thought she'd just tolerated it.'

'No. She said if Rob and I need to go away again, she's happy to stay with you and your daughter.'

'Good, I'm very pleased.'

'I understand she told you both about the abuse she suffered with her mother.'

'Yes, she did. It sounds dreadful.'

'I know. Sorry. But it shows how much Tia trusted you both. She has never told anyone else apart from me and her therapist. Many years ago she confided in someone at school, who then told someone in the class, and before long it was general knowledge. She felt everyone was talking about her behind her back. It added to her school phobia.'

'Oh dear, I am sorry.'

'Hopefully she's over that now. It's a positive sign she was able to successfully stay with you guys. Thanks again. Rob and I enjoyed our night out.'

'Any time.'

'We might take you up on that.'

We said goodbye and I immediately told Paula what Bev had said. She was naturally pleased Tia had enjoyed her stay with us, then said, 'Mum, it's Friday tomorrow, will Riley be staying with us?'

'As far as I know, yes.'

'You don't mind if I'm not here the whole weekend?' she asked. 'I'm thinking of meeting a friend on Saturday and seeing Lucy and Adrian on Sunday. Weekends are the only time I have free.'

'Of course not, love. You make the most of your weekend. It's important you do.'

Paula was a big help, but she had her own life to lead

and respite fostering was my responsibility, although I had consulted her before agreeing to it.

On Friday morning when I arrived at Janie's they were all up, which was good. However, Janie was in a bad mood. It was the first thing Riley said when he opened the front door with Max in his arms.

'Mum's in a mood.'

'Why? What's the matter?' I asked, going in.

'It's Max,' Riley replied flatly.

I followed him into the kitchen-diner where he put Max down. Jayden and Lola were sitting at the table eating their cereal, which was also good. But I could see from Janie's expression she was annoyed.

'It's not my fault,' Riley said to her, and returned to the table to eat his cereal.

'What isn't Riley's fault?' I asked Janie.

'Read this,' she said, and thrust a sheet of writing paper into my hand. 'It must have been pushed through my letterbox last night. I found it this morning.'

I read the handwritten letter.

To the occupants,

I and other residents in the block are concerned that you are allowing your dog to foul the grass at the back of the building. This area is for *all* our enjoyment and *not* to be used as a toilet for your dog. It is irresponsible and a health hazard not to clear up after your dog. It is also against council regulations. If this happens again you will be reported to the authorities.

Regards,

Concerned neighbours

'Oh. Do you know who sent it?' I asked, handing it back.

'No, they didn't have the guts to put their friggin' names on it.'

I could see why Janie was upset. Usually in matters like this I find it's best to deal with it in person, face to face, in the first instance at least. This seemed underhand, and of course it could have been just one neighbour hiding behind the suggestion it was many.

'Whoever sent it is out to get me and stir up trouble,' Janie said, agitated and incensed.

'Janie, I can appreciate why you're upset, but is it true? Have you not been clearing up after Max?'

Janie glared at Riley, who had a spoon in one hand and was patting Max with the other.

'I forget sometimes when I'm in a hurry,' Riley admitted. 'But it's always me who has to do it.'

'It's your job,' Janie retaliated. 'I can't leave Jayden and Lola in here by themselves and walk Max.' Which was true, and I wondered how they were going to manage at the weekend if Riley stayed with me.

While it's reasonable for a child of Riley's age to assume some responsibility for a pet, it seemed that he had more than his fair share. Also, he hadn't been part of the decision-making process on whether to buy a dog or not, when it could have been discussed and agreed who would do what. Pet ownership is a big responsibility and affects the whole family, but Janie had bought Max on a whim.

'I'll remember in future,' Riley grumbled, and petted Max.

I could see how much the dog meant to Riley, perhaps more than anyone else in the family.

'Just make sure you remember,' Janie said in a more conciliatory tone. Then she added, 'There can't have been that much shit, we've only had Max a week.'

Further talk on the matter was halted as Lola cried, 'Mummy, potty!' And Janie rushed to fetch it.

I helped the boys get ready as Janie saw to Lola.

'Has Max been out this morning?' I asked them.

'Yes,' Riley said. 'And I cleared up the mess.'

'Good boy.'

Max wasn't a young puppy so hopefully he would be house-trained before too long. I helped out as I usually did in the morning, then, when the opportunity arose, I asked Janie if Riley was coming to me at the weekend.

'Do you want to go to Cathy's?' she asked Riley.

It shouldn't really have been Riley's decision. Respite had been offered when Janie had felt she wasn't coping. If she didn't need it, doubtless someone else would.

'Can I bring Max?' Riley asked.

Janie didn't say no but looked at me. 'I've got a friend coming for the weekend,' she said. 'It would help me if you could have both of them.'

I'll say at this point that there is nothing in the role of family support worker or respite foster carer that includes looking after the family's pets. My immediate reaction was to say no and (uncharitably) that if I wanted a dog I would have one. But Riley was looking at me imploringly. We no longer had our cat or any other pet, so there was no reason why I shouldn't agree, was there?

'Please,' Riley said.

'All right, just for this weekend.'

'You can come,' Riley told Max, delighted.

Jayden was now looking sad. 'Can I come?' he asked.

'No, love,' I said when Janie didn't. I couldn't just agree to take Jayden without consulting Liv.

'It's not fair,' he said. Janie was still looking at me.

'I have an idea,' I said to her. 'I could collect Riley and Max this evening at five as arranged, then come back early on Sunday, just after lunch, drop off Max and take Riley and Jayden bowling?'

'Suits me,' Janie said.

'Good.'

Jayden was now happy and joined Riley in making a big fuss of Max, so much so that Max weed on the floor. I cleaned it up so the rest of the family could get ready for school and leave on time. Again, it wasn't part of my remit to keep cleaning their floor, but no doubt it would be good practice for the weekend when Max stayed. I made a mental note to check I had plenty of disinfectant.

'Did you see the doctor on Wednesday?' I asked Janie out of earshot of the children.

'Yes, he's adjusted my medication, and it seems to be helping.'

'Good. Nice that you've got a friend coming.' I thought it was good timing, as Janie had been feeling low and then received that letter from her neighbours.

'Yes, I haven't heard from her in ages,' Janie said. 'She suddenly got in touch through –' and she named a social media account.

'Lovely.'

We left the house together. 'See you at five. Have a good day,' I said, and with a little wave I returned to my car.

* * *

Once home, I texted Paula: *Riley will be with us this weekend, and I've agreed to his dog coming. Hope you don't mind xx*

She replied: *OK, but remember I won't be there much as I am going out xx*

I know, love. See you later xx

I then made a list of what I needed to bring from Janie's when I collected Riley and Max later: Max's bowls, his dog food so he had the same brand (important at his age), bed, lead and some of his toys, as well as Riley's weekend bag. I texted the list to Janie and asked if she could think of anything else.

No, she replied.

When I arrived at Janie's flat at 5 p.m. it was nearly dark outside and nothing was ready. Janie's friend was on her way and Janie was in a panic trying to tidy up.

'I didn't think she was coming until tomorrow,' she grumbled, as she threw rubbish in the bin and put used dishes into the sink.

I gathered together Max's belongings as Riley went to pack his bag. Jayden and Lola were sitting on the sofa watching television and eating sandwiches and crisps.

'Dog food?' I asked Janie, having gathered up the items I could see.

'Here,' she said. She paused from what she was doing and took a box of dried dog food from the cupboard under the sink and handed it to me. It sounded nearly empty. 'Sorry, I meant to get more,' she said.

'How often and how much do you give Max?' I asked.

'Riley knows all about that,' she said, preoccupied with clearing up.

Excited to be taking Max with him, Riley quickly appeared with his overnight bag, then helped me pack the car, making sure Max couldn't get out of the flat as we worked. Once we were ready, we returned for Max and Riley put him on the lead. Janie was now peering in the kitchen cupboards.

'I suppose she'll want something to eat,' she moaned, meaning her friend.

'We're off now,' I said. 'See you on Sunday around one o'clock. I'll give Riley lunch first.'

'Yes, see you then,' Janie said.

'Say goodbye,' I told Riley.

'Bye!' he called.

'When are you taking me bowling?' Jayden asked.

'Sunday, love.'

I said a general goodbye and we let ourselves out.

'When was the last time Max went to the toilet?' I asked Riley.

'When I got home from school.'

'OK, hopefully he won't have an accident in the car.'

I didn't have a dog carrier for transporting Max so I'd make do as best I could. I'd already put his bed on the back seat and Riley now lifted Max in, then sat next to him. He began stroking his head and talking to him in a gentle voice. Max's tail was wagging furiously and he kept standing up and sniffing around. Being in my car was a whole new experience for him, with lots of different smells and textures. I waited on the pavement with the rear car door open as Riley slowly calmed Max. After some minutes, Max lay down in his bed.

'Well done,' I told Riley. 'Keep stroking him and talking to him.'

I checked Riley's seatbelt was fastened, then got into the driver's seat. As I started the engine Max stood.

'Sit,' Riley told him.

I waited until Max had settled again, then pulled away. I drove slowly and evenly, avoiding any sudden movements; every so often I glanced in my rear-view mirror.

'You're doing a good job,' I told Riley, and saw him smile, pleased.

I stopped off at a small store on the way home to buy another box of dog food. It was a popular brand so I thought they would stock it. I parked right outside the shop where I would be able to see the car from inside.

'I'm just going to get some more dog food,' I said. 'We can't take Max into the shop.'

'I'll stay with him.'

I would never normally have left a child unattended in a car, and it was a pity Janie hadn't let me know they were nearly out of dog food, as I would have bought some earlier. Possibly there was enough in the box to see us through until tomorrow, but not knowing how much Max ate I didn't want to risk it. I took the box with me into the shop to make sure I bought exactly the same one and was out again in a couple of minutes. Max was sitting in his bed and Riley was still stroking and talking to him.

'Well done,' I said to them both as I got in.

Five minutes later we were home. I parked, opened Riley's door, and he and Max got out. The lead was still on and Riley encouraged Max along our front path. Max kept stopping and sniffing.

'I think Max may want to go to the toilet,' Riley said.

So by the light of our porch and the street lamp Riley waited patiently with Max as he sniffed the path and the garden that flanked it, while I unloaded the car. I put all the items in the hall, then locked the car. Max hadn't been to the toilet and seemed to have lost interest.

'We'll try him in the back garden,' I suggested.

We went indoors, where Max marked his new territory by squatting and weeing on the floor.

CHAPTER SEVENTEEN

BEST FRIEND AND COMPANION

I cleaned up the puddle Max had left in the hall with hot water and disinfectant while Riley stayed with him in the living room. Once I'd finished, I suggested we took Max into the back garden to show him where his toilet was. I didn't know much about toilet training dogs, only what I'd read with Janie on the internet. It had mentioned that as well as taking the dog to their toilet area as part of their routine, you should also do it after they'd had an accident to reinforce the connection of where they should go. Riley waited with Max while I took our coats and shoes to the back door ready. I also put out a cloth to wipe Max's paws when we came back in, as the grass would be heavy with dew.

I switched on the outside light. Its beam illuminated the upper part of the lawn and garden as well as the patio. The sky was dark and overcast, and the air temperature was freezing. If there was a moon it was concealed behind thick cloud cover.

'It's spooky out here,' Riley said, peering into the darkness at the end of the garden and the shadows of the trees.

'Don't worry, you're safe with me,' I said with a smile.

He raised his eyes cheekily and followed Max as he began sniffing around the garden bench.

'Take him onto the grass,' I said to Riley. 'But keep him on his lead. I don't want him disappearing.'

Although our garden was fenced and safe for children – it had to be for fostering and was inspected annually as part of my fostering review – it wasn't necessarily puppy-proof. In the dark Max could pick up and eat something he wasn't supposed to or get stuck in the shrubbery or behind the shed.

He loved sniffing the lawn with all its new smells; his nose was continually down and his tail up, wagging furiously. Max led Riley around the top part of the lawn while I sat on the bench, coat zipped up, taking in the peaceful calm of a night in the heart of winter. Even the birds were silent, presumably hunkered down somewhere warm and waiting for the day to appear.

After about ten minutes Riley said, 'I don't think Max wants the toilet again.'

'No, I agree.'

We returned indoors where I wiped Max's paws before Riley took him off the lead.

'He may need a drink,' Riley said. 'It's important dogs have water.'

'Yes, it is. His bowls are in the hall.'

'I'll get them. Come on, Max,' Riley cried, and, patting his thigh to get Max's attention, he ran out of the kitchen-diner.

Max shot after him and I caught another glimpse of the bond that was developing between them. Not only was Riley showing care and affection towards Max, but the dog was starting to follow his instructions, wanting to please Riley. I went into the hall too, to help bring in Max's bed, toys, boxes of food and so forth.

In the kitchen Max waited by Riley's feet as he filled his water bowl and set it carefully on the floor. Immediately Max began lapping up the water.

'You were right, he was thirsty,' I said. 'Well done. When do you feed him?'

'Soon,' Riley said. 'He still has three meals. I give him breakfast when I have mine and he has dinner when I have mine. Mum gives him lunch when she remembers. It doesn't matter if she forgets because Max is six months old so he can start having two meals a day soon. I read it on the internet on Mum's phone, and a boy at school has a puppy.'

I nodded, impressed by his knowledge, while wondering if Janie was aware that Riley was accessing the internet on her phone and, if so, whether she was supervising it.

At 6 p.m., when Paula arrived home from work, she was greeted in the hall by a very excited Max and Riley. It was just as well I'd forewarned her Max would be there for as soon as she came in, even before she'd taken off her coat, he was jumping up at her, mouth open, panting and slobbering as dogs do.

'This is Max,' Riley told her proudly.

'Hi, Max,' Paula said, and stroked his head. 'Hi, Riley. How are you?'

'He's my dog.'

'Yes, I know.'

I'd stopped what I was doing in the kitchen to go into the hall, hoping Max wouldn't get over-excited and make another puddle. I didn't think Paula would be too impressed.

'Hello, love. Good day?' I asked as I usually did.

'Yes, thanks, and you?'

I nodded.

Eventually Paula got the chance to take off her coat and shoes and then told Riley she was going upstairs to get changed and she'd be down again shortly. Riley and Max began to follow her up, but I called them back. It was all carpeted upstairs, which would make clearing up Max's accidents more difficult, and Paula wanted some peace. The hall downstairs was now laminate flooring, so easy to clean. It ran from the front door to the living room at the back of the house, which Riley now realised would make a good play area. He took one of Max's balls and began rolling it down the hall, encouraging Max to chase after it and 'fetch'. I watched for a while and then returned to the kitchen to put the finishing touches to dinner.

From what I could hear, Max had yet to master the art of fetching a ball, but I was impressed by Riley's patience and perseverance. As I worked I heard him shout, 'Fetch!' then the ball bounce and Max's paws scrabbling on the laminate, followed by Riley's footsteps as he retrieved the ball. He threw it again, 'Fetch, Max!' Then came the sound of the ball bouncing, dog paws and Riley having to get the ball himself. Well done, Riley, I thought, although I hadn't realized how much sound echoed in the hall!

Paula came downstairs and Riley wanted to show her what Max could do. She watched until I called them for dinner, when I told Riley to wash his hands, which he did the first time of being asked. He fed Max and then I served dinner – a cheese and vegetable bake. Before I sat at the table I closed the door to the kitchen-diner so we could keep an eye on Max. He had a sniff around and then got into his bed, which I'd put in one corner of the room. Exhausted from all the activity, he obligingly went to sleep.

'Puppies need a lot of sleep,' Riley told us. 'Alfie says so.'

'Who's Alfie?' I asked.

'The boy at school with a puppy.'

Riley continued to talk about Max and dogs in general, so much so we had to remind him to eat. But it was good to see him so enthusiastic and wanting to learn about dogs. Having Max had given him an interest and a sense of responsibility. Once we'd finished eating, Paula suggested to Riley we could play some board games like we had on his last stay. But as we left the table Max woke and Riley wasn't interested in games, only Max. He began showing us some of the tricks he was teaching him, which, like fetch, were works in progress. I was just wondering if we should take Max outside again when he trotted off into the hall, to the same place where he'd weed before, and now pooped.

'Yuck,' Paula said, covering her nose and mouth with the top of her jersey.

'Shall we take him outside?' Riley asked.

'Yes, on his lead,' I said.

Paula went with them while I cleaned up the mess and washed the floor again. It had never been so clean! I then googled on my phone how often six-month-old puppies did a poop and the answer was three to four times a day. I decided not to tell Paula.

They came in after about ten minutes without Max having gone to the toilet. We settled in the living room, but whereas on Riley's last visit he had needed constantly entertaining or had just wanted to watch television or my tablet, he now had Max, his best friend and companion. He talked about him, petted him, tickled his tummy and behind his ears, rolled around on the floor with him laughing, and told us how much he loved him. It was wonderful to see, and Paula quietly remarked to me, 'I think Max is good for Riley.'

'Yes,' I agreed. 'He is.'

However cooperative and happy Riley had been during the evening, he still liked to have his own way, and when it was time for bed he wanted Max to sleep with him. I'd already explained where Max would sleep and why – in his bed in the kitchen-diner – but Riley had either forgotten or didn't want to know.

'Max sleeps with me at my home,' he persisted, annoyed.

'I don't think he does. His bed is in your kitchen.'

'Yes, but we leave the doors open so he can come in at night.'

This may have been true, as I remembered Janie saying she had taken Max into her bed to stop him from whining on his first night and he'd weed on her duvet.

'It's different here, our –'

'No, it's not,' Riley snapped, before I could get any further.

'Our cat always slept in there,' I continued.

'Don't care,' Riley replied sullenly.

'I promise you, Max will be comfortable in his bed in there.'

'No, he won't. He'll cry.'

'If he does, I'll come down and settle him. I won't let him cry.'

'He doesn't like you,' Riley said, with attitude.

Paula had heard enough and with a small sigh went into the kitchen to make herself a drink. Riley and I had reached an impasse, with Riley refusing to go upstairs and get ready for bed without Max being allowed to sleep with him.

'I'm sorry, Riley,' I said more firmly. 'I don't have animals sleep on the beds. I know it's different in your home.'

'I'll stay down here then and sleep with Max,' Riley replied.

'I think that would be very uncomfortable for you.'

'Don't care.'

'Riley, I understand how much you love and care for Max, but he will be more comfortable down here. Once you're ready for bed you can settle him and say goodnight.' It crossed my mind that perhaps I was being unreasonable, but I knew Max was likely to go to the toilet at some point in the night, and it was true I'd never allowed our pets to sleep in the bedrooms, although I appreciate many people are happy to do so. Also, it was likely that Riley would want to bring Max again, so I had to feel comfortable with the arrangements, as well as reassure Riley.

Paula reappeared with a glass of juice. 'I'll stay with Max while you get ready for bed,' she said to Riley.

Riley looked at Max, who was now fast sleep on the floor.

'Come on, quickly,' I said. 'Or you'll be too tired to take him for a walk tomorrow. I know just the place for walking dogs, and we can practise fetch.'

'Can I hold his lead?'

'Yes, of course. And then we've got bowling on Sunday,' I said, reminding him of the treat. 'So lots of nice things to look forward to, but we all need a good night's sleep first. Otherwise Max will be too tired to play fetch and so will you.'

Perhaps it was something I said or perhaps Riley just ran out of steam, but he slowly stood and, telling Max he wouldn't be long, went into the hall. I followed, leaving Paula with Max. Upstairs, Riley had the quickest bath ever. He hadn't packed much so he dressed in the pyjamas I'd bought. I reminded him to brush his teeth, and ten minutes later we were downstairs again in the living room. Max was still asleep, and Riley carefully picked him up and carried him into his bed in the kitchen-diner without being asked, which suggested I had won his cooperation, in this at least. Max's eyes opened and Riley sat by him and stroked his head until his eyes closed again. He went off to sleep with his head resting on one of his soft toys.

'He's exhausted,' I whispered to Riley. 'You must be too.'

He shook his head. 'I'm not. I'll stay with him.'

We had another shorter conversation about why Riley couldn't sleep with Max, and eventually I persuaded Riley to say goodnight.

'I'm upstairs if you need me,' he said to Max, and kissed his head.

He kissed him again, and then reluctantly came away, and I quietly closed the door behind us. It was now 9.30.

As Riley got into bed I reassured him again that Max would be fine in his bed downstairs and I would listen out for him. 'I've never left a baby to cry and I wouldn't Max,' I said.

By 10.30 Paula and I were in bed too. I'd checked on Max before I'd come up and he'd been fast asleep in his bed. He stayed that way for about twenty minutes, then, as I turned off my lamp, I heard him give some little yappy barks. I lay still and listened. Perhaps it was because the house was suddenly quiet now we were all in bed, or maybe because he was in a strange room? Gradually the little barks grew louder and more insistent. I put on my dressing gown and quietly went downstairs, hoping he hadn't woken Riley.

I slowly opened the door to the kitchen-diner and went in. Max was out of his bed and came to me, tail wagging.

'Come on, back to bed,' I said, talking to him as I would a child who was up at night.

I wasn't expecting Max to stay in his bed as I would a child, just to be reassured and hopefully be quiet. I stroked his head for a few minutes and then came out. I waited on the other side of the door, listening. All was quiet and I returned to my bed.

Fifteen minutes later the yapping began again. It couldn't be ignored and before long it would wake Paula and Riley. I went downstairs, resettled Max and left, again pausing outside the door before returning to my bed. Ten minutes later he was barking again and had woken Paula. She came out of her room as I left mine.

'Don't worry, love. I'll see to him. You go back to bed.'

'Sure?'

'Yes.'

I went downstairs and resettled Max, then returned to my bed. This continued every fifteen minutes or so, and by 1 a.m. I was regretting agreeing to have Max stay. I had far more success resettling children.

Then on my last trip down Max was standing bashfully beside a large puddle. I wondered if that had been the reason he'd been so unsettled. Had he been trying to tell me he needed the toilet? If so, it was real progress, I supposed. Rubber gloves on and with Max watching, I cleared up the mess with hot water and disinfectant, took Max back to his bed, and returned to mine. Thankfully I didn't hear anything further until Riley came out of his room just after 6.30 a.m. He used the toilet and then ran downstairs. I followed, putting on my dressing gown as I went.

'Max has been a good boy,' Riley declared, going into the kitchen-diner. 'He slept all night.'

'I resettled him a few times,' I said. 'But he was fine.' And I hoped tonight he would be even better!

CHAPTER EIGHTEEN

THE PROS AND CONS OF DOG OWNERSHIP

I made sure Riley was dressed before he took Max into the garden. Sometimes at home he went out in his pyjamas, but it was cold and damp. I dressed too, and a little after seven o'clock on that Saturday morning in February we were both outside, coats zipped up, our warm breaths misting in the early-morning air. The grass was laden with dew and the sky had only just lightened on what looked like a fine day. I stood with Riley as he waited patiently for Max to go to the toilet. Max sniffed around the wet grass but seemed to have little idea why he was out there.

'Do you usually take him out before or after his breakfast?' I asked Riley.

He shrugged. 'Sometimes before and sometimes after.'

We waited another five minutes or so, then I suggested we try again later.

'It's hard work having a dog,' Riley admitted as we went indoors. Then he quickly added, 'But I don't mind. I love Max.'

I smiled. 'I know, and it will get easier,' I reassured him. 'Once Max is fully house-trained, he'll know what to do.'

'Mum says it's like potty training a kid. That's why she can't help with Max. She's too busy with Lola.'

'Yes, love, I understand. You're doing a great job.'

He looked relieved.

In the kitchen I wiped Max's paws before Riley took him off the lead, then he gave him breakfast. I shut the door from the kitchen-diner to the hall while I made our breakfast. I didn't want Max returning to the spot in the hall he'd marked as his toilet or relieving himself elsewhere.

Riley and I sat at the table in the kitchen-diner as we ate a breakfast of cereal and toast. I'd offered Riley a cooked breakfast, but he hadn't wanted one.

'Mum has a table now,' Riley remarked.

I nodded.

They hadn't had a table when I'd first become involved with the family. Liv had suggested it, not only as somewhere to eat, but as a place for Riley and Jayden to do their schoolwork and crayoning, etc. I'd helped them buy the second-hand table, which had come with four matching chairs. Most of their furniture was second-hand or had been donated, as it is for many living on benefits long term.

As we ate I kept glancing at Max. If he began sniffing around, I'd take him outside. I felt sure he must want to go to the toilet by now. He hadn't been since before 1 a.m.

Once we'd finished, Riley began playing ball with Max as I cleared away the dishes. As usual when Riley played with Max it was very energetic and noisy, with Max as excited as Riley. I thought of Paula in the room above having a lie-in after a week at work.

'You could take Max outside again, if you like,' I suggested, 'while I finish clearing up in here.'

Riley immediately put on his coat and shoes, clipped on Max's lead and went out the back door. I could see them through the kitchen window as I worked. Riley was running up and down the garden with Max at his side, both having fun and burning off some energy. Suddenly I saw Max stop, squat and go to the toilet. Riley looked at me to make sure I'd seen it, and I gave him the thumbs-up. Nevertheless, he still wanted to tell me, so he appeared at the back door.

'Max did a poop on the grass!' he exclaimed, delighted.

'Good. Hopefully he'll remember for next time.' I took a small disposable bag from a kitchen drawer, went outside and cleared up the mess.

'Can we take Max for a walk on the lead now and teach him how to fetch like you said?' Riley asked.

'Yes, but first you need to have a wash and brush your teeth.'

He groaned but did as I asked.

It was a little after 9 a.m. when Riley, Max and I set off, leaving Paula awake but in bed. Riley looked very proud to be walking his dog along the street, especially when we saw other dog owners who either said hello or nodded, even though they didn't know us. I quickly formed the impression that dog owners were a very friendly group. Some even stopped to chat as the dogs sniffed each other. If they asked about Max, I always let Riley answer and he glowed with pride.

There's an area on the far side of our local park that runs into open countryside, which I thought would be perfect for Max. There was no one else there yet and we began teaching Max to fetch. I threw the ball and Riley, with Max on the lead, ran after it. Riley then encouraged Max to pick up the ball in his mouth with the hope he would carry it back to me. Max didn't, so Riley brought the ball back to me and I threw it again – once, twice, a dozen or more times. I reassured Riley that it would take a while to teach Max tricks, just as it would to house-train him.

We were there for nearly an hour and then Max lost interest and sat down on the grass, refusing to chase after another ball. We returned home, where I made Riley and myself a hot chocolate drink. Paula was up and getting ready to go out. She was meeting a friend for lunch and to go shopping. Before she left she spent a while talking to Riley, whose only conversation was about his beloved Max.

Max was exhausted from all the exercise and sprawled out on the living-room floor and went to sleep. After a while I saw him suddenly wake and leave the room. I went after him. He was heading for his toilet spot in the hall. I quickly picked him up and carried him out of the front door where he pooped in the garden – much better than the hall floor – and I cleaned it up.

Riley and I had lunch around midday and straight afterwards he wanted to take Max for another walk. Coats and shoes on again, and with Max on the lead, we followed the same route as we had earlier, stopping for more games of fetch. There were a few others walking in the area now, some with dogs. A couple of times, after a lot of encouragement, Max picked up the ball in his mouth and Riley and I praised him. Max received more praise on the way home when he stopped at a lamppost, had a good sniff and then weed. It seemed my weekend was revolving around Max's toileting, but Riley was focused and hadn't got into a strop or asked for my tablet all day. That afternoon Riley even remembered he had some homework to do!

'I left my book at school,' he admitted guiltily. 'But I remember what we have to do.' The children had exercise books they were supposed to bring home to write in, together with their reading book.

'It's important to bring home your schoolwork,' I said. 'What is your homework?'

'We have to make up a word search of our own. We've been doing them in class.'

A word search is an activity that involves identifying words hidden in a page of letters set out in a grid. It can be a leisure activity for children and adults too, but also helps improve problem-solving skills and word recognition.

'We'll do it on a sheet of paper,' I said to Riley. 'How big has it got to be?'

'Miss didn't say, but the words have to be about animals. She said to look them up if we didn't know how to spell them.'

I fetched a ruler, a pencil and a sheet of plain A4 paper and set them on the coffee table in the living room. I drew up the children's stool for Riley to sit on.

'It's supposed to be in the book I left at school,' Riley said, not moving, apparently thinking that meant he couldn't do his homework.

'I know, but as you have forgotten your book you can do your homework on this sheet of paper. Better that than not do it at all.' He looked as though he disagreed, which I ignored. 'Sit down, love, and start by ruling out the paper into small boxes. Do you know how to do that?'

'Of course, I'm not thick,' he said, and sat on the stool.

He picked up the pencil and ruler but didn't know how to begin so I pointed to where he needed to draw the outer lines of the box. Once he'd done that, he stopped again, unsure of how to continue.

'Now mark out where you will draw the lines by putting a dot every centimetre,' I said, showing him on the ruler. 'Then the boxes will be the same size when you draw them.' I'd done this activity with other children I'd looked after, and my own. Creating word searches seemed to be a lasting educational favourite.

Riley concentrated on marking out the lines, then, using the ruler, he joined the dots to form a grid as Max slept peacefully on the floor a little way off, occasionally twitching.

'Well done,' I said, once the grid was complete. 'Now you need to think of some animals. 'Did your teacher say how many you need to do?'

'Ten, or more if we want, but I will do ten.'

'OK, think of some animals and I'll help you with the spelling.'

'Dog,' Riley said.

'Good. Can you spell it?'

'Of course. D-o-g,' he wrote in the boxes as he sounded it out.

'Excellent.'

'Cat,' Riley said, and he could spell that too. 'Dinosaur,' he said, which he couldn't spell – not many children his age could. I sounded it out for him. 'Rabbit,' he said.

'Good, you could write it vertically or diagonally, so the words are more difficult to find,' I suggested, and pointed out what I meant.

'That's what Miss said, but I like doing it my way.'

'OK, it's your word search.'

I helped him sound out 'rabbit'.

'Bird' was his next word and he asked how to spell it.

Snake was next. And so we continued. Once there were ten words, he stopped. 'Finished,' he declared, and put down his pencil.

'No, you haven't.'

'Yes, I have, I've done ten.'

'Riley, look at the word search,' I said. 'Isn't there something missing?'

It took him a few moments to realize.

'Doh,' he said, slapping his forehead. 'I haven't put in the other letters.'

'That's right. But don't slap your head, you'll hurt yourself.'

Riley picked up the pencil again and began writing Ts in the empty boxes. After a while I said, 'Choose some other letters to make the words more difficult to spot.'

He wrote a number of As, then Bs, then Cs, then Ds and so on until all the empty boxes were filled.

'Miss said to write the words at the bottom,' he said. 'But I don't think I'll do that.'

'I think you will, love, as it's part of your homework.'

He hesitated, glanced at the dog who was still asleep, then began copying the words from the grid at the foot of the page.

'Good boy,' I said. 'But, Riley, you need to try to remember to take your book bag home with you. It's important you do your schoolwork.'

'It's boring,' he said, which I'd heard from other children who were struggling with their learning.

'I'm sure it can't all be boring, and you want to be able to read, write and count, don't you? Your teacher and TA [teaching assistant] will help you if you're stuck.' I knew Riley had extra support in the classroom from the TA.

'My teacher tells me off,' Riley said.

'For what?'

'Talking when I'm not supposed to and winding up other kids.'

'So don't do it. Behave yourself and you won't get into trouble.'

I'd found before that children who found learning challenging could become disruptive if not engaged with the lesson. Some teachers are better at differentiating work – tailoring it to the child's needs – than others. As I wasn't fostering Riley full-time, I wasn't invited to attend the meetings associated with his Individual Education Plan (IEP). Janie would go.

'Have you got any other homework?' I asked Riley.

'Don't think so,' he said, which probably meant yes.

Again, had I been fostering Riley I would have made sure I knew what homework he had, and that he had it with him.

Riley left the coffee table and began stroking Max.

'I'm going to work with dogs when I'm older,' he said, suggesting he had no need of an education. 'I'll charge people to walk their dogs.'

'So you will need to be able to make appointments and keep accounts.'

'No, you do it all on your phone,' he said, which was probably true.

I praised him for doing his homework, then folded the paper and placed it in an envelope, ready to take with us on Sunday. Paula texted to say she was going to the cinema with her friend so would be home later than planned. We always let each other know if our arrangements changed.

Have a good evening x, I replied.

Thanks, and you x

When Max woke Riley took him in the back garden while I began preparing our dinner. He went to the toilet, which may have just been good timing rather than control, but Riley and I were delighted and made a big fuss of him. That evening Riley sat with Max on his lap as we watched a children's film together. Again, I noticed how much calmer and focused Riley was as he held Max close and gently stroked his fur. The therapeutic value of pets, especially cats and dogs, is now recognized, with some studies showing a decrease in the stress-related hormone cortisol and a rise in the feel-good hormone oxytocin. However, this needs to be balanced against the work and commitment needed to look after a pet, which, as Janie was finding, could be very stressful.

When it was Riley's bedtime he was more accepting of Max sleeping in the kitchen-diner and only asked twice if Max could sleep on his bed. Like the night before, once Riley was ready for bed he came down and said goodnight to Max.

'Sleep tight,' he told him, using the phrase I did. 'See you in the morning.'

And with a final kiss he came away.

'Good boy,' I said. 'We've had a nice day.'

'Yes. I wish it could be like this at Mum's,' he said with a child's honesty.

'It will be, she just needs some help.'

Paula arrived home shortly after Riley was asleep and we spent a while chatting before we went to bed. Max was still sound asleep in his bed, and during the night I only had to settle him once – a huge improvement on the night before. I felt I was finally getting the hang of looking after a dog!

CHAPTER NINETEEN

RILEY IS ACCUSED

On Sunday morning Riley was up early again, eager to see Max. By 7.30 a.m. we were both dressed and outside waiting for Max to go to the toilet, which he did. There'd only been one puddle again during the night. Riley wanted to stay outside and play with Max so I left him in the garden, reminding him not to make too much noise, as it was very early on a Sunday morning when my neighbours might be having a lie-in. He came in when it began to rain and practised making Max sit on command, with some success.

Paula joined us for breakfast and when she asked Riley what he'd been doing he told her about Max and the word search. 'You can do my word search if you want,' he said hopefully.

'Yes, I used to like word searches.'

I fetched the envelope containing Riley's homework and he was delighted when Paula needed time to find some of the well-hidden words.

'I know how to make them,' Riley announced proudly. 'Shall I show you?'

'Yes, please,' Paula said.

I fetched more paper, the pencil and ruler and returned to the table where Riley set about making another word search. I helped him with the spellings and Paula and I praised the end result.

'Miss will be pleased,' Riley said happily. 'I've done more homework than I was told to.'

'She certainly will be,' I agreed.

'I can't wait to show her,' Riley exclaimed excitedly.

Only yesterday school had been 'boring', but now Riley had done something well his confidence and enthusiasm had grown. We usually enjoy what we are good at and are good at what we enjoy. Sometimes if feels safer to avoid or dismiss a new challenge for fear of failing. But as my dear father used to quote: *It's better to have tried and failed than never to have tried at all.*

Aware that Janie struggled with timekeeping, I texted her on Sunday morning to remind her that I'd be there around 1 p.m. to collect Jayden and return Max. She replied: *Can you give Riley something to eat? My friend has eaten all my food!*

I'd already told Janie we'd have lunch before we left, and I thought she was probably exaggerating about her friend. She had a habit of overstating events for dramatic effect, which made gauging the severity of an incident difficult.

That morning Paula spent time with Riley and Max and had lunch with us before going to see Lucy and Adrian. Shortly after she left, Riley and I packed up the car with his and Max's belongings, took Max in the garden to see if he wanted to go to the toilet (he didn't), then set off for his home. I felt the weekend had gone very well but I steeled myself for the question I knew Riley would ask. Five minutes into the journey he said:

'If I stay with you again can Max come?'

I never knowingly make a promise I might not be able to keep, so I replied, 'I'm not sure, love. We'll have to see.'

'Why not?'

'I'd need to discuss it with your mother first and I might have plans where it would be difficult to take Max.'

'What sort of plans?' Riley asked.

'Well, if we went out for the day, for example. Not all places allow dogs, and it wouldn't be fair to leave Max shut in our house all day.'

I glanced at Riley in the rear-view mirror and could see he was deep in thought.

'I don't mind not going out for the day,' he said. 'And Mum won't mind if he stays with me.'

'We'll see,' I said again.

Of course Janie wouldn't mind us having Max for another weekend. She'd been finding it challenging looking after Riley and had then added Max to her family. Although I could now see the benefits of Riley having a dog, I agreed with Liv that it was bad timing.

Riley asked me again if Max could come and stay and I repeated what I'd already said. He was used to his mother giving in to him, so I needed to stand my ground. Riley knew he had to keep Max on the lead until he was safely indoors. He pressed their doorbell and his mother answered, greeting us with, 'Oh, it's you. Here comes trouble.' Then she shouted through to the kitchen-diner, 'They're back!'

Riley let Max off the lead and he shot off down the hall. Riley followed.

'Are we going bowling?' Jayden asked, appearing in the hall.

'Yes, love. Are you ready?'

I put Riley's bag in the children's bedroom, then took Max's bed, etc., through to the kitchen-diner. A woman of a similar age to Janie was sitting at the table.

'This is my friend from school,' Janie said.

'Hi, I'm Cathy,' I said with a smile.

'Hello,' she said in a dour voice. Then to Janie: 'I'm going outside for a ciggy while you see to the kids.'

'You can smoke in here, she's not a social worker,' Janie said.

'No, I'll go outside.'

And for reasons I couldn't explain, I felt that her eagerness to leave was more about not wanting to be with me than exposing the children to smoke.

'Max wees and poos outside now,' Riley eagerly told his mother.

'Sometimes,' I added. 'We've been taking him out regularly and it seems to be working.'

'Mum, you'll have to take him when I'm not here,' Riley added.

'Yes, I hear you,' Janie said, clearly preoccupied. Then quietly to me she said, 'Can you lend me a tenner until tomorrow? My friend wants to order pizza and I've only got three pounds left. She lives on takeaways. We had one Friday and a Chinese last night. She ordered the most expensive thing on the menu with fancy beef.'

We both glanced towards the window, through which we could see Janie's friend smoking and talking on her phone.

'Hasn't she offered to pay for anything?' I asked, concerned.

'No, and I don't like to ask. It's nice of her to visit me after all this time.'

I paused for a moment before I said, 'I'll buy what you need from the supermarket on the way back from bowling, but I don't feel comfortable giving you money to buy your friend another takeaway. You could offer to cook something – pasta?' I knew Janie always had a packet of dried pasta in the cupboard, as many of us do.

She pulled a face. 'I don't like to. She's used to better things.'

I decided that was for Janie to sort out.

'Have Jayden and Lola had something to eat this morning?' I now asked.

'Yes, they finished off the Chinese. There was loads. She ordered a meal for four.'

I nodded. 'What do you want from the shop?'

'A bag of chicken nuggets and chips for the kids and me to have tomorrow. Hopefully she'll be gone by then. I'll pay you when my money comes through.'

'OK.'

'Don't forget to take Max outside,' Riley told his mother.

'Yes, yes, I heard,' Janie replied.

I helped Jayden into his coat and shoes, and we left. I thought about Janie and her friend as I drove. Surely her friend knew that Janie didn't have a job and lived on benefits? Unless Janie hadn't told her? Even so, it seemed selfish to me to spend the weekend with some- one and live on takeaways and not offer to pay. I guessed Janie valued her friendship and didn't like to make a fuss, but she couldn't afford the luxury of regular take-aways.

The boys and I had a fun afternoon bowling. We played two games and then, as we changed out of our bowling shoes, the boys said they were hungry and asked for burgers from the café. I had one too. On the way to Janie's I stopped off at the supermarket and bought the shopping Janie had asked for. I wasn't expecting her to pay for it. I'd helped her out before, as Liv had. A recent survey found that seven out of ten social workers have used their own money to help a family suffering financial hardship by buying essentials, or a birthday present for a child, for example, when they otherwise wouldn't have had one.

It was just after 5 p.m. when we arrived at Janie's and by then her friend had gone.

'I told her I only had pasta and she left soon after,' Janie laughed. 'She wasn't impressed.'

I smiled too. 'But you had a nice weekend?' I asked.

'I guess so. To be honest it was a bit of a surprise, her suddenly getting in touch. I mean, we weren't that friendly at school. She's obviously doing well for herself – better than me.'

'You're doing fine,' I reassured her, and passed her the shopping.

I confirmed I'd see them as usual in the morning and, saying goodbye, I left.

I was surprised when, later that evening, a little after 8 p.m., my mobile rang and Janie's number showed on the caller display. Paula and I had eaten; she was upstairs washing her hair ready for work in the morning.

'Hi, Janie.'

'You know Riley stayed at yours the whole weekend?' she began.

'Yes.'

'Did he have any money with him?'

'Not as far as I know.'

'So he didn't buy anything or show you money?'

'No. Why?'

'It's just that I'm sure I had more in my purse. I know I spent a lot on takeaways, but I don't see how I can just have three pounds left.'

'You think Riley might have taken money from your purse?' I asked uneasily.

'He did once before, but that was to buy me a Mother's Day present so I forgave him.'

'Have you talked to Riley about it?'

'He said he hasn't taken it.'

'Perhaps you spent more than you realized?' I suggested.

'Yes, that must be it,' Janie agreed. 'You know me and money.'

'You've got enough food for tomorrow?' I checked.

'Yes.'

'Was that everything?'

'Yes.'

'See you in the morning then,' I said, and the call ended.

Although Riley's behaviour had given cause for concern, as far as I was aware there'd been no suggestion of him stealing. I hoped I would have been told so I could take precautions – for example, by not leaving my hand-bag lying around. It's difficult if a child habitually steals and it can take a while to regain trust.

I checked my purse and as far as I could see there was nothing missing. I didn't keep much cash now anyway; I used my debit card, and a credit card, which I cleared at the end of each month. Many young children go through a stage of taking things that don't belong to them and the parent or carer teaches them it's wrong. Riley taking money to buy his mother a gift I viewed more as touching, so I didn't give the matter any more thought. I assumed Janie had spent more than she'd realized.

On Monday morning I arrived at Janie's at my usual time and managed to get them out of the door to arrive on time for school. When I arrived on Wednesday a wind was getting up. The worst storm in decades was forecast to hit the UK over the next two days, peaking on Friday. The Met Office had given a red weather warning advising people to stay indoors.

'Some schools are closing!' Janie cried excitably, checking her mobile phone for the latest news feed. 'Nothing from ours yet.' Their school, like most others, emailed parents now rather than sending a letter home with the child.

The children were looking worried, and Riley and Jayden were hyper. I calmed them down.

'Let me know if your school closes and I won't come on Friday,' I said to Janie. I then asked Riley if his teacher had liked his word search.

'Yes, I got a good work sticker,' he said, pleased.

The wind continued to increase during the day on Wednesday and on Thursday Janie texted to say their school was closing early that afternoon and would be closed all day Friday. *Are you collecting Riley on Saturday?*

Yes, I confirmed. *About 10 a.m.*

Like most others who didn't have to go out, I heeded the government warning to stay indoors. I sat at my computer and tried to concentrate as the wind howled outside, tossing bins and other items along the street. Paula had to drive to work that morning and texted to say she had arrived safely but said that some roads were closed due to fallen trees. By the time she returned home that evening the wind had eased, although it was still blustery.

We watched the evening news, which was dominated by storm damage and the clear-up now going on, not just in the UK but across Europe. Like the other extreme weather conditions the world was now regularly experiencing, it was put down to climate change. Very worrying, particularly as governments could be doing a lot more to reduce carbon emissions, preserve forestation and generally clean up the planet.

Janie hadn't mentioned Max staying with me at the weekend but I was half expecting her to ask me when I collected Riley on Saturday morning. Or perhaps she'd just assumed I would be taking him. Janie could make assumptions without checking first, then become upset and disappointed if her arrangements didn't go to plan. I checked with Paula that she didn't mind Max staying, and she didn't. After a busy time the previous weekend, she was planning on chilling this weekend.

Because the school had been closed on Friday, Janie would have had the children all day and probably not gone out. I wondered how she'd coped. I texted before I left home to say I was on my way. The roads I used had been cleared of storm damage, but some of the pavements were still blocked by large branches. I passed a huge tree that had fallen in a front garden.

I arrived at Janie's as planned at 10 a.m. Riley answered the door but was looking very glum.

'What's the matter, love?' I asked, going in.

'Something's happened, but Mum won't tell me what,' he replied.

The poor lad looked as though he had the weight of the world on his shoulders.

'Don't worry, I'll talk to her. Where is she?'

'In her room.'

I could hear the television on in the main room and I checked in there first. Jayden and Lola were sitting on the sofa watching a children's programme. Max was beside them.

'You stay with Jayden and Lola while I talk to your mum,' I told Riley.

He picked up Max to make room on the sofa and sat with him on his lap.

Janie's bedroom door was ajar. I knocked and went in. She was sitting on the edge of the bed, shoulders slumped forward.

'Janie?'

She nodded an acknowledgement but didn't look up.

'What's the matter?'

I went closer and saw she was holding her mobile phone in her hands and gazing at a blank screen.

'What's the matter?' I asked again.

She looked up, tears in her eyes.

'I've been such an idiot. And now the police are involved. That's the last thing I need. Read it yourself,' she said, and thrust her phone at me.

CHAPTER TWENTY

ACCIDENT AND EMERGENCY

I began reading the social media messages on Janie's phone, scrolling back to the beginning of some threads. She sat, quiet and dejected, on the edge of the bed. The sound of the children's television drifted in. It soon became clear what had been going on and why Janie was upset. The so-called 'friend' who'd stayed with her last weekend, who I now knew to be called Isla, was a thief and a liar, and had been scamming her friends. She'd traced many from her class at school through social media and had contacted them with the same story – that she'd been seriously ill and regretted not keeping in touch – then arranged to visit and stay. Not only did she live off them, but she also stole what she could. Those who'd been taken in were outraged and there were a lot of expletives. Sometimes she just stayed for a night or two, but with some she had stayed for a whole week. It wasn't until one person posted on social media about how they'd been deceived that others posted that they had been too. She'd stolen cash, jewellery, clothes, perfume – anything she fancied. Two had been tricked into giving her their card details on the pretence of ordering a takeaway; later they'd found she'd bought other stuff too. When they tried to phone her it wouldn't connect, and since the police had been involved she'd deleted her social media accounts.

'I didn't see those posts until I googled her name,' Janie admitted, clearly blaming herself.

'I'm sure the police will find her,' I said. I'd read a post that said the police were contacting everyone and to contact them if you'd been affected.

'I'm not emailing them,' Janie replied. 'Other than feeling a complete fool, I guess I got off lightly. All she took from me was the money from my purse. I knew I should have been more careful. What really hurts is that I believed she was a real friend who'd bothered to get in touch after all these years.'

I looked at Janie, sad and downcast. I didn't know how to help her. She stood and, putting her phone into her pocket, looked at me.

'Max isn't coming with you today,' she said.

'OK, is Riley still coming?'

'Don't know.'

I went with her into the main room.

'Riley, you going with Cathy?' she asked, her voice sounding flat.

'Can Max come too?' he replied.

'No. I told you, he stays here with me. Liv wants to know I'm looking after him.'

'I'm not going then,' Max replied, not taking his eyes from the television.

'Sure?' I asked, and he shook his head.

'Are we going bowling today?' Jayden asked.

'Tomorrow,' I replied. 'We can all go.'

I was about to leave, but then I hesitated and said, 'You all need a break now. What about if we went to the park?'

'Park,' Lola replied, and came over.

'We haven't got anything else on,' Janie said to Riley, who continued watching television.

'Riley and Jayden, are you coming?' I asked.

Neither spoke. Riley was watching television and Jayden was watching Riley.

'Enough television for one day,' Janie said. 'You've got the park.'

Riley ignored her.

'Now!' Janie said, and she switched off the TV at the plug.

'I was watching that!' Riley shouted.

'Later. You've had it on all morning.'

As Riley leapt from the sofa and began thundering around the room, I was starting to regret offering to take them out at all.

'We can take the dog on a lead,' I suggested.

'I know!' Riley shouted. And he went to fetch his shoes.

Jayden copied him.

Fifteen minutes later we were ready to be outside; the air was fresh and welcome. We walked to the park, which was at the end of their road.

'Are you OK?' I asked Janie.

'I guess so. I just have to come to terms with what has happened.'

'It's up to you, but personally, I would call the police.'

'I'll think about it,' she said.

We were at the park for nearly an hour. I texted Paula and explained what had happened. *You up for visiting Lucy later?*

Yes, if they're free.

I saw Janie home and then went to my house and texted Lucy. She replied saying they were just out at present but to come this afternoon. So Paula and I had some lunch and then went to Lucy's for about 2 p.m. Lucy was unsympathetic when I told her what had happened to Janie. 'She needs to check up on who she is meeting first.'

We spent time with Emma and Theo, then we left around 4.30 to go home. After we'd had dinner I stood at the French windows and looked down the garden. It was a mess. I had a pain in my stomach, which refused to go. The light was fading and I sat on the sofa and nodded off. When I woke about an hour later the pain had gone, although I didn't feel well and went to bed at 8.30. Paula was sympathetic but unable to offer much.

The following morning the pain hadn't returned. I got up but didn't feel like any breakfast. Paula asked how I was and I said, 'OK, I think.'

We decided it was indigestion and continued with our arrangements as planned. I had organized to take Riley and Jayden bowling again on Sunday. 'You don't need my help?' Paula asked.

'No, love. I'll be fine. You do what you want.'

When I arrived at Janie's flat, I found that she was largely over her upset and was concentrating on getting ready. Then suddenly I had to sit down. I wasn't feeling myself. The pain had returned, and I felt hot and sick.

'I can't go out at present,' I said.

'What's wrong?' Janie asked.

'I'm not sure. I've got a pain.'

Janie looked at me. None of them knew what to do.

'Should you go to the hospital?' she asked.

'Just give me about five minutes,' I said. I gradually recovered.

'Are you OK?' Janie asked.

'I think so.'

'Do you want to go home?'

'No, I'll come.'

'Perhaps you're doing too much?' she suggested.

'I don't do as much as I used to,' I replied.

A few minutes later and it was as though the pain was no longer there, but I needed to use the toilet.

'You don't usually use my loo,' Janie said, referring to the fact that it wasn't kept clean.

The children were now looking at me with concern. I went to the toilet and sat down. I had some blood in my urine, but the pain had gone. I made a mental note to phone my doctor first thing in the morning, but I didn't say anything now.

'Are you all ready?' I asked, returning.

'Yes,' Janie said. 'Max can stay here for a short while.'

It was about a quarter of an hour's drive to the leisure centre and they were all well pleased to be there. I don't think Janie would have gone without me.

Happy that the pain had gone, I got bowling shoes for everyone, and Lola ran between us, delighted to be going in with the boys. We played our usual two games and Riley won.

'I can't afford to pay you,' Janie said quietly to me.

'It doesn't matter.'

We ate there and I dropped them all off at home. It was about five o'clock by the time we'd finished.

'I'll see you tomorrow,' Janie said. 'Thank you.'

'Yes, see you tomorrow.'

As I drove away I didn't feel wonderful and about halfway home the pain started again – this time more severe. I drove straight to the hospital, parked in their car park and rummaged in my bag for coins for the meter.

Inside, a large wall display showed a five-hour waiting time. I hesitated before giving my details to the receptionist. I was asked to sit down and had just done so when a nurse called me in. She took my temperature and blood pressure, and examined my stomach. She said it looked like a stone and gave me a painkiller, then asked me to wait outside.

I joined twenty others. The pain in my stomach was getting worse, not better. I began to sweat again. I texted Paula and told her I'd had the pain again, twice, and was now at the hospital. I asked her not to bother the others, although I knew she would. Adrian and Lucy both texted; Adrian offered to come and sit with me.

No, I'm fine. Don't do that, I replied.

I googled what a stone was – a hardened deposit of digestive fluid that can form in your kidney or gallbladder. I didn't know where it had come from, only that it seemed to be getting worse. I read that the kidneys seemed the more likely source, and the size of the stone can range from as small as a grain of sand to as large as a golf ball. People who experience symptoms from their stones sometimes require surgery. Surely, I didn't need that?

The pain began to ease and just before seven o'clock Adrian walked in. He came straight over.

'Lovely to see you. You shouldn't have come.'

'You're all right,' he said, kissing my cheek, and sat next to me.

'I'm afraid there is no news yet,' I whispered. 'But the nurse said she thinks it may be a stone.'

'How on earth did you get that?'

'I don't know. They've given me a very strong pain-killer.'

We sat and waited, and talked mainly about their baby, Sophia, now five weeks old. It was after nine o'clock before I got called to see the doctor. Adrian came with me and we went through two sets of double doors, where the nurse showed us into a cubicle where a doctor was wait-ing. I explained what had happened and confirmed I'd never experienced anything like this before. He made notes as I spoke and then asked Adrian to wait outside while he examined me. The pain had largely gone now but I suspected that was to do with the pain relief, as the area was still sore. The doctor pressed my stomach and I groaned.

He decided that in all likelihood it was a kidney stone, but he wanted me to have an X-ray first. He gave me a form, told me where to go and said to wait outside until someone came for us. Adrian and I followed his instruc-tions to the X-ray department, where we sat down. With no one on hand to give the form to, we waited, and after about ten minutes a nurse appeared and took my form. We waited some more.

'You'll be late getting up for work tomorrow,' I said to Adrian.

'It doesn't matter,' he replied.

We waited for another ten minutes and then an elderly man on a trolley was wheeled out of one of the X-ray compartments. A while later I was invited in while Adrian waited outside where he looked after my handbag. I lay down on the bed and the nurse checked my name and the reason I was there. She then positioned me. It was very high-tech and it had been a long while since I'd had anything so sophisticated used on me. She positioned the monitor, told me to stay still and then went behind a screen from where she worked the X-ray mechanism. It hummed as it moved over me and then stopped. I was told to take a breath and then the process was repeated.

'All finished,' she said, coming out. 'Return to the waiting area, please.'

I explained to Adrian what had happened as we made our way back along the twisting, twining corridors. The numbers waiting in Accident and Emergency had decreased. It was now quarter to ten on a Sunday evening. We sat down and I saw Adrian stifle a yawn.

'Go if you want to,' I told him.

'No, I wouldn't hear of it.'

Half an hour passed before my name was called. The nurse showed us into a consulting room and left. There was no doctor there; it was another five minutes before they appeared.

'Sorry to keep you,' he said, clipping my X-rays onto a lightbox. He switched on the light and appeared to be studying them, then after a while said, 'You have a kidney stone – two to be exact.'

'Oh, I see,' I said, relieved.

Adrian looked relieved too.

'In my view we don't need to do anything. Most kidney stones are small enough to be passed out in your wee and can probably be treated at home. They may cause pain until you pass them, which usually takes one to two days.'

'Thank you,' I said.

'I will get you a leaflet to explain.' He got up and disappeared out of the cubicle, returning with a leaflet, which I glanced at.

'Drink plenty of fluids throughout the day, about three litres, until the stones have cleared.'

'How will I know when they've gone?'

'Hopefully you won't. If your pee is dark, it means you're not drinking enough. I will see you at my outpatient clinic in a month.'

He began writing a prescription, which he handed to me.

'Was there anything else I can help you with?' he asked.

'No, thank you,' I said, and we left the consulting room.

'Well, that's a relief,' Adrian sighed. 'How are you feeling now?'

'A bit nonplussed by it all.'

'The pharmacy's down in the basement,' he said.

It was 10.30 when we arrived at the pharmacy. There was one other person ahead of us. It was silent: no one was at the counter and the office behind looked empty. Adrian rang the bell and waited for what seemed like ages. A woman finally appeared; she held out her hand for the prescription and then disappeared without another word. We sat down again and waited. Adrian checked his phone.

'You can go if you're needed.'

'No, I'll stay. How is your pain?'

'All right at present.'

Ten minutes later the nurse appeared with two boxes of pills – some painkillers and some medicine to help with uric acid – and read out my name. There was only us here now. The other person had gone. We went up to the counter and she insisted on reading out my full name and address. 'Take one tablet twice a day,' she said, referring to the pills for uric acid.

'Thank you,' I said, and we left.

'Can you drive home?' Adrian asked as we made our way outside.

'Yes. I'm fine.'

He walked with me towards my car. It was now 11 p.m. and I just wanted to get home and rest. I was feeling quite tired.

'Have you got work tomorrow?' he asked.

'Yes, but I'll see how I feel,' I replied, and thanked him for all he'd done.

He kissed and hugged me goodnight and looked like a little boy again.

'Text me to say you're home,' he said.

'I will.'

Without further ado I got into my car and drove home. It took a lot of concentration. The pain hadn't returned, but the painkiller they'd given me at the hospital had been powerful.

Paula was up and must have heard my car pull up and park. She opened the front door. 'How are you, Mum?' she asked. 'I've never known you be ill before.'

'I'm fine. I expect Adrian told you all about it.'

'Yes, most of it.'

'It's two kidney stones and I've got to pass them when I go to the loo,' I said, taking off my coat.

I went into the kitchen and poured myself a glass of water, then went up to bed. Paula followed.

'I'll make you a cup of tea,' she said.

'Yes, please.'

By the time she had returned with the tea I was fast asleep.

CHAPTER TWENTY-ONE

MRS BRIGGS

I must have needed the sleep for it was after seven o'clock when I woke. I texted Janie and said I wouldn't be there today. I looked at my family's WhatsApp group, which had been very busy late at night with nineteen messages, none of which I had to reply to any more. I slowly got up and went to the toilet. I didn't feel like doing much today. Paula was up and heard me.

'How are you?' she asked, concerned, as she came down.

'Not a hundred per cent, but getting there,' I replied.

She made me a hot drink and I took it with the tablets I'd been prescribed into the living room. It was a wet Monday morning and the sky was just lightening. I gazed out of the window at the windswept lawn, then I sat down. I was sure I was suffering from the after-effects of my stint at the hospital and the painkillers. I never usually took any and what they'd given me had been very strong. I looked at the ingredients on the packets and decided to go with the ones for helping with the uric acid and to ignore the painkillers.

Paula reappeared on her way out.

'Are you sure you'll be OK?' she asked me.

'Yes, of course love, you go.'

She hesitated. I couldn't remember the last time she'd left for work seeing me in my dressing gown.

'I'm fine, love,' I confirmed.

She kissed me goodbye. I listened to her car pull away. Then I sat on the sofa and sipped my tea. Being unwell had given me a shock. It wasn't like me to be ill. I now spent half an hour on my phone googling how kidney stones were made and the best treatment. Apparently one in ten people get them!

At around 9 30 a.m. I got dressed. It was a slow process and I returned downstairs and must have nodded off again. When I awoke I went into the front room and switched on the computer. I emailed Liv and Rania, saying I wouldn't be going to Janie's today as I was ill. I'd see what I was like on Wednesday morning. Back came an autoreply from Rania, saying she was off sick too. There seemed to be a lot of sickness going around of late. Liv replied wishing me well and saying she was setting up an online meeting with Janie for Thursday at 11 a.m. I made a note. Then I spent time wondering what I would give Paula for dinner. I opened the fridge door and found some slices of quiche.

She texted – all my family did – to ask how I was, and Lucy phoned.

'I'm all right,' I said.

I nodded off again on the sofa. When I came to Paula had come back.

'It seems you're OK?' she asked.

'Yes, why?'

She'd been trying to call my phone, but I hadn't heard it. It was in my handbag and I checked it now. There were nine missed calls from my family.

'I'm sorry. I must have fallen asleep,' I said. 'Can you get yourself something to eat? There is quiche in the fridge. I think I'm going to bed.'

On Tuesday morning I was awake at my normal time and feeling much better, and by Wednesday I was back to normal. I decided to finish the tablets for uric acid – there was a week's supply – then I would go to my doctor. I texted Janie, *I'll be there today*, and left the house by 7.30 to arrive at hers by 7.45.

I rang the bell and Janie answered.

'Hi, stranger,' she said.

I began to tell her all about what had happened to me, but she wasn't interested. She was only half listening, absorbed in shouting at her family and sometimes seeing to their needs.

'We've got a meeting on Thursday,' I said, over the noise.

'I know, Liv phoned me,' Janie said. Then she told the boys off for not doing as they were asked.

I wondered what I was doing there. In the two months plus since I'd been helping Janie I felt I hadn't made any difference, despite me passing on what I felt she needed to know to successfully parent her children. She'd still been taken in – first by Bowie, then by Isla – as well as struggling to deal with all the issues that seemed to beset her and her family.

I continued to help that morning, getting the children ready. Did they have their school books, for example? Riley had forgotten his. But he'd already taken out Max, and the dog was now in his bed.

The living room was a mess, the children's bedroom

was indescribable and Janie's bedroom was a tip. When I used to foster I didn't see the children's home life. They worked to my rules for all our safety. Now, as a family support worker, it seemed that in my absence Janie just did as she pleased. Was my being there encouraging that? Is this what others offering family support did – picked up the pieces? I'd been on training and had done my best, but there'd been no real improvement.

I began clearing up the dishes, I put rubbish in the bins, I cleaned up what looked like dog mess from the wall, and generally tidied up. Janie was hunting for a school sweater for Jayden.

'I told him yesterday to keep it on!' she cried.

She went to the washing machine, which was stuffed full of washing, took out a handful and smelt one of the school sweaters.

'It will have to do for now. I'll get another one from the school.'

'Janie, when was the last time you did your washing?' I asked. There was a bag of washing close by.

'I don't know. At the weekend, I guess,' she said with a dismissive shrug.

She continued rushing around getting the children ready. Lola wanted to go to the toilet so Janie grabbed the potty.

'I've had a solicitor's letter,' she said, 'about giving Bowie contact. He can take a running jump.'

'Do you want me to take a look at it?' I asked.

'No. He'll get fed up and give up. I've binned it.'

I decided not to worry about it. They were ready to leave just on time and I reminded Janie that we had an online meeting at 11 a.m. on Thursday.

'I haven't forgotten, she said.

I watched them go. Other than helping them get out the door on time, I really didn't think I was making a difference.

I was still thinking about Janie as I shopped, wandering up and down the fruit aisle. Was this placement going anywhere? Was it open-ended? Neither Liv nor Rania had given me a timescale for how long it would last. Doubtless, I would get a better picture during the meeting we had tomorrow; if not, I could ask. I was partway through examining a large horned melon when Liv phoned.

'Hello, I wasn't expecting to hear from you until tomorrow,' I said.

'I wanted to speak to you about another matter.'

'Yes?'

I wedged the phone under my chin as she began.

'It's a long story, but there's an elderly lady who lives in the road next to yours. She needs some respite care urgently. Mrs Briggs, number seventy-five. Her carer used to come around at three o'clock, but she's gone now for good.' I heard her sigh as she stopped talking.

'I see. How can I help?'

'Oh, yes. I wondered if you would like to go. You don't have to tell me now. Give me a ring back. Within the hour if possible. Then meet me there. I'll be going at three today.' She sounded in a rush.

'OK. I'll do that. Call you back.'

I tucked my phone into my bag and tried to concentrate on the fruit. What was it I wanted to buy? I looked at the pomegranates. Did Liv want me to go and visit Mrs Briggs every day? I should have asked.

I continued my shopping, going up and down the aisles. I wanted a challenge – something that would captivate me and leave me free to see my family. Visiting Mrs Briggs regularly would do that, wouldn't it? I scooped up what I needed and went to the checkout, where I paid and left the shop. In the car I phoned Liv but, as I learnt from her colleague, she'd gone into a meeting.

'Can you tell her I would be interested in the position in respect of Mrs Briggs? Can she call me back, please?'

'Yes. She'll be pleased. Does she have your number?' her colleague asked.

'She does.'

'I'd better take it down again anyway.'

I recited the number and then drove home, wondering why Liv would be pleased. I unpacked the shopping, and spent some time making a gooseberry tart, all the time thinking about Janie and Mrs Briggs. I had assumed that social care for the elderly was an entirely different department to that for young people. I must have been mistaken. I tried to picture the houses around number seventy-five in the next road but couldn't.

At around 2.30 I got changed into something smart and at 2.45 I left the house to walk to number seventy-five – down my street, along the side road that connected the two roads and then down the road. The front gardens came into view. As I approached the one for number seventy-five I could see it was a bungalow with the front garden badly overgrown. A tall apple tree stood in the midst of a heap of dying brambles, and the front door and windows needed to be repainted. There was no driveway.

It was exactly 3 p.m. and Liv's car didn't seem to be there. I pressed the bell and then saw a key safe box on the wall. I wasn't sure what to do, so I waited, then pressed the bell again, all the while expecting Liv to approach. No one answered or approached. I waited another five minutes and pressed the bell again, with the same result. The house seemed empty. It was as if no one lived there. I walked up and down the front path as I continued to wait. Then, at 3.15, Liv's car arrived. She parked outside and got out.

'I'm so sorry I'm late,' she said, flushed.

'It's OK.'

She pushed her key into the lock and let us in.

I followed her down the hall. It looked old and dark inside, and there was a dado rail separating the lower half of the hall walls from the top – a once-nice bungalow, which needed a good coat of paint and new carpet. A light shone through from the kitchen window in the far-off room. We turned left and went into the living room where an elderly lady sat in a chair with a table across it. 'Someone's been ringing the bell,' she said.

'I'm sorry, that was me,' I admitted.

She looked at me over her glasses. I thought she must be in her late eighties.

'How are you, Gran?' Liv said.

'Gran?' I repeated.

'Oh, yes, sorry. Didn't I say? Mrs Briggs is my grand-mother. Long story short, we've been through a lot of carers with this agency we're using. They come and go, and we have been left with a vacancy this afternoon.'

'So I would be taking over from this afternoon, tempo-rarily?' I queried.

'Yes, for now. Is that all right? There was supposed to be a carer coming this afternoon, but she's called in sick.

I suppose she's ill, but they seem to have a lot of time off. There was one here this morning – I checked – and then another at lunchtime. Then the last one later this afternoon – at any time up to nine o'clock. Did anyone come by this morning and at lunchtime?' Liv now asked Mrs Briggs.

She appeared not to have heard her.

'You're hearing aid,' Liv raised her voice, 'is it up, Gran?'

Mrs Briggs was still looking at Liv, confused.

'What?'

'Your hearing aid. Is it turned up?'

'Oh. Silly me.' Mrs Briggs fumbled to take out the hearing aid. Her bony fingers fiddled with it as she spent a few moments turning it up and then replacing it.

'I can hear you both now perfectly,' she said.

'Good,' I smiled. 'I'm Cathy. Your new carer, for the time being.'

'Not another one!' she replied.

I now saw that the full-length green curtains at the window were nearly closed and the living-room light was on. It made the room gloomy. I wasn't sure whether to say anything or to leave them as they were. Liv was looking at her grandmother. 'Do you need the toilet, love?'

'Not sure. I'd better go while you're here.'

Liv was clearly pushed for time. She pulled the table away and drew over a Zimmer frame. I could see how smartly dressed Mrs Briggs was, but her walking wasn't good. Liv went with her out of the room.

'Do you need a hand?' I asked.

'No. We're OK, aren't we, Gran?'

'Yes,' she replied. 'We are.'

I thought I should be doing something, so I smoothed the cushion she'd been sitting on and straightened the back cushion in the chair. The table that Liv had drawn away had cup rings stained on the varnish.

The room, the whole bungalow, was silent. I could see what looked like an old-fashioned gramophone in one corner of the room, and the television was beside it. One wall was covered with a large display cabinet containing books and china knick-knacks. I went over and looked at some of the titles. A *Reader's Digest* set of twelve books like my mother used to have.

The dust had been allowed to build up in the room. I assumed that, like many in receipt of four-hourly care, Mrs Briggs would receive visits from the carers at around 9 a.m., noon, then 3 p.m. and finally sometime in the evening. They'd have about half an hour to give them their food and do what was needed. It wasn't long enough, I thought.

I didn't like to touch anything, but I was there to help. I gathered together the empty dishes that were on the table and took them through to the kitchen sink. I thought the carers must spend a lot of time in here, as it was spotless. I heard the sound of Liv's voice coming from the bathroom and then as they returned to the living room.

'That's better,' Liv smiled.

Mrs Briggs was walking more easily now from the exercise.

'The carers are due to come again this evening to put her to bed,' Liv said. 'If you could do the three o'clock shift, and I'll phone the agency to make sure someone is coming later.'

'Yes, of course. For today?'

'And for the rest of the week, please.'

Liv was returning Mrs Briggs to her chair. She straightened the back.

'This is the first time I've been in this week,' Liv said. 'I thought it was going too well. I was in twice last week. And I can't remember the week before.'

'So where are your parents? If you don't mind me asking.'

'Mum's right down in Cornwall so all she can do is worry. She offered to have Gran down there to live with her but Gran's adamant she wants to stay here.' She rolled her eyes.

'And you don't have any other help? Your father?'

'He's dead. Many years ago. I've got a useless brother who visits Gran about once every two months if I remind him.'

She looked at her clock. 'Sorry, I'm in a meeting at three-forty-five. I'm already late. Gran usually has a cup of tea about now and a snack if she wants one. There's a biscuit tin in the kitchen.'

'So how long does the carer usually stay?' I asked.

'Half an hour.'

'That's not long. I'll stay for a bit longer.'

'If you can, that would be great,' she said, getting together her belongings.

'I'm going now, Gran, but I'll leave you in the capable hands of Cathy.'

'All right, dear.' She raised her cheek so they could kiss.

'So just to confirm: you're all right to do this for the rest of this week at three o'clock? I need to tell the agency,' Liv said.

'Yes, that's fine with me. But how do I get in?'

Liv put down her coat and bag. 'Sorry,' she said. She quickly took a pencil and paper and wrote down the code for the key safe.

'There you go.'

'Thank you.'

Then she said goodbye and was gone.

CHAPTER TWENTY-TWO

ANOTHER'S HOUSE

It was strange being in Mrs Briggs's house. I wasn't sure what to do.

'Shouldn't you be in the kitchen making tea?' Mrs Briggs asked me as I stood, a little nonplussed, in the living room.

'Yes, I'm going there now. I understand you usually have tea and something from the tin?'

'Yes,' she replied.

'Do you want the curtains closed?'

She looked at them. 'Don't mind.'

'I'll open them then. I like to see the daylight. There's precious little of it.'

She watched me go to the curtains and pull them back. The garden appeared, and it was in a right state – even worse than the front. The grass hadn't been cut for months so was long and straggly, and the leaves from the fall last year had blown into rotting piles of slush. The recent storm damage had left its mark, and clearly no one had had a chance to clear up, or maybe there wasn't anyone to do it. Some statues, which I assumed had once stood proudly on the patio, were strewn across the lawn.

'Your garden needs a good clear-up,' I said.

She looked at me. 'If you say so.'

I wondered how many days the curtains had been partially closed.

'I'll get you that cup of tea now.'

'Milk and one sugar, please.'

'Very good. You don't mind if I have one, do you?'

She seemed surprised. 'No. Have one with me.'

I went into the kitchen and filled the kettle. As it boiled I washed and dried up Mrs Briggs's dishes and placed them with the side plate that stood beside the drainer with her cutlery. That was all that was out; it didn't feel like home, not to me anyway. The kitchen was old, and I thought the floor could have been original.

The kettle boiled, cutting through the silence in the bungalow. I made a cup of tea for us both, then took the lid off the biscuit tin. It was crammed full of half-eaten packets of biscuits. I had no idea what she wanted so I took the tin through to the living room.

'You can have a look at these while I brew your tea,' I said, setting the tin down on her lap.

I returned to the kitchen, finished making the two cups of tea – one with sugar – and took them through.

'Don't you have to go?' she asked, looking at my tea.

'Not for an hour or so.'

She looked at me, puzzled, but didn't say anything.

'Liv didn't explain it well,' I said. 'I live in the next road and am doing some respite foster caring for a family on her books. She's asked me to look in on you at three o'clock for the rest of this week. If that's all right with you?'

'Yes. I used to foster,' she said, taking two jammy dodgers from the tin. 'A long while ago now. That's why Liv became a social worker.'

'I didn't know that.'

She nodded. 'I used to foster children who couldn't be looked after by their own parents. There were very few social workers back then.' She paused and, looking at me, took a bite of her biscuit. 'I'm ninety-four.'

'You're what!'

'Ninety-four,' she repeated, with a smile. 'I know I don't look it.'

'I'd put you at about eighty-four.'

'Well, there you go,' she said, and the conversation continued.

I stayed with Mrs Briggs until she'd had enough of me. It was after five and by then she was getting tired. I washed up her tea things and said I hoped the evening carer would be in soon.

'Me too,' she said. 'Can you close the curtains, please? I'll have to do them myself otherwise.'

I went to the curtains and closed them.

'Do you have everything you need for the evening?' I asked.

'Yes, love. I'm tired.'

'Of course. I'm going now.'

I didn't know how long it would be before the evening carer appeared, only that it would be between six and nine. Mrs Briggs had told me that the carer often came closer to nine and put her to bed while getting her dinner ready. I'd already established that Liv phoned at 9.30 p.m.

'I'll see you tomorrow then,' I said, and kissed her cheek.

She looked surprised. 'Yes, thank you, love. See you tomorrow.'

I went out, leaving Mrs Briggs to her evening fate.

I thought about how her life had changed. I didn't know anyone else who was looked after in their own home. She had mentioned that Liv always phoned her during the evening and how much her life had slowed down in recent years. I felt sad that it had to end this way. She wouldn't get better, only worse.

When I got home I told Paula about Mrs Briggs and that Liv had asked me to help her.

'That was good of you,' she said.

'I suppose it was.'

She looked at me. 'There can't be many who'd have gone round at such short notice.'

'I hadn't really thought about it like that. I enjoyed her company. Perhaps it's a sign of my age!' I laughed.

That evening I thought about Mrs Briggs and wondered what she was doing, all alone in that bungalow. It seemed to me that carers only had enough time to pop in and out without making a significant difference; they were just maintaining the status quo. It was sad; Mrs Briggs deserved more – one of over a million people in the UK who was in receipt of state help.

The next morning I was awake at the usual time, feeling fine. Again, I thought about Mrs Briggs and whether her carer had been. I saw Paula off to work and by 11 a.m. I was sitting in front of my computer waiting for Liv and Janie to appear for our meeting. Online video calls had to some extent replaced the old-style meetings we used to have.

'Hello, Cathy,' Liv said.

'Hi, Liv.' She appeared to be in her office. There was no sign of Janie.

'I just wanted to thank you for all you did yesterday.'

'Oh, you're welcome,' I said.

'I called Gran at nine-thirty, as I do every evening, and she was over the moon with you. She didn't stop talking about you. You were there until after five, I believe?'

'Yes, I was. It was nothing, really. We were talking about Bolton, where my mother used to live.'

'Gran used to live there too.'

'She told me.'

We chattered for a while about Bolton until Liv said, 'Janie's arrived.'

She appeared to be logging in to the meeting on her phone.

'Welcome, Janie,' Liv said.

'Hi, guys.' She sat down. It wasn't in her own home.

'Where are you?' Liv asked her.

'At a friend's. Don't worry, I'm alone. No one else can hear you.'

'All right, it's only a short meeting to see how we're all getting on.'

Janie now stood and disappeared from view to resettle the dog. I couldn't imagine where she was, but I didn't say anything.

'Will you sit!' Janie said, her voice rising.

We waited for the dog to settle. It was sniffing around as though it needed to use the toilet. Liv patiently waited for Janie.

'That's your dog?' she asked after a moment.

'Yes, it is,' I replied when Janie didn't.

Janie was in a kerfuffle and had forgotten she was carrying her phone along with the dog out of the house and into the garden. The screen was panning all over the place. She put the dog down.

'Come on, do your business,' Janie said.

Liv waited patiently for Max to go. When it became clear the dog had forgotten why it was out there, Janie gave up and carried it back in. She set him down on the floor.

'This is the house I'm cleaning on a Thursday morning,' Janie explained. 'But Riley said Max had eaten something bad and mustn't be left alone.'

I saw Liv look at her papers. 'Did I know this – about your cleaning job?'

I certainly didn't.

'Maybe not. I only started it this week.'

'So how many days are you working?' Liv asked, ready to make a note.

'Two – don't want to overdo it,' Janie said, with a small laugh, and she moved Max again.

Liv wrote. 'Thursday and –?'

'Tuesday,' Janie said.

'And the hours?'

'Two hours each day. But don't tell the benefits office, as that's another forty quid each week.'

Liv nodded. 'Let's get on with the meeting then.'

Suddenly another dog appeared – a cross-breed.

'Whose is that?' Liv asked, amazed.

'This is Betsy's dog,' Janie said, making a fuss of the dog.

'Who is Betsy?' I asked.

'The woman whose house this is,' Janie said, as if I should have known.

'Are you ready to begin?' Liv asked. 'Time is ticking by.'

'Yes, I've got to get on the bus to collect Lola – they'll hold onto her for me.'

'Where are you now?' Liv asked.

Janie named a part of town that was about half an hour from the nursery on the bus.

'Let's begin then,' Liv said, a little agitated. 'I know you and I have been seeing each other, but this will give us a chance to consolidate what you've learnt and the opportunity to include Cathy's view. You've been involved for over two months now. How do you think it's going?'

I tried to concentrate as I spoke, but it was very difficult, nearly impossible, for as I began Janie got up and was, I thought, checking on the dogs. I could only see an angled view of the wall. I couldn't imagine how much housework she'd done while looking after the dogs. Janie suddenly let out a scream.

'Oh, Jesus! You dumb dog, that's five times this morning! Sorry, but I'll have to clear this up.'

We waited. This meeting was now all about Janie and her dogs. I knew it wasn't what Liv wanted to hear but I didn't appreciate how badly it was going.

Liv waited and tried again, pursuing a different thread.

'Which improvement do you think you would have identified and made for yourself?' she asked Janie.

We waited again as Janie stopped whatever she was doing with the dogs.

'I guess I'm at school on time now,' she said, her gaze going to the dogs.

'Janie's skills in the morning have improved,' I said. 'I don't think they've been late. But it would be useful if I could know on Friday mornings if the weekend respite for Riley is needed.'

Janie clearly felt got at. 'He doesn't know himself until the evening!' she snapped at me. 'Sometimes he wants to stay with his dog.'

Liv looked helpless.

'Riley has settled because of the dog,' I said. 'He's much more reasonable now. He's only needed the weekend placement once.'

'What do you feel, Janie?'

'I don't know. About what?' She was looking around and trying to wipe up the mess from the carpet.

'This is hopeless,' Liv said curtly. 'I'll rebook this meeting. Goodbye, Janie. I'll be in touch.'

The call ended, but Liv still remained on the line. 'I'm doing too much,' she said. 'I'm going to see my doctor this afternoon. Are you OK to see to my gran tonight? I won't be there.'

'Yes. Of course.'

'Thanks, goodbye.'

'Bye,' I said.

That was the last time I saw Liv. Although I didn't know it at the time, I learnt later that she was signed off sick.

Later that afternoon I went to visit Mrs Briggs and she said she'd been looking forward to seeing me. She rose from her chair and offered to make me a cup of tea. I explained I needed to make her one, which she accepted. Ten minutes later we were snuggled up in the sitting room with tea and biscuits, gazing out onto the garden and worrying about the best way to clear it up.

'Why don't I begin to sweep up the leaves?' I suggested.

'No, you don't want to be doing that.'

'I do.'

I helped myself to another biscuit and finished my cup of tea. She stopped saying I shouldn't do the garden, so I went outside and found a broom in a dusty shed and began sweeping up the leaves – there were plenty and I could see her watching me through the window. She was happy and kept giving me the thumbs-up sign as I worked. The massive sycamore tree by the bungalow didn't have a leaf on it. I spent most of the time sweeping up the leaves from it and putting them into the compost bin, which hadn't been used for years. The last of the leaves I put in disposable rubbish bags. It was nearly an hour later when I packed everything away and returned to the bungalow.

'There, it's nice and tidy for the spring,' I said.

'Yes, indeed. Hurry up, spring.'

I sat with Mrs Briggs talking for another hour before I made a move to go.

'See you tomorrow,' I said.

'Yes, you can come earlier if you want tomorrow.'

'I will have to see,' I said.

I gave her a kiss on the cheek and left. She provided me with what Janie didn't – a stable, loving home life with a wealth of history.

CHAPTER TWENTY-THREE

FÜR ELISE

The following morning Janie was nowhere near ready when I arrived. She may have had a bottle or two of beer the night before – there were some in the kitchen – but I didn't comment. Neither she, nor any of the children, were dressed and Riley wasn't properly awake. He'd been up all night with the dog, who was ill.

'Is he better now?' I asked him, looking at Max. He was in his bed, and his food bowl was in front of him, full. He didn't look well.

'No, I don't think so. He may have swallowed something – one of Lola's toys.'

'What makes you say that?' I asked him, going over to Max.

'There's one missing.'

How anyone could possibly tell that from the mess their flat was in I didn't know. Janie was flitting around in her nightwear. 'We've searched the whole flat and can't find the baby rabbit,' she said, picking up and activating a couple of toys. Everything seemed to make a noise here.

'We'd better take him to the vet's,' I said. 'I can take you to school and then we can go on from there. You'll be back in time for Lola.'

'I know,' Janie agreed. 'And coming right on top of my job loss!'

'Your job loss?' I asked, mindful that everything with Janie was a drama.

'Yes.' She was still looking for the toy.

'You just lost your job?' I asked.

She was hurrying around, telling the children to get dressed and have their breakfast, and saying she needed a coffee.

'Yes, my cleaning job,' she finally replied. 'It lasted two days.' She plugged in the kettle.

'The one you were at yesterday?' I asked.

'Yes. The silly cow. She phoned me late last night after the children were in bed. Well, Riley wasn't. She went on about it like there was no tomorrow. Didn't know whether I was coming or going. Lola, will you get your knickers on, please!'

'So what happened?' I asked.

'She wasn't happy. She said she couldn't see I'd done any work, and that I'd made a mess in the living room. Cheeky bugger. She found a lump of dog shit on her rug, but I didn't know it was there.'

'Oh, I see,' I said. I thought the woman – someone Janie had met in the park – had probably tried her for a couple of days and by the second day had decided to let her go.

'So can we take Max to the vets?' Janie asked, now stuffing Lola into her clothes while I washed up.

'Is Max going to die?' Riley asked.

'I bloody hope not,' Janie said.

'No, love. The vets will check him over, that's all,' I said. 'They'll work out what's wrong with him.'

The chaos continued. I did my best and we left for school nearly on time. Their flat was in a shocking mess as I closed the door. We got in the car. Janie and Max were in the front seat and the children in the back. They took a while to settle. I drove to the school and parked as close as I could. I stayed with Max while Janie saw the children in. None of them had a school bag; Janie had said they'd all been left at school.

'I need this like a hole in the head,' Janie remarked as she returned to the car. 'I've got a new boyfriend now – Guy – I'm meant to be seeing him today.'

I hoped he was better than the last one.

'You have?' I started the car, checking Max was OK on the rear seat where Janie had put him.

She was busy searching her phone.

'I'll have to call him and put him off. Roll on when Lola starts school.'

She made the call. 'I can't see you this morning. Max is ill.'

I couldn't hear his reply, only Janie laughing, then saying, 'No, you don't understand, the dog is really ill. No, I'm not kidding.'

The free vet was about a twenty-minute drive away. I was concerned for Max and kept checking on him in the rear-view mirror. He was just lying there, out of it, as I continued to drive. The new boyfriend phoned again during the drive and immediately Janie's face brightened.

'Hello, mate, I thought I'd just spoken to you.' She laughed.

She listened and then said, 'I'll see you this afternoon. She might go to sleep for a while.'

They said something else, which I didn't understand, then Janie said goodbye and hung up.

'Where does he live?' I asked.

'Not far from the last one,' she said with a laugh.

And that was all she told me. She changed the subject and began talking about the vet. She did a lot of texting as Max slept on.

When we arrived at the vet's I parked the car and Janie carried Max out.

'At least he's asleep,' Janie said.

I looked at the poor dog. Max wasn't good. He wasn't asleep; he was lethargic.

Janie gave her name to the receptionist, who was wearing a face mask. She found Janie's details on their website.

'So this is Max?' she asked.

'Yes.'

'We last saw him for his injections.'

'That's right.'

'How can we help you today?'

'He's swallowed something. We think it's a small toy.'

'I'll ask the vet to have a look at him for you. Please sit down.'

We did as she asked and waited for about fifteen minutes. It was busy, with lots of people coming and going. Eventually Janie got up and went to the receptionist.

'Can you tell me when I'm going to see the vet? I've a child at nursery and my friend has just brought me over. She's going to have to go if you keep me waiting much longer.'

'Those of you who don't have an appointment will be seen just as soon as I have a slot. Or I can book you in for this afternoon?' the receptionist replied.

That wasn't what Janie wanted to hear. 'Do you not know how long the vet's going to be?' she asked.

'No, sorry. Shall I book you in for this afternoon?'

'No,' Janie said, disgruntled, and returned to her chair, not in the best frame of mind.

When Janie decided on a plan of action she expected others to fall in with it and was disappointed when they didn't. Children, her dog, the vet – it didn't matter; it was all the same to her.

'Silly cow,' she said to me, while texting on her phone.

It was another quarter of an hour before a male veterinary surgeon came out and called the dog's name. We stood.

'About bloody time,' Janie said, picking up Max, and she followed him into the consulting room.

'I'm Dr Singh. How can I help you?' he asked. He was only young – probably in his late twenties – and his nurse was even younger.

'He's swallowed something,' Janie said, plonking the dog on the table.

'What sort of something?'

'A rabbit,' she said, her concentration now back on her phone.

'It's a small toy rabbit,' I explained. 'Part of a set. About this big.' I showed him by measuring with my fingers.

He nodded and began examining Max, who yelped and nearly bit him at one point. I assumed vets were used to this. Janie had stopped texting and was now focusing on what the vet said.

'I can feel something,' he said as he prodded and poked some more. His face was serious, and Max went for him again.

'How long has he been like this?' Dr Singh stopped and asked.

'About two or three days,' she said.

He examined the dog some more, but it soon became obvious that Max's stomach was too tender to keep touching.

'I'll have to give him an ultrasound,' the vet said.

'When?' Janie asked.

'Now. Do you think you can wait outside?' he asked.

We left the consulting room and returned to the waiting area. We were there for about ten minutes – time Janie put to good use by texting again – before Mr Singh called us back in. Max must have been feeling so rough that he didn't have the strength to put up any more of a fight. On seeing us, he simply stayed where he was, stretched out on the table.

'Come and have a look at this,' the vet said.

We went over to the ultrasound machine where a large picture of Max's insides loomed.

'You see that?' he said, freezing the screenshot. 'It's a sock, not a toy rabbit.'

I peered closer. 'Oh, yes. I see what you mean.'

Janie was looking at the screen while Max lay on the table being comforted by the nurse.

'It looks like it's been there for more than a few days and I don't think it's going to dislodge by itself,' the vet said.

'So what are you going to do?' Janie suddenly asked, looking serious.

'Operate,' the vet said, and he clicked on some more photos.

'Oh my!' Janie said. These ones were larger and more detailed.

'I think we keep him here, and I'll operate later today,' the vet said.

'Really?' Janie asked. 'What do I tell Riley? His dog is going to be operated on?'

'Yes. You agree to the operation?' the vet asked, clearly wanting to move on to his other patients.

'Yes. What's there not to agree to? You're going to save Max's life.'

I thought she might disagree if she knew the cost.

'I'll get the forms ready,' the vet said. He then disappeared from the room, leaving us to make a fuss of Max.

'He's not very well, is he?' I said to the veterinary nurse.

'No, but Mr Singh will make him better.'

The vet returned and got Janie to sign a lot of paper-work, which she did without reading it.

'I'll phone in the morning,' he said.

'Yes, please. Bye, Max,' Janie said, kissing his cheek.

I also went to the dog and stroked him.

The nurse smiled. I've no idea what she thought of Janie or me.

Back outside, we went to the car and got in. Janie was texting again and carried on doing so all the way home. We'd start a conversation and then she'd stop to text.

'I'll call tomorrow,' I said as we arrived at her flat. 'There is no point in me having Riley tonight.'

'No.'

We said goodbye and I watched her go in. She had a full hour before Lola finished nursery. I didn't for one moment think she would use that time to do her house-work, but that was up to her. I had a relaxing day planned. I was going straight home and then visiting Mrs Briggs. However, at 12.30 a social worker – not Liv – phoned me.

'Mrs Glass?'

'Yes.'

'I'm one of Liv's colleagues. ***** School has just called and asked to speak to her, but she's off sick. You don't know where Janie has got to?'

'No, I don't. I am sorry. Hasn't she collected Lola from nursery?'

'No, not yet.'

'I was with her this morning. I'm afraid I don't know where she is now. You've tried her phone?'

'Yes, so have the school. If Janie should contact you, could you tell her to phone them?'

'I will,' I said, concerned.

About half an hour later Janie phoned from the school. She sounded subdued.

'Are you OK?' I asked her.

'Yes. I'm just collecting Lola now. I'll tell you all about it later.'

'All right. Let me know about the vet's when you hear.'

'Oh, yes.'

'You're sure you're OK?'

'Yes, I am sure.'

So I had to leave it at that.

* * *

I went to see Mrs Briggs that afternoon. It was the last time I would go. I didn't know if I was getting paid to visit her. It was only three days, so it didn't matter if I didn't. I let myself in using the key safe.

'Hello, it's me, Cathy,' I called.

She must have dozed off in her chair until she heard my footsteps in the hall. I walked in and just for a moment she didn't know who I was.

'Oh. It's Cathy,' she said.

'You've got your curtains closed. Shall I open them?'

'Oh, yes, please. That will be the lunchtime carer. She always closes them for me.'

I opened the curtains.

'Tea?' I asked her.

'Yes, please.'

I went into the kitchen and set the kettle on to boil. I'd also made some biscuits that I now arranged on a plate. I knew she liked a biscuit with her cup of tea. She was very grateful when I took them through.

'Have you heard from Liv?' she asked me.

'No. Not yet.'

'She's going to get in touch with you.'

We concentrated on our biscuits. They were rather nice. My signature Cathy Glass shortbread with sprinkles on. She ate three. Mrs Briggs's husband had been a cellist and she liked to reminisce about him. He'd been dead for ten years. I listened to what she had to say about him, nodded, and agreed where appropriate. She said she accompanied him on the piano and suddenly put down her cup and saucer and agreed to play. I helped her to her feet, then followed her into one of the smaller rooms. There was a baby grand piano standing in the centre of the room, which was otherwise filled with boxes ready to go to the charity shop.

'You look like you're packing up,' I said.

'There is so much to do,' she said. 'And so little time to do it in.'

I suddenly felt very sad for her, and concentrated on pulling out the stool and helping her to sit down.

'I haven't played for a long while,' she said, and took a moment to compose herself. She then began playing Beethoven's *Für Elise*. It was enchanting – a really sad piece. Plaintive and deeply melodic with an undefined nostalgic feeling. There were a few mistakes when she sucked in her lips, but she carried on. When she came to the end she sat back, quietly exhausted. The piece had been one of my mother's favourites and I felt its passion now as I did then. I wiped a tear away from my eye. It was a moment before I could speak.

'Wonderful,' I said, and I meant it.

'That's the last tune I played to my dear husband,' she said, and began to rise.

I helped her up.

'I hope you will play that again,' I suggested.

'We'll see. I spent a lifetime playing with my dear husband. And now he's gone.'

She was in a sombre mood today, and wanted to talk about death and dying. 'Do you think there is a heaven?' she asked me.

'I don't know,' I said.

I steered her away from that topic more than once and talked about happier things.

As 5 p.m. approached I said I needed to be going back as Paula would arrive home soon. I kissed her goodbye, said I'd pop in again next week to see her and then left. Some of her mood came with me, and I found it difficult to shake off.

I ate dinner with Paula that evening and told her of my day.

Janie phoned once we'd finished, at about 7 p.m.

'The vet called and Max is going to be fine. You won't guess what they found in his stomach.'

'What?'

'Two toys – they were lodged inside the sock. A crunched-up rabbit, and a glass marble. The vet couldn't believe what he'd found!'

'How did they get in there?' I asked.

'Kids leaving them lying around, I suppose.'

'You've told them to be more careful in the future and to keep an eye on Max?'

'Yes,' she said flatly.

'Are you all right?' I asked.

'You know I was late for school? I mean, I got there over an hour late?'

'Yes.'

'I fell asleep.' She laughed. 'I mean, I had good reason.'

I waited, aware that Janie wanted to tell me something but didn't know how.

'You see, I got into bed about eleven, and by the time we'd finished it was nearly half past, and I was tired out, so I went to sleep and woke up at twelve forty-five.'

'I take it you weren't alone.'

'Well, that's the thing. Guy answered the phone and it was the school. He thought it was one of his mates.'

I could hear children screaming in the background.

'Will you stop it now!' Janie cried at them.

'It was Jayden, not me,' I heard Riley say.

Then Lola began to cry – really scream.

'You'd better go and get them ready for bed. Then, once they're settled, give me a ring back.'

She didn't, and I didn't think any more of it. I went to bed and slept well.

CHAPTER TWENTY-FOUR

AN INJURY

The following morning I tried to call Janie to find out what time we had to collect Max from the vet's. I assumed he was coming home today. It was nearly 11 a.m. before she answered, which made me worry about her and the children. She sounded groggy.

'Are you alright?' I asked.

'Yes. What time is it?'

'Ten fifty-five.'

'Oh, shit. I was supposed to fetch Max by ten. And we're not dressed yet.'

'What's wrong?' I asked.

'Don't go on. I've had a few to celebrate.'

'Celebrate what?'

'I don't know. Anything.'

It must have been more than a few. She still sounded drunk.

'Best phone them now. Have you just got up?' I asked.

'Yes,' she said, and ended the call.

I told Paula I wouldn't be long, that I was going to collect the dog. When I arrived at Janie's her children were quiet and the family still weren't dressed. Lola was watching Saturday-morning television.

'Everything all right?' I asked Janie.

She had her back to me. 'You'd better ask her,' she said, nodding towards Lola.

Lola turned away from the television and looked at me. 'Bump,' she said.

There was a massive lump on her forehead.

'How on earth did she get that?' I asked, going to her.

'I don't know. Don't go on,' Janie replied, rubbing her own forehead.

'What happened?' I asked.

Lola looked at her mother.

'I'm not sure,' Janie said.

'When did it happen?' I asked.

'Last night, I think.'

I looked at the lump.

'When did you find it?'

'When she woke up this morning,' Janie said.

I knew she was lying – she had that look about her – and I didn't know what to do for the best. Jayden and Riley were very quiet.

'Have you sought medical advice?' I asked.

'No, not really.'

'I think we should.'

I hesitated and then phoned 111 – the NHS helpline – on my mobile, as their doctor's surgery would be closed on a Saturday. Janie didn't want to talk to them and busied herself with something else. They answered after a short while and asked me a lot of questions about Janie and her daughter. I answered them as best I could.

'Is the mother there?' the male call handler asked.

'Yes.'

'Can we talk to her?'

She shook her head and drew back.

'No,' I said. 'She's refusing.'

'Hold the line a minute,' he said.

I assumed he was checking what to do. He came back on the line after a moment and said, 'She needs to go to hospital to have the wound checked. Do you have transport?'

'Yes, I can take them in my car.'

'We are advising you to go straight there, as it's difficult for us to assess when the injury took place.'

'Yes, I will do. Thank you,' I said.

I said goodbye and then told Janie I'd phone the vet. Without doubt she was hungover and possibly still drunk. I sat beside Lola as I called. She didn't say much on good days, so was no quieter when she'd been hurt. I explained to the receptionist at the vet's that there had been an accident and this involved taking Lola – Janie's daughter – to casualty, so we would be late collecting the dog.

'Just a minute,' the receptionist said, and put me on hold.

She returned after a few minutes.

'Mr Singh says that is fine but if it's after six to call tomorrow.'

'Thank you,' I said.

I told Janie that the dog could stay at the vet's for today.

She was very quiet and hardly said a word all the way to the hospital – about a twenty-minute drive away. Lola was in the back with the boys, and they were quiet too – perhaps sensing the enormity of what was happening.

I parked in the hospital car park and fed the meter. I let Janie give Lola's name. She was still subdued and was now nursing Lola, refusing to let her walk around in reception.

We were told to go through the double doors and wait in the Children's Emergency Department. It was full. We found room for us all to sit down and waited. After a few minutes a nurse came out of one of the cubicles and read out Lola's name.

'I'll stay with the boys,' I said to Janie.

She stood and carried Lola into the cubicle. The nurse closed the door. I tried to keep the boys amused; I couldn't expect them to just sit there. Jayden wanted to run off and play with another child.

Eventually Janie and Lola reappeared; Lola was walking. They sat down and Janie said nothing.

'What did the nurse say?' I asked. 'The doctor will want to see her as soon as he's available. But you were in there a long time. She would have examined Lola at least.'

'Yes, she did. I need to get some water,' Janie said.

'The children need some food,' I said, and I looked around.

There was a vending machine against one wall, but Janie didn't have any money, so I gave her some of mine. She went over and bought packets of crisps for them all and a bottle of water for herself, then spent some time on her phone. Once the children had finished their crisps, I kept them amused. Even little Lola was restless. I sensed Janie knew – as I did – that this visit to the hospital would go against her. She was quieter than normal, perhaps thinking about her options – what to say? She kept Lola close to her, but then seemed to forget about her and let her wander off. I brought Lola back and checked her forehead. The swelling was no bigger.

It was over an hour before Lola was called to see the doctor. He came out through the double doors. I waited with the boys while Janie went in with Lola. We were there for about three-quarters of an hour, during which time the boys wouldn't sit still, before Janie came out with Lola. It was obvious she wasn't going to tell me what had happened, so we collected up the children's coats and made our way towards the door.

'Janie, what happened?' I asked.

'Yes, it's fine.'

'What do you mean, "it's fine"?'

'I told him what I told you and he said not to worry,' she replied testily.

'Is that all he said?' I asked.

She was texting again. 'He said if she goes drowsy to bring her back.'

'Anything else?'

'No.'

I didn't say anything further. I took the boys' hands as they were going to be left to cross the car park alone.

'Can we go to the vet's now?' Janie asked as we got in my car.

'Yes.'

I felt a bit like a taxi driver. It was now 2.45 p.m. and I was mindful that the children hadn't had anything to eat, except for the packets of crisps, but Janie didn't want to stop off for food. She wanted to collect the dog and go home ASAP.

'You'd better wait in the car,' she said to the children

and me when we got to the vet's. I assumed she'd thought she'd be in and out quite quickly.

After about fifteen minutes, when there was still no sign of her, I suggested we went in. The car park was at the side of the building and as soon as we stepped in we could hear Janie's voice. She was arguing with the receptionist.

'You tell me why I'm still here!' she demanded.

I looked at Janie, then at the embarrassed faces of those waiting. Janie had no idea how to behave. The children were looking at their mother. Lola went over.

'Oh, you've come in,' she said, suddenly realizing we were there.

I was going to intervene and see what the argument was about when the receptionist suddenly left her seat.

'I'll fetch Dr Singh now,' she said.

'Yes, you do that!' Janie retorted.

I went up to Janie. 'What's the matter?' I asked her.

'She won't give me my dog. The silly cow.'

'But it's *my* dog!' Riley said, wound up by his mother.

I thought Janie was acting weird. She had been all morning. I'd seen her behave in a similar way before, but as I didn't have access to Janie's case files I had no idea where it came from. I also thought it likely that Mr Singh had no intention of keeping her dog. He operated on animals free of charge.

Suddenly he appeared from one of the rooms, the receptionist by his side. She went to her desk while he came to us.

'Is there a problem?' he asked.

'Yes. I want my dog.'

'A nurse is going to fetch him.'

'Good. I'm due home now,' she said. 'I'm late.'

So I assumed Janie had someone coming this afternoon and her plans had been plunged into disarray by me arriving and taking Lola to the hospital. It was now nearly 3 p.m.

As we waited a nurse arrived with Max, who was wearing an Elizabethan dog collar to stop him from chewing his stiches. He looked so sad. The children went to him to make a fuss, but Janie took hold of his lead and headed out of the surgery. I saw the receptionist raise her eyebrows as she printed out the paperwork for someone – namely me – to sign. I did so and then dropped £10 in the community collection box. It was the least I could do.

Outside, Janie was trying to get into my car, which wouldn't open until I'd unlocked it. Max had his head down and was clearly irritated by the cone collar. He didn't like it one little bit. I unlocked the car and Lola got in the back seat with the boys.

'Are you all right?' I asked her.

She nodded plaintively.

I got in and drove us to their home. It was well after three by the time we got there.

'Don't forget to give the children something to eat,' I said to Janie as they all got out.

Janie raised her arm in acknowledgement and continued into the building. I sat for a moment, a sinking feeling enveloping me.

I had felt for some time that Janie's situation could go either way. Now, I had a sudden feeling that it was taking a turn for the worse. Perhaps it was to do with her lack of consideration for the children or her unwillingness to share with me what the doctor had said to her. Clearly, she had something on her mind that she didn't intend to share. I hoped it would pass by the following morning and Janie would be herself again – whatever that meant; I wasn't sure. She had flashes of irrational behaviour that I felt could ignite and send her off the rails.

Presently, I started the car and drove home.

I arrived back later than Paula had anticipated, and collapsed, exhausted, on the sofa in the living room.

'I just need a cup of tea, love,' I said when she asked if I was alright.

She made me a tea and brought some biscuits. I realized then that I hadn't had anything to eat or drink all day.

'Thanks, love,' I said. 'That's great.' And I ate the biscuits quietly.

Paula sat with me for a bit but when she realized I wasn't going to give anything away she went to her room. I stayed where I was, lost in thought.

It was 5 p.m. when Liv phoned that Saturday evening.

'Hi,' she said. 'How are you?'

'I'm OK. How are you?'

'I'm getting there, thank you. I've been signed off by my doctor for a month.'

'Oh, I see.'

'I think it's exhaustion,' she said. We then spent a few minutes talking about her health before she said, 'I wanted to ask you something.'

'Yes?'

'Can you still visit Gran? She likes you going in. All you have to do is pop in from time to time.'

'Yes, of course. I had intended to, about once a week.'

'Great. I'll let her know.' And she began to wind down the conversation.

'Liv, before you go. I need to mention to you something about Janie.'

'Yes?'

'It might not be anything, but I went over to Janie's this morning to take her to the vet's, and there was a large lump on Lola's forehead. I phoned 111 and they suggested we take her to the hospital. We were there for a long time. Janie went in to see the nurse and the doctor alone and didn't say much when she came out. Then we went straight to the vet's to collect the dog.'

'Oh, poor Lola,' she said. 'What was the matter with her?'

'I'm not sure. It was a large lump and Janie didn't offer any explanation. She just said the doctor said it was fine, which clearly it wasn't.'

'You don't think Janie could have done it?'

'I think it was an accident, but I'm not sure.'

'I haven't got the case files, so I can't help much, I'm afraid. I only took the case over when I joined the department a few months ago. I don't know the case history well.'

'All right,' I said.

'Thanks again for all you did for Gran.'

'You're welcome.'

We said goodbye and I put down the phone, deep in thought.

I didn't want to make a fuss so I didn't phone Janie again. I was a support worker and there was no need to. It didn't stop me from thinking about her, though. She was alone in the house with a poorly dog and Lola – who'd done real damage to her forehead, somehow.

I resisted my instinct to phone her until the follow morning – Sunday – at 9.30. It went through to voice-mail. I tried again at 10, with the same result. Then again at 10.30. This wasn't like her. I then made the decision to drive to Janie's. I tried again before I left at 11 a.m. Her phone was off as I left my house.

My heart was racing and I was feeling uncomfortable as I drove. It was a Sunday, so the roads were quiet. I arrived, parked outside and cut the engine. The house seemed still and hushed. I went up to their front door, where I'd stood many times before, and pressed the bell. I waited. I pressed the bell and waited some more. I then came to the conclusion that there was no one in. So where the hell was she with her phone off?

I walked around the back where we took Max and peered in through the window. No one was there. Then I saw Max, who saw me looking in and began to bark. I peered in through the kitchen window. It looked a mess, as it always did. There were children's cereal bowls on the table surrounded by crisp and biscuit wrappers. Max was still barking furiously. Could Janie have gone out to buy a new phone? That was the only reason I could think of for her not being in, in which case I would look pretty silly. Then, as I was looking through the window, I saw Riley come into the kitchen. He stopped in his tracks and stared at me, his face a mixture of incredulity and shock. Max was standing there jumping and barking. I knocked on the window.

'Riley, is your mother there?'

He didn't answer and just stared at me.

'Go to the front door,' I shouted, and made an accompanying gesture.

He continued to stare at me and then disappeared. There wasn't anywhere for him to go but into the hall and to one of the two bedrooms. Max stopped barking as soon as I left the back window. I went to the front door and rang the doorbell, unsure of what to think. No one answered. I opened the letterbox and peered in.

'Riley!' I called.

There was no reply.

'Riley!'

Jayden appeared.

'Hi, love. Is Mummy there?'

'No.' He rubbed his eyes and began to cry. 'I want her.'

'Jayden, listen to me, love: is Lola with you?'

'No.'

Then Max, realizing I was at the front door, shot down the hall towards me, barking. His plastic cone collar rebounded off the wood.

'Jayden, do you know where Mummy has gone?' I asked through the letterbox.

He shook his head.

The dog was still barking. Riley joined his brother in the hall.

'Riley, can you open the door for me, love?'

Unable to make the decision, he just stared at me.

'I want Mummy,' Jayden said. Riley nudged him.

'I know you do, love. When did Mummy leave?'

'Last night,' Jayden said.

My heart sank.

'Do you know where she's gone?' I asked. Max was still trying to get at me, his cone banging on the hard wood of the door.

Neither of the boys answered.

I had to think what to do. These were two young children. Riley was seven and Jayden was five, and they'd been left alone overnight and were now not letting me in.

'Mum left us pasta,' Riley said. 'And she told us not to answer the door.'

'I understand,' I said. 'But I'm different, aren't I?'

'Go on, let her in,' Jayden said.

'No,' Riley replied, clearly following his mother's instructions.

'Has your mother told you what time she will be back?' I asked.

'Four o'clock,' Riley said.

It was now 11.30 a.m. I couldn't leave two young children in the house by themselves for another four hours.

'If you aren't going to let me in, I will have to call the police,' I said.

Both boys looked at me, horror-struck, but neither of them moved or said anything.

'Has this happened before?' I asked.

Riley shrugged, while Jayden nudged his older brother. 'Let her in, please.'

I waited. Nothing happened. So I took out my phone.

'OK. We'll let you in,' Riley said, and he slid the chain from the door lock.

CHAPTER TWENTY-FIVE

ARRESTED

I went in, closing the front door behind me. Max came up to me and barked loudly, then lost interest and headed down the hall. I looked at Riley and Jayden. Riley was dressed, but Jayden wasn't. He was still in old and grubby nightwear.

'We'd better get you dressed,' I said, and led him to their bedroom.

It was a mess. There were day clothes and toys – many of them broken – all over the beds, together with some crisp and biscuit wrappers. I looked in the drawer where I knew Jayden kept his clothes. All I could find was a top that was too small and pants that had been over-washed, but at least they were clean.

'Come on. Let's get you dressed. Good boy.'

He began silently stripping off his night clothes. I waited unit he'd finished. I was silent, thinking, and Riley was quiet too. He didn't speak until Jayden was dressed.

'What are you going to do with us?' he asked at length.

'I'm not sure yet,' I said softly. 'What have you had for breakfast?'

'Pasta,' he replied.

I scooped up Jayden's dirty nightwear and took the boys into the kitchen. It was impossible to get any more into the washing machine – it was overflowing. The kitchen was a tip. I took the lid off the pot on the stove. It had the remains of pasta sauce in it.

'When did you have this?' I asked.

'Last night and this morning,' Riley said.

Jayden wanted a hug so I put down his dirty night clothes and picked him up. I sat on the sofa and held him close.

'I want Mummy,' he said.

'I know you do, love.'

'Are you going to get her?'

'Be quiet,' Riley hissed. 'We'll be in trouble.'

'It's OK,' I replied, and swallowed hard.

These children had been alone in the house all night.

'What time did Mummy go out?' I asked.

No one replied, then Riley said, 'It was about six o'clock, I think.'

'Do you know where she has gone?' I asked.

'To spend the night with Guy.'

'Has she done this before?' I asked.

They both went quiet, then Jayden nodded.

'You need to shut it,' Riley said.

'It's all right,' I said, and held Jayden close.

I sat with them, thinking what to do for the best. I knew what I should do. I tried Janie's number, but she wasn't answering her phone.

'Do either of you want anything to eat or drink?' I asked them.

They both shook their heads.

'Has Max been out for a walk?'

'Yes,' Riley said.

We sat quietly for a moment, then I tried Janie's number one last time. If she'd been on her way home, perhaps I could have waited. Perhaps. She didn't answer, so I took the next step. Keeping Jayden on my lap, I phoned the police.

I felt my heart rate increase as I waited for the handler to take my call.

'I've found two young children, aged five and seven, alone in a flat. I'm their support worker,' I told them.

'And you are?'

I gave my name and contact details.

'And the boys are alone?'

'Yes, their mother has gone. I don't know where she is, but she left at six o'clock last night and isn't contactable until four o'clock today.'

'Yes, she is,' Riley interjected. 'She phoned last night.'

'But not this morning?'

He nodded.

'Did you hear that?' I asked the call handler.

'Yes, I did. So the children haven't spoken to their mother since last night?'

'That's correct.'

'And their address, please?'

I gave it to her.

'And you can stay with them until the police arrive?'

'Yes,' I said.

'I'll get someone to you.'

'Thank you.'

It was about fifteen minutes before a police car arrived. When the officers knocked on the door Max shot straight to it. I held him back. It was a man and a woman.

'Hello,' the male officer said to the dog who was jumping up at him. 'Can we come in?'

'Riley, can you take Max, please? Sorry,' I said.

Riley took the dog, which allowed the officers to come inside.

They came through to the kitchen where Jayden was standing, waiting.

'Hello, lovelies,' the female officer said.

Jayden said nothing and looked close to tears. Riley began to stroke Max.

The officer wanted to know Janie's full name, and my full name and address, although I'd given it to the call handler on the phone. I explained my role and that I wasn't supposed to be there at all. That I'd discovered the children by accident when their mother wasn't answering her phone.

'Why isn't she answering?' the male officer asked.

'I've no idea.'

They took down a lot of details. Were there any others in Janie's family who lived close by who could sit with the children until Janie returned?

'No.'

'What about people in the block of flats?' they asked.

'Not as far as I know.' I felt they were missing the point.

'The children have been left alone from six o'clock last night until four o'clock today. That's assuming Janie is back by then.'

The two of them spoke a few words out of earshot, then the female police officer said she was going outside to speak to someone from the car. The male officer stayed and talked to Jayden and Riley. When he couldn't get anything out of them, he spoke to me. I explained again what I was doing there. The female officer was gone for about fifteen minutes and then returned.

'Janie is on the line now,' she said. 'Can she speak to you?'

I took the phone.

'I've told them it's a misunderstanding and you are looking after the children,' Janie said. 'Can you help me, please?'

'I've already told them something different.'

She sounded very het up and excitable. 'I'll be back in half an hour,' she said, and there was desperation in her voice. 'Go on, please wait. Please.'

'I can wait for half an hour,' I said.

I handed the phone back to the female officer.

'I've agreed to stay for half an hour,' I said.

The officer nodded and went outside to continue the conversation.

I looked at the children and then the male officer.

'I've agreed to stay until she returns. She said she will be about half an hour,' I said.

'Olive would have called it in to the social services,' he replied.

I nodded.

The female police officer, Olive, then returned from outside.

'So your mother is on her way back,' she said to the children with a smile.

Riley nodded sombrely and looked at us as though he was in trouble. Jayden let out a small sigh. He clearly hadn't liked being alone in the house all night with Riley in charge.

The female officer kept popping into the hall to take more calls as we waited. She and the male officer exchanged a few words. I concentrated on the children and finally got them interested in a game, although my heart wasn't in it any more than theirs was.

I heard Janie before I saw her. The front door was open – the female police officer must have been outside when Janie approached with Lola.

'What do you think you're doing?' she said, loud and aggressive. 'They're my kids and I can leave them with a friend for a bit.'

'Are you Janie Watson?' we heard the female officer ask.

'Of course I am. I'm here, aren't I? I've been out for a while.' She continued into the flat, barging past the female police officer and into the living room.

Janie had really wound herself up. She was angry and said a rough hello to Jayden and Riley – maybe that was how she usually spoke to them when there was no one else there; I didn't know. Then she pulled off Lola's coat. 'She's sopping wet. I'll have to change her,' she said.

'I'll come with you,' the female officer said.

'No, you won't.'

Janie tried to stop her but then gave up and they both went into the children's bedroom. Jayden went too. Riley stayed with Max.

I knew this was serious: it was bad, leaving two children in the house all alone and overnight.

'How long before the social services are here?' I asked the male officer.

'It can be any time,' he said.

We could hear Janie and the female officer arguing, and then, after about ten minutes, Lola and the female officer came back into the living room. Janie was highly agitated. She was stomping around, moving things and then moving them back.

'When are you going?' she demanded of them.

'We're not, and if you don't calm down, I'll arrest you,' the female officer said. 'You've already left your children alone overnight, which is illegal. Supposing someone had come to the house? Or there'd been a fire or an accident?'

'Well, there hasn't been, has there? I'm here now to look after them. So you can go!'

It was obvious that Janie wasn't in any fit state to look after the children, and they were becoming scared. I didn't know what to do. I'd never been in this position before. I'd only ever brought children to my home after the police and social workers had been called. The female officer tried talking to Janie again, and when she just got rudeness in response, she'd had enough.

'I'm going to arrest you if you keep talking to me like that,' she said.

'No, you're not!' Janie cried.

There was then a scuffle. Lola and Jayden cried out. The male officer joined in, and it took all their strength to bring Janie under control. She was fighting and crying out, then the female police officer began reading her rights: 'You do not have to say anything, but it may harm your defence if you do not mention when questioned something which you later rely on in court. Anything you do say may be given in evidence.'

They marched her, shouting, all the way to their car, leaving me horrified and shaken. I'd never seen an arrest before.

CHAPTER TWENTY-SIX

HOME

I went to Lola, who was the most affected by what had happened, and tried to comfort her. She was crying, and the boys were agitated and looking pretty miserable too. I assumed one of the police officers would come back into the flat before long.

'I want Mummy!' Lola cried, and kept trying to run after her. Max was going mad.

'It's OK, love,' I reassured her as the dog barked.

'I want Mummy!' she cried again.

'I know you do, love.' I held her on my lap and rocked her.

'Has Mummy been arrested before?' I asked the boys.

Riley nodded.

'For what?' I asked him.

'Taking food from a shop.'

'Recently?'

'She's been doing it for years,' he said. 'She would have gone to prison before, but they kept letting her off because of us.'

The male police officer finally returned; he was talking to someone on his phone. The dog started barking again.

'It's the social worker,' he said, and handed his phone to me. I tried to silence the dog.

'I want Mummy,' Lola said again.

I held her close as I took the call. 'Mummy, Mummy,' she cried.

The male police officer went to take her from me, but she clung to me as though she was afraid of police officers. I cuddled her as I tried to speak to the social worker.

'Hello?' I said.

'Are you all right?' she asked, hearing the commotion.

'Yes.'

'I'm trying to get someone to you now. Are you Cathy Glass?'

'Yes, I am.'

'I'm a senior social worker from the out-of-hours team. You used to be a foster carer?'

'That's right. I still am – respite only.'

'Why did you stop fostering?' she asked.

'I retired – well, semi-retired.'

'And why are you looking after Janie Watson?'

'I am supporting her.'

'Oh, I see.'

'Can we have the television on?' Jayden asked.

'Yes, let him,' the social worker said. 'I am trying to find someone who can take the children. You definitely can't?'

'No.'

She said goodbye and I passed the phone back to the officer, who disappeared outside. I was still expecting Janie to reappear. She didn't. It was another ten minutes before the male police officer came back into the room.

'We're going to take Janie to the police station. Someone will be in touch. They have your number.'

'All right,' I said, not knowing what to say.

He said a friendly goodbye to me and the children (they didn't reply), and he left. Max followed him down the hall to check he'd gone and then returned, exhausted. Their home was suddenly very still and silent. I had no idea what was going on in the social services. It was after four o'clock now on a Sunday afternoon. I supposed that the duty social worker was trying to get in touch with someone. The children were starting to play up and Max suddenly began barking loudly.

'He wants to go outside,' Riley said.

'Are you sure?'

'Yes.'

Riley found his lead among the rubble in the flat and took him outside. As I watched them through the window in their kitchen-diner, my thoughts were tumbling all over the place. They weren't out there for long but Max did a wee. Riley praised him and then looked at me. I realized that he wanted adulation so I clapped.

'Who's a good boy? You're a good boy,' he said as he came in.

'I'm hungry,' Jayden announced.

I settled them in front of the television and searched through the cupboards. There was nothing apart from a frozen pizza and some out-of-date stuff. I took out the pizza and put it in the oven. I had no idea what time the social worker would come, so while the children were watching television I telephoned Paula.

'I'm stuck at Janie's. Long story but she's been arrested and the social workers are on their way. There is no one else to look after the children for now. I assume they are looking for someone.'

'Do you want me to come?' she asked.

'Yes, please, if you haven't got anything on.'

'I'll be straight there. What's the address?'

I gave it to her.

It was half an hour later when Paula rang the doorbell, by which time the children were eating pizza. I hadn't had a phone call during that time, so I told her as much as I knew. She looked worried and made a fuss of the children. Riley and Jayden just looked at her, then carried on watching the television. Lola, who was still upset, stopped crying and went to her.

'I hope you've had something to eat,' I told her.

'Yes, thank you.'

A quarter of an hour later the front doorbell rang again. Max shot down the hall, barking. Lola was now eating her pizza – fiddling with it, really – and Jayden was looking in the fridge for any dessert. I'd already told him I'd have to buy something.

I went to answer the door, holding Max by his collar. I knew the woman at the door was a social worker even before she said, 'Cathy Glass?'

'Yes.'

'I'm Julie Evans, social worker. I've been asked to visit this address.'

'Yes, of course. Come in.'

I held Max back.

She came in and went through to the kitchen where Paula had taken Lola onto her lap. The boys were still watching television. I let Max go and he quickly settled.

'Would you like a drink?' I asked automatically.

'Yes, a tea, please. I haven't had one all day.'

I went to the kettle and tipped out the stale water. It felt strange, offering someone a drink when I was in someone else's home.

'I'm Julie Evans,' she said to Paula. 'Who are you?' She took out her laptop from her bag.

'I'm Paula. Cathy's daughter. I've just come over to help,' she said.

Julie began making some notes and stopped to take her tea.

'Thank you so much,' she said gratefully. 'Now, Janie is known to us and I understand she has just been arrested. I haven't got the details of that yet. Can you tell me what happened?'

I told her, finishing with: 'I assume she'll be back before long?'

'I don't think so, but I'll check. I'll phone through to the office when I've finished here. Liv is Janie's social worker?'

'She is, but she's off work ill for a month.'

The boys were half watching television. Lola was snuggled up close to Paula, who was listening.

'You don't know who's standing in for Liv?' Julie asked.

'Sorry. I don't.'

Julie typed.

'In case the children can't be found a home for tonight, can they come to you? Just while we get all this sorted out? You are a foster carer, aren't you?'

Three children … I thought, but I asked, 'Until tomorrow?'

She nodded.

'Yes. All right then.'

'It might not be necessary,' she added.

Then she received a number of phone calls and kept saying to us, 'I've got to take this.' But unlike the police officers she didn't leave the room. Nearly an hour went by and she said, 'I thought I'd found someone to take the children, but they've just accepted a family of four.' At that point, with the time going by, I felt I should offer to take the children.

The phone went again. She answered and said, 'Go ahead.' She listened and then said, 'OK. Thank you for letting me know.' Then to us she said, 'Janie won't be coming home this evening. The police are keeping her overnight.'

'I can have the children for one night,' I offered.

'That's sorted then. Let me check I have your address.'

A minute later she read it out.

'Yes, that's correct,' I said.

'All right, children. You're going to Cathy's for tonight. You'll see Mummy tomorrow.'

'I'll be taking them to school then?' I checked.

'I assume so,' she said.

'What about the dog?'

'He'll have to go with you too. Is that manageable?'

'I suppose so. Isn't it?' I glanced at Paula, who nodded.

As Julie finished typing her notes I thought of the room that had been Riley's, and the guest room that had no one sleeping in it at present. The dog would sleep where it had before. It was doable.

'Has Janie got her front door keys with her?' Julie asked.

'I've no idea,' I said, and had a quick look around. I couldn't see them.

'She must have,' I said.

Julie now packed away.

'Can I use the toilet?' she asked.

'Yes, of course, it's in the bathroom.'

I hadn't thought to check the toilet was in a decent state. I heard it flush a number of times and then Julie came out.

'It wasn't clean,' she said.

'I am sorry,' I said.

'No worries.' She smiled. 'I'll be off then. You've got your daughter to help you. Good luck.'

And with that, she left us to it. I guessed the reason she was happy to do this was because I'd been a foster carer for thirty years. Nevertheless, I looked around and felt out of my depth. There were three children in front of me and it was nearly six o'clock. I knew we had to get going now. It was only one night, after all, I told myself.

'You stay here with the children,' I said to Paula. 'I'll pack what they need.'

I went into their bathroom first. The bath and the sink were grubby, and then I lifted the toilet seat – it was disgusting! I couldn't see any disinfectant, so I went to the kitchen and took a bottle from there. There was no long-handled toilet brush. I flushed it, then ripped off some toilet paper, wiped the seat and under it, then flushed it away. I squirted the disinfectant under the rim and left the toilet like that. It was better, but not perfect.

I took the single facecloth, which was grubby. There were no others, so I assumed they all shared one. I went through to the children's bedroom and looked at the mess. I tidied up a bit and straightened the duvet covers so they were ready for when Janie came home tomorrow. I began hunting in the children's drawers for changes of clothes. There were no school clothes. I couldn't find any. Then I thought of the washing machine. I went into the kitchen-diner where the children were watching television.

'Everybody all right?' I asked.

Paula looked at me and nodded. The boys didn't answer, but Lola said, 'I want Mummy.'

Paula hugged her.

I pulled out the contents of the washing machine, found the school uniforms for Riley and Jayden, then took the rest of the dirty washing in bags. I'd do it for Janie so it was ready for tomorrow. I was feeling guilty now. I'd never imagined she'd get taken in by the police. I hoped she was all right.

I now hunted for the children's shoes and found them spread over the floor in their kitchen-diner. I gathered them up and put them by the front door ready for the off, then I returned to the living room.

'Riley,' I said. 'Can you take the dog outside before we leave, please?'

He didn't reply.

'Riley, can you take the dog out, love?'

He didn't move so I asked again, and when there was no response I switched off the television.

He flew at me and switched it on again, clearly frightening Lola. I glanced at Paula, who was looking unsettled. Jayden was watching his elder brother. Had I overreacted? He seemed like a different child to the one I knew.

'Riley,' I said calmly.

He didn't respond. He was completely transfixed by the television.

'Riley,' I tried again.

When there was still no reply I said, 'Jayden and Lola, time to go. Say goodbye to Riley.'

Riley snapped out of it.

'I'm coming,' he said, and quickly switched off the television. I breathed a sigh of relief.

The children came to the front door with me and there we put on their shoes.

'Can you take Max out, please?' I asked Riley again.

He did so. Paula and I got the children's coats on, then took them to my car.

'Where are we going?' Jayden asked.

'To my house, love. Do you remember I explained? Just for one night.'

'Where's Mummy?' Lola asked,

I hesitated and then said, 'She's with a police officer.' Which she accepted. We got them into the back of the car, fastened their seatbelts, then loaded the bags of clothes into the boot. Riley finished seeing to the dog.

'Did he go?' I asked him.

'Yes.'

He then helped me load up the other dog stuff.

'Good boy,' I told him.

'Where am I sitting?' he asked.

'In the back with the others.'

He climbed into the back of my car. Thankfully the child's seats were still in place. Paula checked I had everything I might need for one night, and then got into her car. I went back and closed the front door to the flat.

Max was sitting on Riley's lap.

'Are you all OK?' I asked him.

'Yes, if he'd just sit still.'

'Sit, Max,' I said, and waited until he sat.

No one looked very happy, and Lola looked sad. 'We will soon be at my house,' I said. She gave a small nod.

I started the car, and we followed Paula home; all the while I was thinking of Janie in a police cell.

Paula parked in front of our house and I parked on the drive. It was nearly a quarter to seven. I checked my phone before I got out and saw I'd missed a call from Adrian. I'd reply later.

Paula had left the hall light on and the heating was on low.

'Come on, children. Let's get you indoors quickly,' I said. It had started to rain and the night was foul.

Lola was nearly asleep on her feet but seemed to wake up when I put the lights on. Riley rushed into the living room, dragging Max along with him. I turned up the heating. Jayden and Lola had never been in my house before.

'You stay with the children, Mum, and I'll see to the car,' Paula told me.

Gratefully, I gave her my car keys.

There was plenty going on to keep me occupied. Riley had left the living room and was now in the kitchen-diner where the toy cupboards were. He flung open a few doors and took out a large blue car that made a noise. He began running it around the floor. Jayden wanted it and then began to cry when he couldn't play with it. He was tired too.

'Come on, there are lot of things in the cupboard,' I said. I hunted around and found a similar orange truck.

Straight away, Riley wanted it.

'No,' I said, firmly. 'You are playing with that car.'

'Don't want it,' he said, and slammed it down.

He ran upstairs, followed by his dog, and into his bedroom, then came down again.

'There's a spider in there,' he shouted. 'On the wall!'

'I'll deal with it,' I said wearily.

I went up to his bedroom, disposed of the spider through the window, then returned downstairs. The children had gone mad in the short time I'd been upstairs. Lola was wandering around crying. Riley had let Max off his lead, and he now shot out of the front door.

'Max! Come here!' I shouted. He was sniffing around Paula, who grabbed him and brought him back in.

'That's it,' she said, setting down the bags and passing me the car keys.

'Thank you so much.'

We then both looked at Max, who was quietly squatting in the hall.

'Welcome home,' I said, and we both managed a small smile.

CHAPTER TWENTY-SEVEN

STILL NO NEWS

I cleared up the mess in the hall, put the washing machine on, then settled the children in the living room, while I prepared food. They were hungry – it was a freezer meal of sausages, beans and chips. Once it was ready, I called them in. Paula looked exhausted.

'Yummy,' she said as we all sat down.

Suddenly my house was full of children all wanting something. Riley wanted the tomato ketchup, Jayden wanted the salt and Lola just sat there, wanting her food cut up, which I did. They ate it all, had a drink, and as they finished I left Paula watching them while I went upstairs. I wanted to check the guest bedroom to make sure there was nothing breakable in there. It was fine and I made up the double bed.

I assumed that Lola was still in nappies at night, so I'd taken a couple from Janie's place. It was then I realized I hadn't packed a favourite toy for any of them. Riley wouldn't be bothered, but I knew that Jayden and Lola might be. I found some spare cuddly toys in my supply and put a heap of them in the middle of the bed.

As I returned downstairs I could hear Paula talking loudly to them. I could tell they'd left the table. Paula was trying to get them to help her clear away. Only little Lola was interested. I looked into the living room, which was a complete mess, and I then went into the kitchen-diner. Max was nowhere to be seen.

'Has anyone seen Max?' I asked.

Jayden and Riley stopped what they were arguing over and began hunting around. Eventually we found him, snuggled behind the sofa and next to the radiator, fast asleep.

'He can stay there,' I said. But already Riley had woken him.

'Come on. Let's play,' he said.

He began throwing a dog toy into the air and expecting Max to catch it.

'I need to take Lola up now,' I said.

'Are we staying here tonight?' Jayden asked.

'Yes, love, then tomorrow I will take you to school.'

'Will Mummy be there?' he wanted to know.

'I'm not sure,' I replied honestly.

'I hope she is,' he said.

I did too.

I took Lola up first and spent some time getting her ready for bed. It was all new at my home for her, and I talked her through the process of squirting toothpaste onto her brush and then washing with her flannel. It was too late for a bath. I checked she still wore a nappy at night and she nodded.

I tucked Lola into her bed, ignoring the noise that was coming from downstairs, which Paula was trying to settle. I gave her a cuddle and, having said goodnight, I then called down to Jayden. Riley and Max came up too.

'No, the dog stays downstairs,' I said to Riley.

They all shot downstairs again. I went down and had to bring Jayden upstairs alone. Lola was out of bed now and in tears, so Paula came up and resettled her. I had no idea what Riley was doing downstairs. It seemed fair to me to put the children to bed in an ascending order, so I continued with Jayden.

As I got him ready for bed, then steered him into his and Lola's bedroom, he sneered at the fact he was sharing a bed with Lola, then at the cuddly toys. Lola had found two she liked and was snuggling up to them. I had no idea what the children were like at bedtime at home. I only went in for the morning routine.

'Thanks, love,' I said to Paula, who was now upstairs again giving Lola a cuddle.

Jayden wanted to look in all the wardrobes before he got into bed, then he climbed in beside Lola.

'Haven't you got any bunk beds?' he asked.

'No, love.'

He pulled a face but then snuggled down, keeping well away from Lola as if it was a game. I resettled them both.

'Are you two OK?'

Lola nodded.

'You know where Riley sleeps?' I checked.

'He's slept here before,' Jayden said.

'That's right, love.'

I'd just said goodnight to them both when Jayden got up again, wanting to use the toilet, even though he'd only just been. As I waited outside the door I thought about Janie. I wondered what she was doing and if she had calmed down now. It was my fault she'd been taken away and I felt bitterly sorry.

Jayden came out of the toilet and I sent him back to wash his hands.

'Is Riley coming up now?' he asked.

'Yes, love.'

Paula had gone down and was telling Riley it was time to get ready for bed. I could hear them. They were at the foot of the stairs arguing the point. I left them to it and resettled Jayden. Lola was still awake, watching what was going on.

I left Jayden lying quietly and went downstairs. Riley was no longer at the foot of the stairs but in the kitchen-diner, taking out the entire contents of the toy cupboard. The toys were everywhere, and as fast as Paula packed them away, admonishing Riley, he got out them out again.

'Come on, clear up now, Riley,' Paula kept saying. And he got another game out.

'Bedtime,' I announced in a loud voice.

'No, it's not!' he said in an equally loud voice.

Max was sniffing everything he took out.

'It's after nine o'clock,' I told him.

He turned and, without warning, ran out of the kitchen and upstairs. The dog followed him – straight into Lola and Jayden's bedroom. Riley stopped and reversed back like a large truck. Max, wound up, was yapping. Jayden was sitting up in bed laughing loudly. Lola was pretending to be asleep.

'I want Max downstairs now,' I hissed.

Riley ran out of the room and downstairs, followed by Max. Jayden laughed all the louder.

'Be quiet,' Lola said, her eyes still closed. I guess that was how she dealt with them at home.

Paula was halfway down the stairs, not best pleased. I went down and told Riley that Max was to stay down here. Riley made a noise like a siren and ran upstairs again. I caught Max, though, and shut him in the kitchen-diner.

'What do you want me to do?' Paula asked.

'Stay down here with Max,' I said.

I went upstairs where I met Riley on his way down.

'Riley, that's enough for one night!' I said.

'I want Max,' he retorted. Riley hesitated on the stairs and looked at Jayden, who was now out of bed and watching, about to start laughing again.

'Can you come and get ready?' I said to Riley. 'Now, please.'

'I always say goodnight to Max.'

'He does,' Jayden added.

'You can do it once you are washed and dressed,' I said.

He thought about this for a split second, then ran into the bathroom where he had the quickest wash ever. He quickly changed into his nightwear and, leaving his clothes in the bathroom, ran downstairs to the kitchen-diner where he threw open the door. Jayden followed him down. Lola began to cry.

It took ten minutes to settle Lola, then I went down to bring up Riley and Jayden. They said a final goodnight to Max and all three children were in their beds by 9.40 p.m. I was exhausted.

I went slowly downstairs. Paula had cleared up the dinner things and packed away the toys.

'Thank you so much, love,' I said. 'It will be straight out the door tomorrow morning.'

'Thank goodness for that.'

'I'd better text Adrian now,' I said, and went into the living room with Paula.

I've got three children for the night! I'll phone you tomorrow evening, unless it's anything urgent? x

He replied: *Nothing urgent. Three children?*

I'll tell you all about it another time. Night night. Love Mum x

Paula and I sat and looked at each other. We were both shattered, but the house was quiet.

'Will they let Janie out first thing tomorrow morning?' she asked.

'I would think so,' I said.

Paula and I discussed what had happened – Janie's upset, which had meant the police had taken her into custody. Paula thought, as I did, that the children would be back home by lunchtime the following day. Max was in with us and every so often he'd get up and begin sniffing around. Paula was immediately on her feet and took him in the garden, where he did a large poo. We'd clear it up in the morning.

We were both shattered and stumbled up to bed at 11 p.m. We couldn't help but look in on the children, who were all fast asleep, sleeping like angels. We left their bedroom doors open so I could hear them if they got up. I checked on them around 2.30 a.m. and then I woke with my alarm at 6.30 a.m. Half an hour later I was washed and dressed. The children were still asleep, so I went downstairs, ready to start the new day.

With some trepidation I opened the door to the kitchen-diner. Max shot out of his bed and came over to me, tail wagging frantically. I looked around the room – I couldn't see anything – then I clipped on his lead and took him outside, where he went for a big wee. It was just getting light.

I returned indoors and gave him his breakfast. I was worried about what the day would bring. Janie was sure to be annoyed with me, but I hoped it wouldn't last and we could carry on as we had been.

I heard a noise come from upstairs and immediately went up. Jayden and Lola were awake now and out of bed and went in to wake Riley. They weren't used to not sharing a bedroom. The house was full of noisy children again, wanting to know where their mother was. I reassured them they would see her today. I didn't know if Janie was going to collect Lola at lunchtime; I assumed I would be told this morning.

'Come on, get dressed,' I said.

I'd taken their dry clothes from the washer-dryer and arranged them at the foot of their beds the evening before. Lola's nappy was still dry and I praised her for it.

'I want Mummy,' she said.

'You'll see her later,' I replied.

'This morning?' she asked.

'I don't know yet. I doubt it. I'm waiting to hear from your social worker.'

Riley came out of his room and gave Lola a big hug. Bless him.

'You get dressed, love,' I told him.

Paula was in her room getting dressed. I helped Lola and we all went downstairs to the kitchen-diner. Paula was already just ahead of us.

'Hello, munchkins,' she said to them.

They looked at her and then Jayden asked me, 'Is she your daughter?'

'Yes, love.'

Paula got herself breakfast while I saw to the children. I knew what they ate from watching breakfast at Janie's. I gave them their cereal – not the same one but it was close – and then a pile of toast. Little Lola especially tucked into the toast and was still eating when Paula came in to say goodbye.

'You'll see me again, I expect,' she said to Riley.

He pulled a face. 'When?'

'If you stay here, I meant.'

She left and I continued getting the children ready for school.

I estimated that we needed to leave the house by 8.20 a.m. to get to school on time. Sure enough, by eight o'clock we were all upstairs getting ready. Max was not part of this and stayed down in the kitchen-diner. We were all downstairs again by 8.15, ready to leave the house, when Lola wanted the toilet. I left Jayden and Riley in the hall and took Lola upstairs. Then Jayden wanted to go. I suspected it was a bit of nerves because I'd never known them do this at their home.

By 8.30 we were in the car and Max was shut in the kitchen-diner. The children had plenty of questions; Lola's was always, 'Will I see Mummy?'

'You will see her today, but I don't know when,' I replied.

I didn't think she was going to have a good morning, but what could I do about it?

We arrived at school and as I parked some parents were coming out of the school building, having already taken their children in. At least Jayden and Riley had their school books with them – I'd made sure of it. I took the boys into school, then took Lola through to her classroom. I introduced myself to the nursery teacher.

'Will you be collecting her at lunchtime?' she asked me.

'I don't know yet.' I could see that didn't help, so I then said, 'Yes.' I could always come with Janie.

She nodded and Lola went in with her.

It was 9.30 by the time I arrived home and I expected to hear something from the social services soon. I took Max outside again but he didn't go. He wandered about and looked lost without the children. He kept sniffing by the front door, then sat down and weed on the floor where he'd been before.

An hour later and I still hadn't heard from the social services. Then, at 11 a.m., I received the call.

'It's Debbie Cruikshank,' she said. 'I understand that you have Janie's children?'

'Yes, that's correct.'

'Thank you for taking them. That's a relief. One less thing for me to do …' and she continued.

'I'm sorry to interrupt but it was just for one night – taking the children, I mean.'

There was silence on the other end of the phone for some time, then she said, 'I'm just reading the report from yesterday.' I waited some more. 'It's ambiguous,' she said. 'It suggests you are looking after them permanently.'

'Permanently? I don't understand.'

'Well, at least until the court hearing is over with.'

'Court hearing?'

'Yes, we're going to apply to have the three children – that's Riley, Jayden and Lola – taken into care permanently. You haven't been told?' she said.

'No, I haven't.'

'Oh, I see. Well, I am sorry you have been overlooked. Does that alter anything for you?'

'Yes, it does, I'm afraid. I've been acting as their support worker. I agreed to have Riley for respite at the weekend, but that was all. I can't possibly look after all three of them long term!'

'Oh, I see,' she said. 'I'd better get back to you then.'

She ended the call straight away and I had the feeling she was very young, perhaps still in training. I sat down and thought. I couldn't take all three children; I knew my limitations. It would be impossible. I needed to stand my ground. I appreciated there was a shortage of foster carers, but even so. This had just been badly organized.

Fifteen minutes later someone called Mavis phoned.

'I understand you can't take Janie's children?' she began.

'That's correct. I am sorry. I retired from fostering last year. I have been a support worker to Janie.'

'Where are Janie's children now?'

'In school. I've got to get Lola soon. She's at nursery.'

'I see. And you definitely can't take them?'

'No, I am so sorry,' I said.

Mavis said she'd be in touch and we said goodbye.

I had just enough time to get into the car and drive to school. What a cock-up, I thought. Janie's children were being taken into care, but why now? Clearly there'd been other stuff going on that I wasn't aware of, and the incident over the weekend was the last straw. As a support worker I wouldn't be told, unlike when I fostered, when usually I was invited to meetings, so I knew what was happening.

I arrived at school, parked the car and collected Lola. She was disappointed to see me.

'Where's Mummy?' she asked, bewildered, as we walked away.

'I'm not sure at the moment,' I replied, and left it at that.

I got her into the car and headed home.

I made Lola some lunch, and at 2 p.m. the phone rang again. 'It's Mavis,' she said. 'Are you able to take the children to the Family Centre this afternoon?' That was where contact was held.

'They're in school,' I said. 'Well, the boys are.'

'We'll make it after school. What time suits you?'

'From four.'

'Four-thirty then.' I knew that when children were first taken into care the social services liked to arrange a visit that day. 'Any news on where they will be staying tonight?' I asked.

'That's not for me to sort out. It's someone else.' I assumed they were still looking. 'I'll chase it up and get back to you.'

'Thank you,' I said.

At 3 p.m., when Lola and I left the house to collect the boys from school, I still hadn't heard anything more.

CHAPTER TWENTY-EIGHT

PHIL AND MEGAN

I explained to Lola in the car that we were going to collect the boys, then go to the Family Centre to see her mother for a short while. She just stared at me, not understanding. I too was feeling pretty hesitant, unsure of how Janie would be with me. Usually, I met the parent(s) at the end of the session when I collected the children, or sometimes at the start. And of course Liv, the social worker we'd been working with, who would normally have been present at the start of the first session, was off sick. I cringed at the possibility of meeting Janie with just the contact supervisor there.

Riley and Jayden were surprised to see me when they came out of school.

'I thought Mum was coming,' Riley said, his face setting.

'You're going to see her at the Family Centre,' I said, as brightly as possible. 'Have you ever been there before?'

'No.' We crossed the playground as I explained how contact at the Family Centre worked.

'It's like a house with lots of living rooms in it,' I said. 'You will be seeing your mother in one of the rooms. It will have a sofa, table and chairs, and lots of games and toys. Other children will be seeing their families in the other rooms. There are six in all. A contact supervisor will be with you the whole time to make sure you're all right. They usually sit at a table making notes.'

I opened the door and let them into the car. I'd taken many children I'd fostered in the past to the Family Centre to see their parents, and I knew that to begin with it could be difficult for everyone. Feelings run high: the children are upset, and the parents are angry that their children are in care. The only way they can see them is in supervised contact at the Family Centre for a few hours a week.

I strapped the children into their seats in the back of the car and got in. I began to drive to the Family Centre, about twenty minutes away. The children had fallen silent and I knew they were worried. I couldn't reassure them today, not properly. I parked in one of the bays and cut the engine.

'Is this it?' Riley asked.

'Yes, love.'

I got them out, and held Lola's hand as we walked up the path to the security-locked main door. I pressed the buzzer. The closed-circuit television camera above us was monitored in the office. A few moments later the door clicked open and we went in. I gave the children's names to the receptionist. She was sitting at her computer behind a low security screen on our right. There was no sign of Janie.

'It's for Janie Watson,' I clarified.

'Can you sign the Visitors' Book? Then you can go to room three. It's along the corridor and turn right.'

'Thank you,' I said. 'I know where it is.'

Janie would have got here earlier to have the house rules explained to her. She would also have to sign a written agreement that outlined the arrangements and expectations for contact.

We walked along the corridor and turned right. I knew where the room was from all the years I'd been bringing children here. We arrived at the door and it was closed. I knocked and a woman came to open it. She looked flustered.

'The children are here,' she called to Janie.

She let them in and I caught sight of Janie standing in the far corner of the room. She'd clearly been crying but now looked more angry than upset. The children rushed to her.

'Are you able to collect them at five-thirty?' the woman asked me.

'Yes, I can do. Sorry, who are you?'

'Mavis.'

She began to close the door as Janie hugged her children.

I was relieved it hadn't been any worse.

I needed to get some food shopping, mainly for the children. It was now 4 p.m. so I assumed the children would be staying with me tonight. I hadn't heard anything to the contrary and I didn't think the social services would move them now; it was getting too late. I got in the car and drove to a small grocery shop, where I bought what I needed and returned to my car. I'd just got in and was about to drive away when my mobile rang.

'Hello, is that Cathy Glass?'

'Yes.'

'This is Julie Evans. We met yesterday at Janie's. I've taken over temporarily from Liv.'

'Yes, I remember.'

'You've got Janie's children?'

'Yes – well, not at this moment. They are in contact.'

'With Mavis?'

'Yes.'

'She's asked me to phone you as she can't at present. Can you keep the children tonight?'

'Yes, I can.'

'Good. I need to ask you a few questions about your home?'

'Go ahead.'

'It's four bedrooms?'

'Yes.'

'So the children can have a room of their own each?'

'No. I have Paula living with me. I put Jayden and Lola in one room and Riley has his usual bed in the other room.'

There was a pause before she said, 'Lola is three and Jayden is five?'

'Yes,' I said, and then realized what I'd done. Opposite-sex children of Lola's and Jayden's ages couldn't share the same bedroom. It's generally considered inappropriate by the social services. 'I'll be separating them tonight,' I said, and she moved on.

How could I have been so stupid? I hadn't been thinking. I thought about my mistake as Julie continued asking me for a few more details about my house, but my thoughts were with Jayden and Lola. Riley would have to go in with Jayden to keep within the council's rules on bedtime sharing whether he liked it or not. It would only be for one night.

Julie was only on the phone for about five minutes; she said goodbye, then I drove back to the Family Centre still feeling miffed. I parked and texted Paula to say that the children were staying another night and we'd have to change their bedrooms. I explained why. Then I waited until 5.30 to go in.

'You can go straight through,' the receptionist said as I signed in.

'Thank you.'

I went along the corridor and turned right. The door was shut. I checked my watch and waited until it was a couple of minutes past 5.30, then I knocked. I couldn't hear anything.

'Come in,' an unfamiliar voice called.

I gingerly opened the door.

There was just the contact supervisor present, and she said to me, 'Mavis had to go at five.'

I nodded and looked at Janie, who was involved in an elaborate tidy-up. She was strutting around the room throwing children's play activities into their respective containers.

'I am so sorry,' I said to her.

She just continued to clear up the mess her children had made, as the parents are supposed to. The contact supervisor looked at her and then at me. I didn't know what to do as Janie carried on cleaning. The boys looked as though they appreciated that they were going home with me. Lola, bless her, didn't have a clue.

I waited, unsure of what to say or do, as Janie kept going, growing more agitated as she went. Then suddenly she shouted at me.

'You can get out!' And she slammed a toy into its box.

I looked at the contact supervisor.

'Did you hear me? You can go now!' Janie shouted again at me.

'I don't think that's going to help,' the contact supervisor said evenly.

'And you can shut up too!'

Janie was livid now and I wondered what the rest of contact had been like. She carried on packing up as I waited patiently by the door.

'Get out! Now!' she cried and began towards me.

'I'll wait outside,' I said to the contact supervisor, and I disappeared out the door. I went to reception to wait.

Ten minutes later the contact supervisor came out with the children.

'The manager is talking to Janie,' she said. 'They have contact again tomorrow.'

I nodded, thanked her, thought that it wouldn't affect me, and then took Lola's hand in mine. We signed out of the Visitors' Book and left. We went straight to my car where I got us all in. I was keeping an eye out for Janie, but she didn't appear so she must have left some time after us.

The children were very quiet going home in the car and Lola looked close to sleep. About halfway home Riley asked, 'Is it your fault we are all in care now?'

'No, love. It's no one's fault.' Then I added, 'I've got to change your bedrooms tonight.' And I explained the reason.

Paula had got home just ahead of us and welcomed us at the door. She said she had cleaned up the dog mess in the kitchen-diner and I rolled my eyes and thanked her. I checked whether Lola wanted to use the toilet – she didn't – and then left the children watching television with Max while I made dinner. Paula was in and out of both rooms, then called them to the table when dinner was ready.

Towards the end of the meal I left the children eating and went upstairs to change the bedrooms so that Riley was sleeping in with Jayden, and Lola was by herself in what had been Riley's room. I didn't know if Lola had slept in a room by herself before – certainly she hadn't since Janie had been given the council flat.

The children didn't have that many things – very little had come from home, and it was mainly Riley's stuff – so a quarter of an hour later it was done. I went downstairs, gave the children dessert, and then began taking them up to bed in age-ascending order with Lola first. She wanted to know why she wasn't sleeping with Jayden. I explained that I'd got it wrong and because she was a big girl she had to have her own bedroom.

I gave her a bath and got her dressed. Lola was still wearing a nappy at night, I took her to the toilet before putting it on and then took her into her new bedroom. It was all right to begin with, she seemed contented, but when she realized I was going she began playing up and repeatedly got out of bed. She wouldn't go to sleep even though I kept resettling her. Then, after about half an hour, when I thought she was finally asleep, I brought the boys up – one at a time. They both had a bath, and by the time they were ready it was 8.30 and it had gone quiet in Lola's bedroom. I tucked Riley in and checked on Lola – she was still wide awake! I resettled her again and told her that the boys were asleep now. She closed her eyes and eventually I crept from her room. I went downstairs, where I finally took the washing from the washer-dryer.

When I went up to check on the children at 9.30 I found all three fast asleep in the large bed in Jayden and Riley's bedroom. I carefully lifted Lola out – she stirred but didn't wake – and carried her through to her own bedroom where I tucked her in. I waited a while to make sure she was asleep and then went downstairs. Paula had cleared up.

'Thank you so much, love,' I said.

'That's alright, you've got a lot on.'

'I have indeed.'

We settled in the living room with a cup of tea.

'Will we hear from someone soon about taking the children?' Paula asked me.

'I hope so,' I said. 'I know three is a lot, but it's not beyond the capabilities of some couples. We'll have to wait and see.'

As it turned out I got a phone call from the social services the following day telling me that they had found somewhere for the children to stay, although they would not be moved until the end of the week. The couple – Phil and Megan Dumbarton – currently had three foster children and two dogs so didn't mind taking Janie's children and dog. They were at present involved in the placement of their three foster children, who were going to live with an aunt. The social worker gave me the Dumbartons' details and I phoned them. We talked about Janie and her children's needs, and I arranged for them to come and visit on Friday. Their current foster children were leaving that day so Janie's would come to them the next.

When I realized how far they were coming I was shocked. It was nearly an hour away.

'Are the children going to the same school?' I asked Megan.

'Yes,' she said. 'It's part of the agreement. Janie doesn't want them moved.'

'What about if they stay in care long term? Will they stay with you?'

'Maybe,' was all she said.

On Friday morning I sat the children down and explained that they were going to meet Megan and Phil Dumbarton; they were coming to say hi tonight – after the children had seen their mum at contact – and would then return tomorrow to take them home with them.

'Are we allowed to bring the dog?' Riley wanted to know.

'Yes, love, you are.'

They didn't really have any more questions – what could they ask? Lola took her brother Jayden's hand for a while until it was time to get ready for school.

Over the course of the week since Janie's outburst at contact on Monday, I'd sensed she was growing more accepting of her fate. On Friday at the end of contact I said, 'Goodbye. Take care.' She knew, as I did, that it would be our last meeting.

She nodded and replied, 'Goodbye.'

It was the first word she'd said to me all week.

I'd agreed with Megan that the children would have something to eat on Friday after school and she and Phil would come to visit them after – around six-thirty – just for half an hour. It was a rush for us after contact, but it

275

had been for them too – their three children had just gone. They were in fact slightly late – there'd been a hold-up on the motorway. When they arrived the children were sitting in the living room waiting for them. I made the Dumbartons a cup of tea and they talked about their house and what they liked to do in their free time. To begin with the children didn't really say much. Lola was ready for bed, then Phil began going through his photograph album on his phone, and they all wanted to see.

'Hold on! Just a second,' he said, and he turned his phone so they could all see.

They sat on the sofa, surrounding Phil, and looked at the pictures he showed them. They were of their house and garden. I was interested too. It was a large, rambling Victorian house, five bedrooms, with a long, narrow garden. As Phil talked to them Megan explained to me and Paula that their two birth children – two boys – had both gone to university. One had come back to live with them, the other one hadn't. He was still in Liverpool. They'd started fostering about five years ago and hadn't looked back.

They were a really nice couple. Lola didn't say much beyond, 'Will Mummy come with us?'

Megan looked at me.

'No, love,' I said. 'It's just for you and your brothers. But you will still see her as you do now.'

'When can I go home?' she asked.

'I don't know yet,' I said.

The poor child looked continuously bewildered. I didn't know what the social services' plans were for them; I wasn't their foster carer, so I wouldn't be told.

Megan and Phil stayed for about half an hour. They made a fuss of Max and talked about their dogs and going on long doggy walks. Then they said they'd better be off as they had their children's rooms to clear out ready for tomorrow.

'Will we have a room each?' Riley wanted to know.

'Yes, love,' Megan said.

I read in her words that they'd miss the children who'd just left and were, in part, accepting Janie's children to get over their loss.

I put Lola straight to bed after they'd gone. It took a while. Then it was Jayden's turn, and he began asking about their move.

'When are we going?' he wanted to know.

'At ten o'clock tomorrow morning.'

'Will we still go to school tomorrow?' he asked.

'It's Saturday tomorrow, love. There is no school.'

'Oh,' was all he said.

I then gave him a bath, got him ready for bed, and we said goodnight.

Downstairs, Riley was busy petting Max as well as arguing with Paula.

'You ask Mum!' she said as I walked into the room.

'Can Max sleep with me tonight?' Riley wanted to know. 'Go on, please, just for tonight.'

'No, love,' I said. 'He's comfortable in his bed in the kitchen-diner. It's time for your bed.'

He ignored me, patting him a while longer. His face was set.

'Come on, love,' I said to him. 'Time to go upstairs. It's your last night so don't spoil it.'

'Max wants to go out into the garden,' he said, annoyed, and got up.

'Go on then,' I said.

I waited for him in the kitchen-diner until he returned.

'Did he go?' I asked.

'Maybe,' he said with a shrug.

I knew enough of Riley to know when he'd got himself into one of his moods. This meant he wasn't going to talk to us, not in any meaningful way. I knew it was going to take him time to go to bed. I began cajoling, then persuading and finally threatening that if he didn't go up soon he'd be downstairs by himself. He went up, slamming his feet hard on the staircase, then stomped across the landing, and finally began getting ready for bed. I went up after him. He didn't want to have a bath but did brush his teeth, then got in beside Jayden, who was already asleep.

It was after 9 p.m. by the time I'd said goodnight and come out. I went downstairs with Riley's dirty washing. When I returned a quarter of an hour later to check on the children everyone was fast asleep. I looked in on Lola first and pulled up her duvet, which had slipped down, then at Jayden and Riley. I thought that if I'd been ten years younger, I could have coped indefinitely with all three of them, but not now. It was just too much.

CHAPTER TWENTY-NINE

A PHONE CALL

The following morning we were all up early. It was the start of March, a new phase in our lives, where the air was fresh and reassuring. I didn't know what was going to happen to the children, but I knew they were going to a good home where the standard of care was exemplary.

However, Lola was in tears again by the start of breakfast.

'I want Mummy,' she wailed. 'I want to go home.'

'You'll see Mummy again on Monday,' I said. 'Then Tuesday, Wednesday, Thursday and Friday.'

'I want Mummy,' she repeated over and over again. Then she went and sat on Jayden's lap for a cuddle and he pushed her off.

I told him off. It was only 8 a.m. and I could see they wouldn't settle indoors so I suggested we took Max out for a walk.

'I don't want to,' Lola said.

Paula was up and dressed. She too was feeling glum. I asked her if she would stay with Lola while I took the boys and Max for a walk. Max had already been outside that morning. She agreed. So after breakfast the boys got ready while Paula sat in the living room and read a story to Lola.

It was a fine day, almost spring-like, and we walked for almost an hour. It wasn't long before the boys started asking questions.

'It's strange for us, going,' Riley said at one point. He was in a better mood now.

'It's strange for me too,' I said.

'How long will we be staying with them?' Jayden wanted to know.

'I'm not sure yet, but it will probably be for a few months.'

'Why can't we stay with you?' Jayden asked.

'Because I'm too old to look after three of you,' I said with a smile.

'So when will we go back to Mum's?' Jayden asked.

'We might not, ever,' Riley replied, and he looked incredibly sad.

Once we got home, it was only a matter of a quarter of an hour before the carers were due. I gave the boys a drink and something to eat. Lola didn't want anything. I then checked their bedrooms for any stray items, but they were clear. We were all sitting in the living room, with Max fast asleep, when any further questions were stopped by the ringing of the doorbell. The children looked at me, alarmed, realizing that this was it.

I went to answer the door and sure enough it was Phil and Megan, bright and breezy.

'Come in,' I said.

'Are these all their bags?' Phil asked, stepping in and looking at their small amount of luggage.

'Yes. They haven't been with me for long,' I reminded him.

'I'll load them into the car then.'

The children had come out of the living room in a procession.

'Hi,' Megan said. 'Don't you look smart.' They did, dressed in new casual clothes I'd bought them.

Max had come out too and I called to Riley to take care of him.

'We can stow him in the back first,' Megan said to Riley.

Riley looked confused.

'Do you want to come out and see where the dog goes?' she asked him.

He nodded and quickly put on his shoes and coat.

'Would you like a tea or coffee?' I asked.

'No, thank you. I'm fine. I don't know about Phil.'

She asked him on his next trip into the house from the car, but he didn't want one either.

'We'll set off once we're packed,' he said. 'Thanks, Cathy.'

Once he'd finished loading their car, which didn't take long, I checked the children didn't want to use the toilet, and then got them into their coats and shoes. Paula helped me. It was now time for them to say goodbye and leave. I thought of all the other children who'd left me in the past as I kissed them goodbye. Only Lola hugged me, and told me she wanted her mummy.

I went with them to the car. Max was sitting by himself in the very back of Megan and Phil's Land Rover. He looked as lost as the children did. They got in. Megan fastened their seatbelts and closed the rear door. We then waved and waved until they were out of sight.

'I hope they get on all right,' I said as Paula and I returned indoors. 'It's Janie I'm really worried about.'

'Why?' Paula asked.

'I am sure she didn't deserve this.'

Paula looked at me doubtfully and then said, 'From what you have told me about her, I'm not surprised the social services have taken her children into care.'

'I don't think she's ever intentionally hurt them,' I said. I liked Janie. She was just always in such a mess.

Paula didn't reply but then said, 'I was going to have a relaxing day today.'

'You've earned it,' I said, and we left the conversation at that.

I thought about the children looking out of the windows of their nice new Land Rover as Phil drove them to their new home. An hour later I thought about them arriving and settling in to their rooms. One each – how lucky were they. I thought about them sitting down to their meals. Megan and Phil would be shattered by the end of the day, and by the end of the week they would have established their new routine, which would include contact with their mother.

I spent the rest of that morning clearing out the children's bedrooms and then wrote up my fostering/ support worker notes, all the while thinking about Janie. I wondered what she was doing all alone in that flat. If she was alone. Then at 2 p.m. I told Paula I was going to visit Mrs Briggs for an hour or so. Paula was chilling in her room. It was over a week since I'd seen Mrs Briggs and before I left I went into the back garden and picked her a bunch of daffodils that were just coming into bud. Then I called upstairs to say goodbye to Paula and left.

It was still a lovely early-spring day, and as I walked my thoughts kept returning to Janie. She was among the many thousands of people who had their children taken into care each year in the UK. How was she doing? I couldn't imagine it would be very well.

I rang Mrs Briggs's doorbell out of politeness, then used the key safe for entry.

'Hello!' I called, going in.

The living room was in darkness, as the lunchtime carer had drawn the curtains so Mrs Briggs could have a sleep.

'Hello, Mrs Briggs?'

She came to. 'Oh, I wasn't expecting you,' she said with a smile.

I gave her a moment to recover, then opened the curtains.

'That's nice,' she said.

'Have you got a vase?' I asked her. 'I've picked these from my garden.'

'How lovely. In the kitchen, pet.'

Once she'd fully woken, she was as bright as a button. I placed the flowers in water and she showed me where she wanted them in the living room, not far from her. I made us tea, which we had with one of her favourite biscuits from the tin. We talked about many things, including Liv. She'd popped in that morning and was recovering well. I wasn't sure if she'd been made aware of the changes to Janie and I didn't bring it up. Mrs Briggs continued to talk about anything that came to mind, especially her dear husband, for nearly two hours. Then I washed up our tea things and said I needed to be going. It was a pleasant way to spend the afternoon and I said

I'd pop in again next week. She thanked me and insisted she walk me to the door, where we kissed goodbye.

On Sunday I had all the family round. They came for dinner. Theo and Sophia were growing fast. Emma had lots to tell me about school and wanted to show me some of her work. It was a lovely day, but of course talk of what I'd been doing over the past few weeks came up.

'Are you fostering again?' Adrian asked pointedly.

'No, love. Just helping out.' I explained some of Janie's sad story.

Adrian gave me an indulgent nod and changed the subject. The others had moved the conversation on by now.

They didn't stay late, and as we all kissed goodbye we said we'd meet up again very soon.

That evening, after we'd done the washing-up and Paula was in her bedroom, I sat in the living room and decided at last to phone Janie.

'What the hell do you want?' she said, her voice immediately rising.

'Janie, listen to me. Please.'

She hung up.

I waited a few moments, then phoned her back. It went through to voicemail and I left the following message: 'I know you're angry with me, but this could give you the breather you need to get your children back. I feel bad. I don't want you to lose your children for good. You let them down once. Can you phone me please to discuss?'

I ended the call and put down the phone.

* * *

On Monday afternoon I answered the phone and it was Janie, but she was still angry and upset with me.

'You're right! I didn't deserve this. I know I didn't. I miss my children badly.' And she burst into tears.

I waited for her to finish crying, then she had a go at me.

'I thought you were my friend! You were my only friend. I've got no one else to talk to now.' She was crying again.

I waited some more and then asked: 'Are you seeing your children?'

'Yes.'

'How many times a week?'

'Five. That bloody centre is closed at the weekend so I just phone them.'

'Yes, I know. How are they?'

'They miss me a lot. But not as much as they should. They are settled in with their new carers, who I don't like one little bit. They're an hour's drive away. I won't get them back now. I know I won't.' She was close to tears again, so I paused.

'What has happened so far? I mean, during last week when they were with me.'

She thought for a moment. 'I had a meeting with two social workers. Not Liv, she's ill. They explained why the children were in care and one visited me. I don't know what happens now.'

'How long are they in care for?'

'I don't know. How would I know that?' she cried passionately.

'You wouldn't necessarily. Have you seen a solicitor?' I asked.

'No, do you think I should?'

'It depends on what type of care order the social services have applied for.'

'It's a Section 20. That's why I had to sign the forms. I told them that Lola's father had some contact with her sometimes.' Under a Section 20, the children are taken into care by voluntary agreement with the person with parental responsibility.

'I see. So the court isn't involved?'

'No. The social workers keep giving me more paperwork, but when I phone to query something there is no one free to talk to me.' I heard her voice break. I thought of all the paperwork having a child in care meant.

'Are you free to meet me tomorrow?' I asked.

'Yes – well, apart from contact. Why?'

'So you are free tomorrow morning?'

'Yes, I am.'

'I'll come round to you at ten-thirty if that's all right.'

She hesitated, then said, 'See you at ten-thirty then.'

'And, Janie, I want you to have all the paperwork ready.' I knew what state she lived in. 'Plus any references to websites the social services may have given you.'

'All right. Do you think I can get my children back?'

'I honestly don't know at present.'

We said goodbye and ended the call, and I took a few deep breaths.

I went straight to my computer in the front room. Instead of concentrating on my writing, I researched Section 20, printing out what was of interest. I then researched those people who'd fought for their children and got them back. There were plenty. I had thought long and hard about how many families in the UK were doing it alone and failed to get their children back. It was appalling.

I spent a long time researching what the social services had to say on their websites, which didn't amount to a lot. They were all saying the same thing. Then I researched solicitors' websites and also charities. They all said something similar. In the end, after about two hours, I stopped and closed the computer screen. I'd had enough for one day.

Paula had come home by now. I asked her about her day, but didn't tell her what I'd been doing. While she got changed I made dinner and then we ate together. I was still thinking about Janie and what I could do (if anything) for her. It was a gamble and I wanted it to pay off. At present I simply didn't know enough about her situation to make a calculated guess as to whether we could get her children returned to her or not. Even though it was a Section 20, if she just took them she ran the risk of the social services taking her to court.

I had an early night but didn't fall asleep until well after midnight. I was thinking about Janie alone in that house. It was strange for us, having had the children leave. What must it be like for her? Eventually, I dropped off and slept through until 7 a.m. Paula was up and I felt a sense of renewed hope. A new day had begun, and I intended to help Janie in any way I could.

CHAPTER THIRTY

A BIG CLEAN-UP

As I drove to Janie's home that Tuesday morning I felt a stab of fear. She could be very volatile and unpredictable – I'd experienced that before – and it was something she'd have to work on. Supposing she'd thought about my offer to help overnight and decided she didn't want it? Supposing she hated me and didn't want anything to do with me? Then I'd leave and never go back.

I parked outside her home at 10.30, took a deep breath, checked my face in the interior mirror, then got out. The sky was overcast and drizzle was in the air. I walked slowly up the path to her home and pressed the bell. I waited, but no one answered for a long while. Then Janie came to the door. She didn't say hello, but left the front door open for me. She didn't speak, so I followed her into the kitchen-diner – where she let rip.

'What do you want?' she asked aggressively. 'I've been up all night thinking about you and what I've lost. You're horrible and I hate you.'

'I've come to help you if I can.'

'To help me!' she cried. 'You're the one who's caused this mess!'

'No, Janie. You did. You left your children alone all night. It wasn't me who did that but you. And clearly other stuff has been going on too. I don't know it all. You have no one to blame but yourself. Yes, I could have said nothing and waited for the social services to come. Then they would have taken away your children for good.'

'You don't know that for sure!'

'You may have done it again and got away with it, but eventually you'd have been caught.'

'You can't possibly know that!' she shouted.

'I do, Janie!'

'No, you don't. I'm a good mother to my children. I always am.' She was close to tears now.

The room was still and we both took a moment to recover.

When I spoke again it was quieter.

'Look, Janie, please sit down and let me try to explain the situation to you.'

She hesitated, looked like she might disagree, then moved a heap of rubbish from the chair at the kitchen table and sat down.

'Can I turn the television off?' I asked her.

'It's company for me.'

'I'll turn it down then.'

I found the remote under another pile of rubbish. I guessed she'd stayed up with the television on for most of the night. I turned it down, then sat opposite her. The house was quiet with no children around. I couldn't help but notice that it was in a right state – even more so than usual. She hadn't cleared up for most of last week.

'Your children are in care under a Section 20,' I said. 'That is a good sign.'

289

'But the social worker said if I didn't cooperate then they could apply for a court order. She was horrible and annoyed with me.'

'I think you may have upset her.'

'It's possible,' Janie admitted.

'Can you get out all the paperwork you've been given for me to look at?'

'I've got it here. Somewhere.' She began rummaging through the letters and other detritus she had on the kitchen table. Eventually she pushed a pile of envelopes towards me.

'Is it all right if I read them?' I checked, for they were confidential.

'Yes, you go ahead. I can't read very well.'

I began going through them.

'Do you want tea?' she asked, her manner greatly improved. 'I'm getting a cuppa for me.'

I nodded, then looked up at her. 'How well can you read?'

'Not good at all,' she replied, going to the kettle. 'I was the class dunce.'

'Do the social services know you can't read well?'

'I honestly don't know. I don't think I've ever told them. I keep it to myself.'

'Have you even looked at these letters?' I asked.

'Some of them. I opened them, but I can't make sense of much of it.'

I made a mental note of her inability to read clearly, then continued to read the letters as she made tea. I read through the wodge of paperwork and eventually she set a cup of tea down beside me.

'Well?' she asked at length, also sitting.

'You will have an assessment for parenting, and I believe you have signed to say they can approach the police, and your doctor?'

'If you say so. What exactly is a Section 20?'

'It's an agreement between a parent and a local authority that can mean you don't have to go to court. It allows for the local authority to continue with a care plan. From what I've read it can include referrals to parenting classes. Most importantly, a Section 20 does not give the local authority parental responsibility. At all times, parents have the right to withdraw their consent to a Section 20. Should they do so, the child should be returned to the parents immediately. But,' I continued, 'it does mean that the local authority can go to court and ask the judge for an Interim Care Order. To be honest, I am surprised they haven't gone down this path with you.'

It sounded like a criticism and she took it as one.

'What the hell do you mean?' she thundered, slamming down her mug of tea.

'I am sorry. I didn't mean it to sound as though you are to blame. But when there are a lot of things going on and you have history, which I think you will agree is the case, it's unusual. Perhaps it's because your social worker is off ill at present and they are short-staffed.'

'So that means they could still apply for a non-Section 20?' she asked, calming down.

'Yes, they could.'

'How long do they last?' she asked.

'As far as I can work out there is no time limit on a Section 20. Although the courts have been criticized when agreements have been considered to have gone on for too long. But it doesn't say how long online.'

I stopped and looked at Janie. 'Are you understanding why I'm saying this?'

'I think so. They didn't tell me all this last week, although I wouldn't have understood anyway.'

'No.' I took another sip of my tea and continued with the reading.

'Have you gone to a parenting class yet?' I asked. 'Only it's mentioned in this letter.'

She shook her head. 'I keep putting it off.'

'Where's the original letter about the classes?'

She stood and rummaged in some more paperwork, muttering, 'I think I might have thrown it away … Oh, here it is.'

She brought it to me and I read it through.

'There's no point in me going to it now. I haven't got my kids,' Janie said.

'No, but you might have one day.'

'God, I hope so. Do you really think I will?'

I looked up from the letter I was reading. I was trying to keep her as focused as possible without giving her any false hope. I knew from my research that some families with help had succeeded in getting their children back.

'Anything else I should know?' I asked her.

'Yes,' she said, anger returning to her eyes. 'Those bloody foster carers. They are doing my head in.'

'Why?'

'They said yesterday my kids are badly behaved and keep having accidents. I don't believe them. I've reported them. They leave them in the garden and Riley has an accident – what do they expect?'

'I would expect Riley to have a number of minor accidents in the garden,' I said. 'What sort of injuries has he sustained?'

'Well, he has a bruise on his knee for one thing.'

I waited. 'And what else?'

She couldn't think of anything. 'I don't like them,' was all she said.

I inwardly sighed. 'That may be, but, Janie, you have to work with them. It will help you long term. Can you do that?'

I could tell she didn't want to from her refusal to reply.

'If they are on your side, they will view your actions in a positive light. Can you try to get along with them for me, please?'

'All right,' she said, after a moment's silence. 'But they are not you.'

The statement hung in the air and I let it pass.

'Anything else?' I asked.

'No, I don't think so.' She finished her tea.

'You're not drinking heavily?' I asked.

'No,' she said. 'Not heavily.' I looked around and couldn't see any beer cans.

'You've got the social worker coming on Thursday,' I said. 'Will you be all right with them?' I still hadn't decided if they needed to know I was still involved. My present thinking was that they didn't.

Poor Janie had dealt with the social services for long enough. She nodded. 'I'll be fine.'

'How about we make a start on clearing up then?' I suggested.

'I'll leave it for now, thank you.'

'When are you going to do it?' I waited for a reply.

She shrugged. 'OK, you win.' She stood and looked around. 'I don't know where to begin,' she said. 'It's a hell of a mess.'

'Yes. It is,' I agreed, and stood also. 'But we have to start somewhere.'

We began where we were – in the kitchen-diner – clearing up the mess, throwing away what wasn't salvageable, sorting any other mail and papers into heaps. I was amazed at how quickly it had built up into such a state, but there was no reason for Janie to clear up now. We moved on to the children's clothes that were lying around. Some were old and by Janie's admission didn't fit any more. They weren't good enough to recycle so we binned them. Then we wiped all the surfaces and got out the floor mop.

I then ran water into the washing-up bowl and cleaned all around the sink and other surfaces before starting on the fridge. There was nothing much in it, but it still needed a good clean. I threw away a lump of mouldy cheese and an egg that was over a month out of date. During the last week Janie must have eaten whatever she had. The freezer was empty apart from a half-eaten bag of chips. I stopped and looked at Janie.

'What are you going to have for your dinner tonight?' I asked her.

'I don't know,' she shrugged.

I opened the cupboards that Janie had wiped clean. I found some coffee, pasta and an open box of tea bags.

'I'll take you shopping now and buy what you need. Get your coat on,' I said.

I expected her to resist but she looked beaten. She simply did as she was told, and we did a whistle-stop tour of the local grocery shop, then returned home. I made us a sandwich lunch, and we spent ten minutes eating. Janie was quiet; she could only talk about her children and my heart went out to her.

With lunch over and the kitchen-diner more or less clean, I washed the floor in the hall. Then I joined Janie in the children's bedroom. I stood for a moment at the door, unable to believe the mess it had got into in a week! Janie had been using it as a dumping ground. She hadn't sent any of the children's belongings to me or the new carers. It was all in here. There were clothes and largely broken toys over the bed and surfaces, and even jammed onto the windowsill.

'Have your children got anything with them now?' I asked.

'Only what they stand up in,' she said. 'I'm not giving those carers my stuff.'

'Look, Janie, you'll get it all back in time. It's never the carers' to own, but it might be nice for your children to have some of their things with them while they are there.'

She huffed and was going to say something, then thought better of it. She picked up some toys and put them into a bag. We worked for an hour, sorting the toys and clothes. Then she made a point of checking the time. It was nearly two o'clock.

'We've got a little way to go yet,' I said. 'I'll come back tomorrow.'

'Why?'

'You've got the social services coming on Thursday,' I said. 'You want it spotless.'

'They'll know it's not me.'

'But you want it to be you from now on, don't you?'

She shrugged and the two of us continued working. The sheets on the bed were grubby so we stripped those and fished out what was beneath the bed. We cleared out the built-in wardrobe – there was a lot of rubbish the children had put in there so we repacked it. As 2.30 approached I said I needed to go soon as I had a call about another family who needed some help.

'I hope you don't shop them,' she said, which I ignored.

After a few moments she said, 'What do you think I should take to contact for the children to play with?' She'd picked up the bag she'd previously used for some of their toys.

'What do they usually play with?' I asked.

She hesitated and didn't know. 'They usually watch television, but the carers don't know that,' she said.

I found her a selection of toys for all three children and put them into two bags. I had to go soon.

'I'll put these by the front door,' I said, 'so you don't forget them.'

I returned and gathered up the washing from the beds and took that through to the kitchen. I put it beside the washing machine to wait for the previous load to finish. I then picked up the information sheet on parenting classes and put it in my bag. We'd agreed that I would chase this up, as it seemed to be unclear whether the classes had already started or not and where they were held.

'Same time tomorrow?' I said.

'What shall I say to the carers when I see them tonight?' she asked. 'I haven't really spoken to them. In fact, I went for them on the phone.'

'Oh, Janie, you don't want to be creating a scene. Just ask them how your children are settling in,' I suggested.

'And if they need anything at all. Listen to what they tell you.'

She gave a vague, dispassionate nod and looked completely out of her depth. Having children in care was new to her, as it is for most people. I hugged her before I left and came away feeling low. Janie had lost her children into the care system. Whether we could win them back again remained to be seen.

CHAPTER THIRTY-ONE

I'LL GET THEM MYSELF!

On Wednesday I was back at Janie's at 10.30 and I began by asking her how the contact had gone.

'OK,' she said. 'Just the female carer was there. I think her name is Megan.'

'Did you talk to her?'

We were in the kitchen-diner; I couldn't believe how clean and tidy it still was.

'Yes, I did, a bit,' she said. 'I gave the children their toys and they were pleased with me.'

'Good. Did you see Megan at the start or end of contact?'

'Both,' she said. 'But I'm still not sure about her.'

'That's all right,' I said. 'As long as you keep it to yourself. Now, the parenting classes,' I continued, sitting down. Janie sat too. I'd noticed she wasn't someone who could sit for long. 'I've booked you a place starting next week. It took a while, so I don't want you to miss it. It's on a Wednesday morning. It will give you a chance to meet other mothers and also help your parenting skills.'

She pulled a face. 'I've thought about it,' she said. 'Do I have to go? I mean, it's not going to do me any good, is it? I haven't got my kids now.'

'No, but this is one of the ways you can try to get them back,' I said. 'I've already explored the process.' She didn't reply. 'OK?'

'If you say so. Only the social services are going to do a parenting assessment on me as well.'

'I know, that's very different – I'll explain it later. It is important you go to the classes, Janie. I've spent a lot of time on the phone this morning getting you in.'

'I've said I'll go,' she snapped.

I showed her the parenting assessment form from the college, which I'd purposely printed out for her. Right at the top on the first page was the question: *Do the parents/carers have any communication/learning difficulties?*

She looked at these lines, didn't have a clue how to read them, then concentrated on the ones below, which asked for her children's names. 'That's my kid's names,' she said. 'I can fill that in.'

'Yes, then what?'

She looked down. 'I don't know,' she said with a shrug.

'If you can't read basic forms without help,' I said, 'what are you going to do?'

'Same as I've always done, I guess.'

'Which is what?'

'Get someone to read them to me, if I have anybody to ask,' she added.

I looked at the form again. 'It continues by asking about your preferred time for attending the support classes. Then the reasons for wanting to attend.'

'Because the social services are making me do it,' she said.

'That's the reason I'll fill in for you,' I replied.

'That's fine' she said.

I read through the rest of the sheet and the last part of the form was for a social worker to fill in. There was no way Janie could have filled in this form alone. I stopped and looked at her.

'Have you ever notified anyone at the school or the social services about your disability?' I asked.

'No! Of course not,' she exclaimed.

'I think you should,' I said again.

'I'll think about it,' she said. 'We've got my bedroom to do now if you've finished.'

I kept my gaze on her for a moment and then put the paperwork for the parenting classes on the now-clean table.

'Don't forget it,' I said. 'It's ten weeks starting on Wednesday.'

I followed her into her bedroom, worried she didn't have the right attitude.

Part of me had thought she might at least have made a start on clearing up in here.

'I didn't have a chance last night,' she said. 'I went to see my new boyfriend.'

So we got on with sorting it out.

'Are the social services going to start your parenting assessment when they visit tomorrow?' I asked as we worked.

'I haven't a clue,' she said.

'Well, in case they do, we need to talk about it.' I'd found before that you could talk to Janie more easily if she was doing something else.

'It's about your parenting being good enough. It doesn't have to be perfect, just good enough. The social worker they send will have a checklist online that she will go through. It will last approximately twelve weeks and be about fifty hours long.'

'Twelve weeks! That's three months. So I won't be getting my kids back during that time?'

'I doubt it,' I said, and I paused to let this information sink in. 'Your assessment will start with basics like providing for your children's health – do you take them to the dentist and doctor when they are ill?'

'Yes,' she stated categorically.

'Ensure their safety?' I asked. 'I know there have been some incidents in the past.'

'What are you talking about?' she demanded.

I decided to leave this topic alone until she'd had a session with her social worker. It was to give Janie some idea of the type of thing she would be asked, but it was hopeless at present.

We concentrated on clearing out the bedroom, but I did also ask her about boyfriends. She admitted she had one, that was all she would say. She was an attractive woman and I didn't think she'd have any problem getting a boyfriend. Whether he was suitable or not remained to be seen. I knew with Janie that I needed to say something a number of times before it hit home, so I ended by saying: 'Just keep him away from your home.'

'Will do,' she said.

I found the most bizarre things in Janie's bedroom. The marble jar for one.

'The kids kept taking it off the shelf in the kitchen,' she said. She also had an unopened box containing a magnetic stacking toy.

'It's Lola's birthday next month,' she told me.

'That's lovely,' I said.

I assumed she'd bought it, rather than stolen it, but I didn't ask.

'I don't suppose they will be home by then,' she said.

'No,' I agreed. 'I don't suppose they will.'

Gradually, Janie was getting an understanding of what was involved. We worked for nearly two hours. We even wiped down a wall that had mould growing on it. The bedding needed a wash, so we took that through to the washing machine. Then we went back and raked out under her bed. Among other things, there were about a dozen beer bottles shoved beneath. Janie seemed to leave things where they fell.

'What are you going to do all day?' I asked her, looking at my watch.

'I've applied for cleaning work for the weekend,' she said. 'I start on Saturday.'

'Well done.' I was pleased.

The social worker came the following day. It wasn't one Janie or I had met before. It took Janie some time before she would accept anyone new. When she told me about the meeting afterwards, she mentioned that he'd asked about the children's fathers and what contact they had. She said he'd talked about her children's health and how they fitted in at school. She'd said she didn't know but had assumed it was fine. He was impressed by the fact that Janie had cleaned and tidied the flat, although there were no children there, and he had made a note. Of course, he couldn't make a comparison to how it was before, and Janie didn't tell him how bad it was. Instead, she said she had proudly opened the cupboard doors – all sparking clean.

'I hadn't got much food in as there is just me here,' she'd told him.

The social worker had made another note. I hoped he was writing good things. It was so difficult to know. He was due to visit again the following week.

The parenting classes started that Wednesday and, as with most new things, Janie still wasn't sure whether to go or not. She did go, after a lot of persuasion from me, and when she returned I phoned her to ask how it had gone.

'It was all right,' was all she said; she wouldn't be drawn further, and I wondered how much she'd actually learnt.

Janie continued to see her children five days a week while I picked up the threads of my old life and the social worker wrote his report. She'd cried when they'd talked about the night she'd left her children unattended at home, not fully appreciating what she'd done. It did seem like it was a one-off incident.

The puppy, Max, became ill. It had developed a limp. Megan took it to their vet and he said it had been born with one leg shorter than the others, and that this was becoming more pronounced as he grew. He said it was like that from birth and the breeder would have known from the start. I'd always thought there was something wrong with the way the dog walked and had put it down to the breed. The vet said they'd observe it for now but to bring him back if he deteriorated, in which case they'd operate. I felt sorry for Janie.

'I can't even buy a proper puppy!' she exclaimed.

Quietly, I wondered how many foster carers would be happy to have a dog stay – Riley's best friend – if the children weren't returned to Janie.

We got the end-of-term report from the school at Easter and it was clear the children were all receiving additional support for their learning. 'They didn't need support when I had them!' Janie exclaimed, annoyed.

I thought for a moment and then asked her, 'Would you have known about it if they did, though?'

She was about to say something indignant back but then stopped herself.

'I don't suppose so,' she said. 'I never went to the parent–teacher interviews.'

Over the coming weeks I began helping another family who needed support, as well as visiting Mrs Briggs. But I still saw Janie twice a week. I helped her read all the information she received about her children and to reply to it where necessary. One notice said that her child bene-fit had now stopped as the children were no longer with her. I said we'd have to phone the number and get it back if they were returned to her care. She needed that money. There was also a letter from the police, advising her that they would not be prosecuting on this occasion following her arrest. It didn't give a reason. I read both letters out to her – she could only pick out some words – and hoped for the best.

I could see that Janie was lonely all by herself during the months of assessment. She was staying in bed a long time and I thought it might be detrimental to her overall well-being. Some of the parenting classes had been post-poned so continued into a fourth month. At the end Janie went to the teacher and asked her to write to the social services and tell them how well she'd done. The teacher said she would.

Liv returned to work briefly but went to work with another team, and the man who'd written Janie's report left; he was an agency employee. Then it all went quiet; we didn't hear anything from the social services. Janie phoned repeatedly asking the same question: 'When am I getting my kids back?'

Another week went by and I could see that Janie was losing it. It had been nearly five months now, and I said I'd phone the social services, but the people I spoke to I'd never heard of. I explained I was helping Janie Watson and when could she expect a decision? They said they didn't know and someone would call me back. No one did. I tried again with the same result. Janie was being failed on all sides.

Janie began drinking again and I warned her against it. There was nothing else I could do. She got into the habit of phoning the social services every day and begging them to let her have her children back.

'I'll get them myself!' she said to me, and I think she meant it.

Then two days later, on a Wednesday, she phoned me: the social services had said she could have them back that weekend, and she should go to a meeting at the social services the following day. We were over the moon, delighted – we couldn't believe it.

'I would just have kept fighting for them,' she said, satisfied.

Why did the social services make that decision? It's possible they were aware of all the changes Janie had made in her life, and that she was genuinely sorry for her mistakes. Also, as she was on a Section 20, someone at the social services might have felt it was easier to return the children than not. I don't know. But Janie had won hers back.

I reminded her of all the things she had yet to improve on.

'Yes, but it was you who said that parenting doesn't have to be perfect, just good enough.'

'I know. But you can still aim for perfection.'

Although I knew there was no way she would.

CHAPTER THIRTY-TWO

A NEW BEGINNING

Janie didn't have any friends, just people that came and went. Since I'd got to know her I thought I knew why. She couldn't read or write, she had a very abrupt manner sometimes, had some repetitive movements that couldn't be controlled and didn't do as you would expect. There were a lot of other things she didn't know or understand. I'd persuaded her to see a doctor for a diagnosis. When she returned she told me he was going to refer her to a specialist, but in the interim he thought she could be autistic, which explained a lot.

The children were due home on Saturday, and on Sunday I was invited to visit them. It was mayhem in that modest flat from the second I walked in. During the five months they had been at Megan and Phil's they'd changed in appearance and acquired a lot of things. The carers also returned all their old clothes in bags, which I suggested to Janie we left as they were and took them straight to the charity shop.

Little Lola eyed me suspiciously – five months was a long time in a child's life and she didn't know what to make of me. She'd begun receiving speech and language therapy while away and the expectation was that it would continue. Jayden and Riley were still receiving a lot of extra help with their learning at school.

Max seemed to recognize me and trotted over for a stroke, or perhaps he did that to everyone.

'He's not good,' Riley told me. 'He might need an operation when he's older.'

'I know. Your mother told me.'

Had they the least idea how much it had taken to get them returned? I wondered.

Janie hadn't unpacked the children's things, so I helped her with some of that. I thought that their flat would be a tip again before long. The children seemed wary of me, perhaps thinking that they would have to stay with me again. I reassured them as best I could.

Janie had her children back but there was a supervision order in place, which meant that the social services would monitor her and offer advice and direction as needed. A social worker was due to visit the following week to see how they were getting on. I cautioned Janie to be courteous and helpful.

I stayed for about two hours, then left the chaos of the flat. I hadn't been officially informed of the return of Janie's children; I was there as a friend. I can only hope that for Janie and her children family life returns to normal – whatever that might be. I continue to visit them once a week and will do so for as long as I'm needed.

If you, too, would like to help keep a family together as a support worker, there are a number of roles you can apply for. Some are voluntary and others are paid. Just google family support worker jobs.

For the latest on the children in this book and others in my fostering memoirs, please visit https://cathyglass.co.uk/updates

SUGGESTED TOPICS FOR READING-GROUP DISCUSSION

Why has Cathy been assigned to help Janie?

Janie leads a cluttered life. Give some reasons that you think might explain why.

Janie has a number of new partners in a very short space of time. Why do you think this might be? Is she looking for something?

Cathy agrees to take Riley for respite care at the weekends. What does this achieve?

Janie does things without thinking, such as getting a dog. Why was it not a good time to do this?

Janie is naive and easily taken in. Give some examples and discuss.

Max is a calming influence on Riley. Why do you think this is?

Riley needs a lot of time and patience that Janie doesn't have. Discuss.

When Janie's children are removed by social services it seems inevitable. How did Janie get them back?

The five months the children spend in care is a long time in their lives, but is it long enough for Janie to have made the necessary changes in her life?

Janie has learning difficulties and is eventually diagnosed with autism. How might this previously undiagnosed condition have affected her parenting?

CHRONOLOGY

If you would like to read, or re-read, my books in chronological order, here is the list to date:

Cut	*Hidden*
The Silent Cry	*Mummy Told Me Not to Tell*
Daddy's Little Princess	*Another Forgotten Child*
Nobody's Son	*The Child Bride*
Cruel to be Kind	*Can I Let You Go?*
The Night the Angels Came	*Finding Stevie*
A Long Way from Home	*Innocent*
A Baby's Cry	*Too Scared to Tell*
The Saddest Girl in the World	*A Terrible Secret*
Please Don't Take My Baby	*A Life Lost*
Will You Love Me?	*An Innocent Baby*
I Miss Mummy	*Neglected*
Saving Danny	*A Family Torn Apart*
Girl Alone	*Unwanted*
Where Has Mummy Gone?	*Unsafe*
Damaged	*Helpless*

The titles below can be slotted in anywhere, as can my Lisa Stone thrillers: http://lisastonebooks.co.uk/:

The Girl in the Mirror	*Happy Adults*
My Dad's a Policeman	*Happy Mealtimes for Kids*
Run, Mummy, Run	*About Writing and How*
Happy Kids	*to Publish*

This list is also on the books page of my website: https://cathyglass.co.uk/true-stories-cathy-glass/

Cathy Glass

———

One remarkable woman, more than **150** foster children cared for.

Cathy Glass has been a foster carer for 30 years, during which time she has looked after more than 150 children, as well as raising three children of her own. She was awarded a degree in education and psychology as a mature student, and writes under a pseudonym. To find out more about Cathy and her story visit **www.cathyglass.co.uk**.

Unsafe

Damian longs for home and, with Cathy's help, is overcoming his many issues and nearing a return

But when his mother's new boyfriend arrives, Cathy becomes deeply concerned.

Unwanted

Lara was seven when she was put into foster care after her mother died from a drug overdose

The care system failed Lara and now she is failing her son . . .

A Family Torn Apart

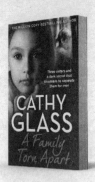

Angie and Polly are loved and looked-after by their parents, so why are they brought into foster care?

But as they settle with Cathy, and start to talk of life at home, it becomes clear something is badly wrong.

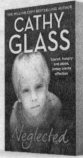

Neglected

The police remove Jamey from home as an emergency and take him to foster carer Cathy

But as Jamey starts to settle in and make progress a new threat emerges, which changes everything.

An Innocent Baby

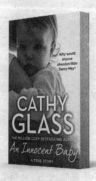

Abandoned at birth, Darcy-May is brought to Cathy with a police escort

Her teenage mother wants nothing to do with her, but why? She is an adorable baby.

A Life Lost

Jackson is aggressive, confrontational and often volatile

Then, in a dramatic turn of events, the true reason for Jackson's behaviour comes to light . . .

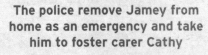

A Terrible Secret

Tilly is so frightened of her stepfather, Dave, that she asks to go into foster care

The more Cathy learns about Dave's behaviour, the more worried she becomes …

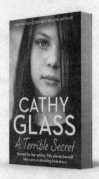

Too Scared to Tell

Oskar has been arriving at school hungry, unkempt and bruised. His mother has gone abroad and left him in the care of 'friends'

As the weeks pass, Cathy's concerns deepen. Oskar is clearly frightened of someone – but who? And why?

Innocent

Siblings Molly and Kit arrive at Cathy's frightened, injured and ill

The parents say they are not to blame. Could the social services have got it wrong?

Finding Stevie

Fourteen-year-old Stevie is exploring his gender identity

Like many young people, he spends time online, but Cathy is shocked when she learns his terrible secret.

Where Has Mummy Gone?

When Melody is taken into care, she fears her mother won't cope alone

It is only when Melody's mother vanishes that what has really been going on at home comes to light.

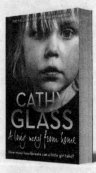

A Long Way from Home

Abandoned in an orphanage, Anna's future looks bleak until she is adopted

Anna's new parents love her, so why does she end up in foster care?

Cruel to be Kind

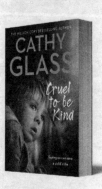

Max is shockingly overweight and struggles to make friends

Cathy faces a challenge to help this unhappy boy.

Nobody's Son

Born in prison and brought up in care, Alex has only ever known rejection

He is longing for a family of his own, but again the system fails him.

Can I Let You Go?

Faye is 24, pregnant and has learning difficulties as a result of her mother's alcoholism

Can Cathy help Faye learn enough to parent her child?

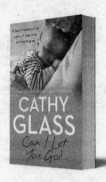

The Silent Cry

A mother battling depression. A family in denial

Cathy is desperate to help before something terrible happens.

Girl Alone

An angry, traumatized young girl on a path to self-destruction

Can Cathy discover the truth behind Joss's dangerous behaviour before it's too late?

Saving Danny

Danny's parents can no longer cope with his challenging behaviour

Calling on all her expertise, Cathy discovers a frightened little boy who just wants to be loved.

The Child Bride

A girl blamed and abused for dishonouring her community

Cathy discovers the devastating truth.

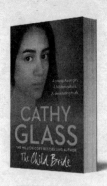

Daddy's Little Princess

A sweet-natured girl with a complicated past

Cathy picks up the pieces after events take a dramatic turn.

Will You Love Me?

A broken child desperate for a loving home

The true story of Cathy's adopted daughter Lucy.

Please Don't Take My Baby

Seventeen-year-old Jade is pregnant, homeless and alone

Cathy has room in her heart for two.

Another Forgotten Child

Eight-year-old Aimee was on the child-protection register at birth

Cathy is determined to give her the happy home she deserves.

A Baby's Cry

A newborn, only hours old, taken into care

Cathy protects tiny Harrison from the potentially fatal secrets that surround his existence.

The Night the Angels Came

A little boy on the brink of bereavement

Cathy and her family make sure Michael is never alone.

Mummy Told Me Not to Tell

A troubled boy sworn to secrecy

After his dark past has been revealed, Cathy helps Reece to rebuild his life.

I Miss Mummy

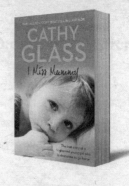

Four-year-old Alice doesn't understand why she's in care

Cathy fights for her to have the happy home she deserves.

The Saddest Girl in the World

A haunted child who refuses to speak

Do Donna's scars run too deep for Cathy to help?

Cut

Dawn is desperate to be loved

Abused and abandoned, this vulnerable child pushes Cathy and her family to their limits.

Hidden

The boy with no past

Can Cathy help Tayo to feel like he belongs again?

Damaged

A forgotten child

Cathy is Jodie's last hope. For the first time, this abused young girl has found someone she can trust.

Run, Mummy, Run

The gripping story of a woman caught in a horrific cycle of abuse, and the desperate measures she must take to escape.

My Dad's a Policeman

The dramatic short story about a young boy's desperate bid to keep his family together.

The Girl in the Mirror

Trying to piece together her past, Mandy uncovers a dreadful family secret that has been blanked from her memory for years.

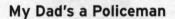

About Writing
and How to Publish

A clear, concise practical
guide on writing and the best
ways to get published.

Happy Mealtimes
for Kids

A guide to healthy eating
with simple recipes that
children love.

Happy Adults

A practical guide to achieving lasting
happiness, contentment and success.
The essential manual for getting
the best out of life.

Happy Kids

A clear and concise guide to
raising confident, well-behaved
and happy children.

CATHY GLASS WRITING AS
LISA STONE

www.lisastonebooks.co.uk

The new crime thrillers that will chill you to the bone . . .

THE MURDER ROOM

Your house should be the safest place in the world. Shouldn't it?

THE GATHERING

Can old friends still be trusted?

THE COTTAGE

Is someone out there?

TAKEN

Have you seen Leila?

THE DOCTOR

How much do you know about the couple next door?

STALKER

Security cameras are there to keep us safe. Aren't they?

THE DARKNESS WITHIN

You know your son better than anyone. Don't you?

Be amazed
Be moved
Be inspired

Follow Cathy:

/cathy.glass.180

@CathyGlassUK

www.cathyglass.co.uk

Cathy loves to hear from readers and reads
and replies to posts, but she asks that no plot
spoilers are posted, please. We're sure
you appreciate why.